Practical Java Machine Learning

Projects with Google Cloud Platform and Amazon Web Services

Mark Wickham

Practical Java Machine Learning: Projects with Google Cloud Platform and Amazon Web Services

Mark Wickham
Irving, TX, USA

ISBN-13 (pbk): 978-1-4842-3950-6   ISBN-13 (electronic): 978-1-4842-3951-3
https://doi.org/10.1007/978-1-4842-3951-3

Library of Congress Control Number: 2018960994

Managing Director, Apress Media LLC: Welmoed Spahr
Acquisitions Editor: Steve Anglin
Development Editor: Matthew Moodie
Coordinating Editor: Mark Powers

Cover designed by eStudioCalamar

Cover image designed by Freepik (www.freepik.com)

Distributed to the book trade worldwide by Springer Science+Business Media New York, 233 Spring Street, 6th Floor, New York, NY 10013. Phone 1-800-SPRINGER, fax (201) 348-4505, e-mail orders-ny@springer-sbm.com, or visit www.springeronline.com. Apress Media, LLC is a California LLC and the sole member (owner) is Springer Science + Business Media Finance Inc (SSBM Finance Inc). SSBM Finance Inc is a Delaware corporation.

For information on translations, please e-mail editorial@apress.com; for reprint, paperback, or audio rights, please email bookpermissions@springernature.com.

Apress titles may be purchased in bulk for academic, corporate, or promotional use. eBook versions and licenses are also available for most titles. For more information, reference our Print and eBook Bulk Sales web page at www.apress.com/bulk-sales.

Any source code or other supplementary material referenced by the author in this book is available to readers on GitHub via the book's product page, located at www.apress.com/9781484239506. For more detailed information, please visit www.apress.com/source-code.

Printed on acid-free paper

Table of Contents

About the Author

Mark Wickham is a frequent speaker at Android developer conferences and has written two books, Practical Android and Practical Java Machine Learning. As a freelance Android developer, Mark currently resides in Dallas, TX after living and working in China for nearly 20 years. While at Motorola, Mark led product management, product marketing, and software development teams in the Asia Pacific region. Before joining Motorola, Mark worked on software projects for TRW's Space Systems Division. Mark has a degree in Computer Science and Physics from Creighton University, and MBA from the University of Washington, and jointly studied business at the Hong Kong University of Science and Technology. In his free time, Mark also enjoys photography and recording live music. Mark can be contacted via his LinkedIn profile (*www.linkedin.com/in/mark-j-wickham/*) or GitHub page (*www.github.com/wickapps*).

About the Technical Reviewer

 **Jason Whitehorn** is an experienced entrepreneur and software developer. He has helped many oil and gas companies automate and enhance their oilfield solutions through field data capture, SCADA, and machine learning. Jason obtained his Bachelor of Science in Computer Science from Arkansas State University, but he traces his passion for development back many years before then, having first taught himself to program BASIC on his family's computer while still in middle school.

When he's not mentoring and helping his team at work, writing, or pursuing one of his many side projects, Jason enjoys spending time with his wife and four children and living in the Tulsa, Oklahoma region. More information about Jason can be found on his website at *https://jason.whitehorn.us*.

About the Technical Reviewer

Preface

It is interesting to watch trends in software development come and go, and to watch languages become fashionable, and then just as quickly fade away. As machine learning and AI began to reemerge a few years ago, it was easy to look upon the hype with a great deal of skepticism.

- AlphaGo, a UK-based company, used deep learning to defeat the Go masters. Go is a Chinese board game that very complicated due to a huge number of combinations. Living in China at the time, there was a lot of discussion about the panicked Go masters who refused to play the machine for fear that their techniques would be exposed or "learned" by the machines.

- An AI Poker Bot named Libratus individually defeated four top human professional players in 2017. This was surprising because poker is a difficult game for machines to master. In poker, unlike Go, there is a lot of unknown information, making it an "imperfect information" game.

- Machine traders are replacing human traders at many of the large investment banks. The rise of the "quant" on Wall Street is well documented. Examining the job opportunities at investment banks reveals a trend favoring math majors, data scientists, and machine learning experts.

- IBM's Watson can do amazing things, such as fix the elevator before breaks, adjust the sprinkler system in the vineyard to optimize yield, and help oilfield workers manage a drilling rig.

Despite the hype, it was not until confronted with problems that were very difficult to solve with existing software tools that I began to explore and appreciate the power of machine learning techniques.

Today, after several years of gaining an understanding about what these new techniques can do, and how to apply them, I find myself thinking differently about each problem I encounter. Almost every piece of software can benefit in some way from machine learning techniques.

Developing machine learning software requires us to think differently about problems, resulting in a new way to partition our development efforts. However, change is good, and using machine learning with a data-driven development methodology can allow us to solve previously unsolvable problems.

In this book, I will describe what I have discovered along my journey. I hope that it can help you in your future software endeavors.

Objectives

The book will meet the following objectives:

- Introduce readers to the exciting developments in the AI subfield of machine learning (ML). The book will summarize the types of problems machine learning can solve. Without machine learning, such solutions would be very difficult to accomplish.

- Help readers understand the importance of data as the critical input for any machine learning solution, and how to identify, organize, and architect the data required for ML. Strategies and techniques for the visualization and preprocessing of data will also be covered using available Java packages. The book will help readers who know Java to become more proficient in data science.

- Explore how to deploy ML solutions in conjunction with cloud service providers such as Google and Amazon.

- Focus exclusively on Java libraries and Java-based solutions for ML. The book will NOT cover other popular ML languages such as Python or C++.

- Focus on classic machine learning solutions. The book will not cover implementations for deep learning, which use neural networks. Deep learning is a topic that requires a complete text of its own for proper exploration.

- Provide readers an overview of ML algorithms. Rather than cover these algorithms from a mathematical viewpoint, the book will present a practical review of the algorithms and explain to readers which algorithm to select for a particular problem.

- Introduce readers to the most important Java-based ML platforms. The book will provide a deep dive into the popular Weka Java environments. The book will show readers how to port the latest Weka version to Android.

- Java developers have the advantage of easily transitioning to the Android Mobile platform. The book will show readers how to deploy ML apps for Android devices using the Weka API.

- One of the fastest growing sources of data is sensor data. Embedded devices often produce sensor data, enabling a significant opportunity to deploy ML solutions for these devices. The book will show readers how to implement ML solutions for sensor data using Java.

Audience

This book is intended for the following audiences:

- Developers looking to implement ML solutions for Java platforms

- Data scientists looking to explore Java implementation options

- Business decision makers looking to explore entry into machine learning for their organizations

The book will be of most value to experienced Java developers who have not implemented ML techniques before. The book will explain the various ML techniques that are now feasible due to recent advances in performance, storage, and algorithms.

The book will explain how these new techniques allow developers to achieve interesting new functionality that was not previously possible with traditional development approaches.

Conventions

Figures and Tables

Each chapter in the book uses a mix of figures and tables to explain the chapter's concepts. Figures and tables include identifiers with a chapter-derived sequence number displayed below or above them.

Figure P-1 shows an example figure.

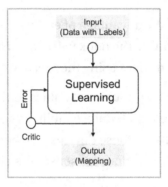

Figure P-1. *Sample Figure*

Table P-1 shows an example table.

Table P-1. *Sample Table*

Cluster Algorithms	Classify Algorithms
DBSCAN	Random Forest
EM	Naive Bayes

Technical Italics

The **technical italic font** represents technical terms. This includes Android-specific terms, URLs, or general technical terms. Reference URLs are sometimes included within each chapter.

Code Listings

Code examples in the book use a fixed-width font with line numbers. They represent key code discussed in the text that immediately precedes or follows the block.

Listing P-1. Sample Code Listing

```
01  // Define the dataset
02  newInstance.setDataset(dataUnpredicted);
03
04  // Predict the new sample
05  try {
06      double result = mClassifier.classifyInstance(newInstance);
07      String prediction = classes.get(new Double(result).intValue());
08      Toast.makeText(this, prediction, Toast.LENGTH_SHORT).show();
09  } catch (Exception e) {
10      // Oops, need to handle the Weka prediction exception
11      e.printStackTrace();
12  }
```

In order to help you locate the code within the associated project resources, the filename associated with the code block is included in the text preceding the code block.

Longer code blocks include the name of the project and source code file below them. Code blocks in the book are not always complete. Refer to the actual project source code to see the full code implementation.

Key Ideas or Points

Emphasized key points or ideas use the following format:

> *Three megatrends have paved the way for the Machine Learning revolution we are now experiencing:*
>
> *1) Explosion of data*
> *2) Access to highly scalable computing resources*
> *3) Advancement in algorithms*

Trademark and Software License

Android is a trademark of Google Inc.

Java is a trademark of Oracle Inc.

Eclipse is a trademark of The Eclipse Foundation.

Raspberry Pi is a trademark of the Raspberry Pi Foundation.

Weka is a trademark of The University of Waikato.

Software in this book written by the author carries the Apache 2.0 license, and you are free to use and modify the code in its entirety according to the terms of the license.

The Weka software is licensed under the GNU GPL 2.0 license.

The software written by the author includes the following Copyright notice:

```
01  /*
02   * Copyright (C) 2018 Mark Wickham
03   *
04   * Licensed under the Apache License, Version 2.0 (the "License");
05   * you may not use this file except in compliance with the License.
06   * You may obtain a copy of the License at
07   *
08   * http://www.apache.org/licenses/LICENSE-2.0
09   *
10   * Unless required by applicable law or agreed to in writing, software
11   * distributed under the License is distributed on an "AS IS" BASIS,
12   * WITHOUT WARRANTIES OR CONDITIONS OF ANY KIND, either implied...
13   * See the License for the specific language governing permissions and
14   * limitations under the License.
15   * For full details of the license, please refer to the link referenced
        above.
16   */
```

The software projects in the book can be downloaded by clicking the Download Source Code button located at the book's apress.com product page at **www.apress.com/ 9781484239506** or from the author's GitHub page at

https://github.com/wickapps/Practical-Java-ML

The Google Cloud Speech API Android project presented in Chapter 3 is copyright by Google Inc. and available on the Google GitHub page.

Summary of Projects

The book uses projects to demonstrate the key topics within each chapter. Table P-2 shows a summary of all projects in the book.

Table P-2. *Summary of Projects in the Book*

Chapter	Type	Source Code	Project Description
2	Desktop Browser	*d3_visualization.zip*	D3 Visualization: This project demonstrates how to produce data visualizations on the desktop browser using the D3 JavaScript library.
2	Android	*android_data_vis.zip*	Android Data Visualization: This Android app loads data and displays a visualization of the data within a WebView control. The application uses the D3 JavaScript library and demonstrates several useful visualizations for machine learning.
3	Android	Google Cloud Platform GitHub	Google Cloud Platform Cloud Speech API: This Android application demonstrates access to deep learning functionality through a publicly available API.
6	Eclipse	*android_weka_3-8-1.zip*	Weka Android Port: This Eclipse project ports the latest Weka version (stable 3.8.1) to Android, creating the *Android-Weka-3-8-1.jar* file. Android apps can then use the Weka API for loading, classifying, and clustering applications.
6	Android	*model_create.zip*	Weka Model Create: This Android project demonstrates how to load data files into Android and create a model for classification.

(*continued*)

Table P-2. (*continued*)

Chapter	Type	Source Code	Project Description
6	Android	*model_load.zip*	Weka Model Load: This Android project demonstrates how to load a pretrained model into Android. The model can classify samples. The app includes time stamping for model performance evaluation.
6	Raspberry Pi	*old_faithful.zip*	Raspberry Pi Old Faithful: This clustering project uses the Old Faithful geyser dataset and a Weka clustering model created in Chapter 5 to implement a clustering application for Old Faithful on the Raspberry Pi device.
6	Android	*activity_tracker.zip*	Android Activity Tracker: This large-scale classification project uses the PAMAP2_Dataset classification model from Chapter 5 to implement an Android Activity Tracking app.

A summary table showing the project details and key project files precedes each project in the book; see Table P-3. Note that not all of the project files are included in the summary table.

Table P-3. *Sample Project Summary Table*

Project: Creating Models

Source: *creating_models.zip*

Type: Android

Notes: A simple Android app to demonstrate use of the Android Weka API to create a classification model

File	Description
app->src->main->libs Android-Weka-3-8-1.jar	External jar file for the Android Weka library
app->src->main->java MainActivity.java	All of the project source code is in this Android activity.

Abbreviations

The book frequently uses abbreviations for the following terms:

- AI: Artificial intelligence

- DM: Data mining

- ML: Machine learning

- CML: Classic machine learning

- DL: Deep learning

- NLP: Natural language processing

- MLG: Machine learning gates, a methodology for developing ML apps

- RF: Random forest algorithm

- NB: Naive Bayes algorithm

- KNN: K-nearest neighbor algorithm

- SVM: Support vector machine algorithm

CHAPTER 1

Introduction

Chapter 1 establishes the foundation for the book.

It describes what the book will achieve, who the book is intended for, why machine learning (ML) is important, why Java makes sense, and how you can deploy Java ML solutions.

The chapter includes the following:

- A review all of the terminology of AI and its sub-fields including machine learning

- Why ML is important and why Java is a good choice for implementation

- Setup instructions for the most popular development environments

- An introduction to ML-Gates, a development methodology for ML

- The business case for ML and monetization strategies

- Why this book does not cover deep learning, and why that is a good thing

- When and why you may need deep learning

- How to think creatively when exploring ML solutions

- An overview of key ML findings

1.1 Terminology

As artificial intelligence and machine learning have seen a surge in popularity, there has arisen a lot of confusion with the associated terminology. It seems that everyone uses the terms differently and inconsistently.

1

© Mark Wickham 2018
M. Wickham, *Practical Java Machine Learning*, https://doi.org/10.1007/978-1-4842-3951-3_1

Some quick definitions for some of the abbreviations used in the book:

- Artificial intelligence (AI): Anything that pretends to be smart.

- Machine learning (ML): A generic term that includes the subfields of deep learning (DL) and classic machine learning (CML).

- Deep learning (DL): A class of machine learning algorithms that utilize neural networks.

- Reinforcement learning (RL): A supervised learning style that receives feedback, but not necessarily for each input.

- Neural networks (NN): A computer system modeled on the human brain and nervous system.

- Classic machine learning (CML): A term that more narrowly defines the set of ML algorithms that excludes the deep learning algorithms.

- Data mining (DM): Finding hidden patterns in data, a task typically performed by people.

- Machine learning gate (MLG): The book will present a development methodology called ML-Gates. The gate numbers start at ML-Gate 5 and conclude at ML-Gate 0. MLG3, for example, is the abbreviation for ML-Gate 3 of the methodology.

- Random Forest (RF) algorithm: A learning method for classification, regression and other tasks, that operates by constructing decision trees at training time.

- Naive Bayes (NB) algorithm: A family of "probabilistic classifiers" based on applying Bayes' theorem with strong (naive) independence assumptions between the features.

- K-nearest neighbor (KNN) algorithm: A non-parametric method used for classification and regression where the input consists of the k closest training examples in the feature space.

- Support vector machine (SVM) algorithm: A supervised learning model with associated learning algorithm that analyzes data used for classification and regression.

Much of the confusion stems from the various factions or "domains" that use these terms. In many cases, they created the terms and have been using them for decades within their domain.

Table 1-1 shows the domains that have historically claimed ownership to each of the terms. The terms are not new. Artificial intelligence is a general term. AI first appeared back in the 1970s.

Table 1-1. *AI Definitions and Domains*

Term	Definition	Domain
Statistics	Quantifies the data. DM, ML, DL all use statistics to make decisions.	Math departments
Artificial intelligence (AI)	The study of how to create intelligent agents. Anything that pretends to be smart. We program a computer to behave as an intelligent agent. It does not have to involve learning or induction.	Historical, Marketing, Trending.
Data mining (DM)	Explains and recognizes meaningful patterns. Unsupervised methods. **Discovers the hidden patterns** in your data that can be used by **people** to make decisions. A complete commercial process flow, often on large data sets (Big Data).	Business world, business intelligence
Machine learning (ML)	A large branch within AI in which we build models to **predict outcomes**. Uses algorithms and has a well-defined objective. We generalize existing knowledge to new data. It's about learning a model to classify objects.	Academic departments
Deep learning (DL)	Applies **neural networks** for ML. Pattern recognition is an important task.	Trending

The definitions in Table 1-1 represent my consolidated understanding after reading a vast amount of research and speaking with industry experts. You can find huge philosophical debates online supporting or refuting these definitions.

Do not get hung up on the terminology. Usage of the terms often comes down to domain perspective of the entity involved. A mathematics major who is doing research on DL algorithms will describe things differently than a developer who is trying to solve a problem by writing application software. The following is a key distinction from the definitions:

> *Data mining is all about **humans** discovering the hidden patterns in data, while **machine learning** automates the process and allows the **computer** to perform the work through the use of algorithms.*

It is helpful to think about each of these terms in context of "infrastructure" and "algorithms." Figure 1-1 shows a graphical representation of these relationships. Notice that statistics are the underlying foundation, while "artificial intelligence" on the right-hand side includes everything within each of the additional subfields of DM, ML, and DL.

> *Machine learning is all about the practice of **selecting** and **applying** **algorithms** to our data.*

I will discuss algorithms in detail in Chapter 3. The algorithms are the secret sauce that enables the machine to find the hidden patterns in our data.

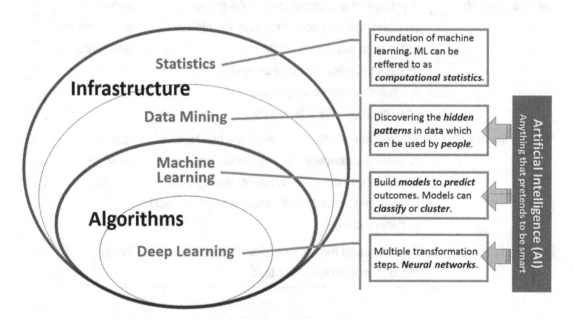

Figure 1-1. *Artificial intelligence subfield relationships*

1.2 Historical

The term "artificial intelligence" is hardly new. It has actually been in use since the 1970s. A quick scan of reference books will provide a variety of definitions that have in fact changed over the decades. Figure 1-2 shows a representation of 1970s AI, a robot named Shakey, alongside a representation of what it might look like today.

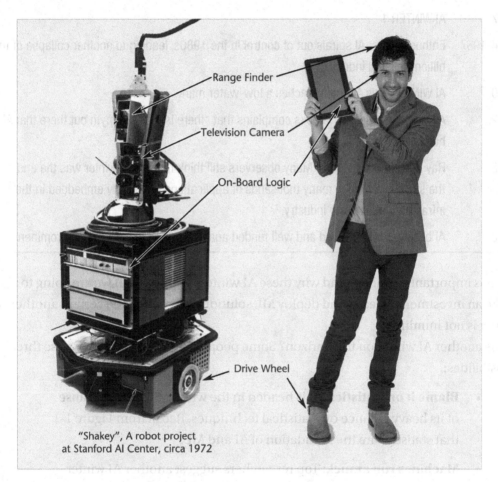

Range Finder

Television Camera

On-Board Logic

Drive Wheel

"Shakey", A robot project
at Stanford AI Center, circa 1972

Figure 1-2. *AI, past and present*

Most historians agree that there have been a couple of "AI winters." They represent periods of time when AI fell out of favor for various reasons, something akin to a technological "ice age." They are characterized by a trend that begins with pessimism in the research community, followed by pessimisms in the media, and finally followed by severe cutbacks in funding. These periods, along with some historical context, are summarized in Table 1-2.

Table 1-2. *History of AI and "Winter" Periods*

Period	Context
1974	The UK parliament publishes research that AI algorithms would grind to a halt on "real world" problems. This setback triggers global funding cuts including at DARPA. The crisis is blamed on "unrealistic predictions" and "increasing exaggeration" of the technology.
1977	AI WINTER 1
1984-1987	Enthusiasm for AI spirals out of control in the 1980s, leading to another collapse of the billion-dollar AI industry.
1990	AI WINTER 2 as AI again reaches a low-water mark.
2002	AI researcher Rodney Brooks complains that "there is a stupid myth out there that AI has failed."
2005	Ray Kurzweil proclaims, "Many observers still think that the AI winter was the end of the story ... yet today many thousands of applications are deeply embedded in the infrastructure of every industry."
2010	AI becomes widely used and well funded again. Machine learning gains prominence.

It is important to understand why these AI winters happened. If we are going to make an investment to learn and deploy ML solutions, we want to be certain another AI winter is not imminent.

Is another AI winter on the horizon? Some people believe so, and they raise three possibilities:

- **Blame it on statistics**: AI is headed in the wrong direction because of its heavy reliance on statistical techniques. Recall from Figure 1-1 that statistics are the foundation of AI and ML.

- **Machines run amuck**: Top researchers suggest another AI winter could happen because misuse of the technology will lead to its demise. In 2015, an open letter to ban development and use of autonomous weapons was signed by Elon Musk, Steven Hawking, Steve Wozniak, and 3,000 AI and robotics researchers.

- **Fake data**: Data is the fuel for machine learning (more about this in Chapter 2). Proponents of this argument suggest that ever increasing entropy will continue to degrade global data integrity to a point where ML algorithms will become invalid and worthless. This is a relevant argument in 2018. I will discuss the many types of data in Chapter 2.

It seems that another AI winter is not likely in the near future because ML is so promising and because of the availability of high-quality data with which we can fuel it.

Much of our existing data today is not high quality, but we can mitigate this risk by retaining control of the source data our models will rely upon.

Cutbacks in government funding caused the previous AI winters. Today, private sector funding is enormous. Just look at some of the VC funding being raised by AI startups. Similar future cutbacks in government support would no longer have a significant impact. For ML, it seems the horse is out of the barn for good this time around.

1.3 Machine Learning Business Case

Whether you are a freelance developer or you work for a large organization with vast resources available, you must consider the business case before you start to apply valuable resources to ML deployments.

Machine Learning Hype

ML is certainly not immune from hype. The book preface listed some of the recent hype in the media. The goal of this book is to help you overcome the hype and implement real solutions for problems.

ML and DL are not the only recent technology developments that suffer from excessive hype. Each of the following technologies has seen some recent degree of hype:

- Virtual reality (VR)

- Augmented reality (AR)

- Bitcoin

- Block chain

- Connected home

- Virtual assistants

- Internet of Things (IoT)

- 3D movies

- 4K television

- Machine learning (ML)

- Deep learning (DL)

Some technologies become widespread and commonly used, while other simply fade away. Recall that just a few short years ago 3D movies were expected to totally overtake traditional films for cinematic release. It did not happen.

It is important for us to continue to monitor the ML and DL technologies closely. It remains to be seen how things will play out, but ultimately, we can convince ourselves about the viability of these technologies by experimenting with them, building, and deploying our own applications.

Challenges and Concerns

Table 1-3 lists some of the top challenges and concerns highlighted by IT executives when asked what worries them the most when considering ML and DL initiatives. As with any IT initiative, there is an opportunity cost associated with implementing it, and the benefit derived from the initiative must outweigh the opportunity cost, that is, the cost of forgoing another potential opportunity by proceeding with AI/ML.

Fortunately, there are mitigation strategies available for each of the concerns. These strategies, summarized below, are even available to small organization and individual freelance developers.

Table 1-3. *Machine Learning Concerns and Mitigation Strategies*

ML Concern	Mitigation Strategy
Cost of IT infrastructure	Leverage cloud service providers such as Google GCP, Amazon AWS, Microsoft Azure
Not enough experienced staff	Even if we cannot hire data scientists, ML requires developers to start thinking like data scientists. This does not mean we suddenly require mathematics PhDs. Organizations can start by adopting a data-first methodology such as ML-Gates presented later in this chapter.
Cost of data or analytics platform	There are many very expensive data science platforms; however, we can start with classic ML using free open source software and achieve impressive results.
Insufficient data quality	There exists a great deal of low quality data. We can mitigate by relying less on "social" data and instead focusing on data we can create ourselves. We can also utilize data derived from sensors that should be free of such bias.
Insufficient data quantity	Self-generated data or sensor data can be produced at higher scale by controlling sampling intervals. Integrating data into the project at the early stages should be part of the ML methodology.

Using the above mitigation strategies, developers can produce some potentially groundbreaking ML software solutions with a minimal learning curve investment. It is a great time to be a software developer.

Next, I will take a closer look at ML data science platforms. Such platforms can help us with the goal of monetizing our machine learning investments. The monetization strategies can further alleviate some of these challenges and concerns.

Data Science Platforms

If you ask business leaders about their top ML objectives, you will hear variations of the following:

- Improve organizational efficiency

- Make predictive insights into future scenarios or outcomes

- Gain a competitive advantage by using AI/ML

- Monetize AI/ML

Regardless of whether you are an individual or freelance developer, monetization is one of the most important objectives.

> *Regardless of organizational size, monetizing ML solutions requires two building blocks: deploying a **data science platform**, and following a **ML development methodology**.*

When it comes to the data science platforms, there are myriad options. It is helpful to think about them by considering a "build vs. buy" decision process. Table 1-4 shows some of the typical questions you should ask when making the decision. The decisions shown are merely guidelines.

Table 1-4. *Data Science Platform: Build vs. Buy Decision*

Build vs. Buy Question	Decision
Is there a package that exactly solves your problem?	Yes: buy
Is there a package that solves many of your requirements? This is the common case and there is no an easy answer.	Undetermined
Is there an open source package you can consider?	Yes: build
Is the package too difficult to implement?	Yes: buy
Does your well-defined problem require deep learning?	No: maybe build
Is analytics a critical differentiator for your business?	Yes: maybe build
Is your analytics scenario unique?	Yes: build
Is a new kind of data available?	Yes: build
Does your domain require you to be agile?	Yes: build
Do you have access to the data science talent your problem requires? Do not sell yourself or your staff short; many developers pick up data science skills quickly.	No: buy

So what does it actually mean to "buy" a data science platform? Let's consider an example.

You wish to create a recommendation engine for visitors to your website. You would like to use machine learning to build and train a model using historical product description data and customer purchase activity on your website. You would then like to use the model to make real-time recommendations for your site visitors. This is a common ML use case. You can find offerings from all of the major vendors to help you implement this solution. Even though you will be "building" your own model using the chosen vendor's product, you are actually "buying" the solution from the provider. Table 1-5 shows how the pricing might break down for this project for several of the cloud ML providers.

Table 1-5. *Example ML Cloud Provider Pricing* https://cloud.google.com/ ml-engine/docs/pricing, https://aws.amazon.com/aml/pricing/, https:// azure.microsoft.com/en-us/pricing/details/machine-learning-studio/

Provider	Function	Pricing
Google Cloud ML Engine	Model building fees	$0.27 per hour (standard machine)
	Batch predictions	$0.09 per node hour
	Real-time predictions	$0.30 per node hour
Amazon Machine Learning (AML)	Model building fees	$0.42 per hour
	Batch predictions	$0.10 per 1000 predictions
	Real-time predictions	$.0001 per prediction
Microsoft Azure ML Studio	Model building fees	$10 per month, $1 per hour (standard)
	Batch predictions	$100 per month includes 100,000
	Real-time predictions	transactions (API)

In this example, you accrue costs because of the compute time required to build your model. With very large data sets and construction of deep learning models, these costs become significant.

Another common example of "buying" an ML solution is accessing a prebuilt model using a published API. You can use this method for image detection or natural language processing where huge models exist which you can leverage simply by calling the API with your input details, typically using JSON. You will see how to implement this trivial case later in the book. In this case, most of the service providers charge by the number of API calls over a given time period.

So what does it mean to "build" a data science platform? Building in this case refers to acquiring a software package that will provide the building blocks needed to implement your own AI or ML solution.

The following list shows some of the popular data science platforms:

- **MathWorks**: Creators of the legendary MATLAB package, MathWorks is a long-time player in the industry.

- **SAP**: The large database player has a complete big data services and consulting business.

- **IBM**: IBM offers Watson Studio and the IBM Data Science Platform products.

- **Microsoft**: Microsoft Azure provides a full spectrum of data and analytics services and resources.

- **KNIME**: KNIME analytics is a Java-based, open, intuitive, integrative data science platform.

- **RapidMiner**: A commercial Java-based solution.

- **H2O.ai**: A popular open source data science and ML platform.

- **Dataku**: A collaborative data science platform that allows users to prototype, deploy, and run at scale.

- **Weka**: The Java-based solution you will explore extensively in this book.

The list includes many of the popular data science platforms, and most of them are commercial data science platforms. The keyword is commercial. You will take a closer look at Rapidminer later in the book because it is Java based. The other commercial solutions are full-featured and have a range of pricing options from license-based to subscription-based pricing.

The good news is you do not have to make a capital expenditure in order to build a data science platform because there are some open source alternatives available. You will take a close look at the Weka package in Chapter 3. Whether you decide to build or buy, open source alternatives like Weka are a very useful way to get started because they allow you to build your solution while you are learning, without locking you into an expensive technology solution.

ML Monetization

One of the best reasons to add ML into your projects is increased potential to monetize. You can monetize ML in two ways: directly and indirectly.

- **Indirect monetization**: Making ML a part of your product or service.

- **Direct monetization**: Selling ML capabilities to customers who in turn apply them to solve particular problems or create their own products or services.

Table 1-6 highlights some of the ways you can monetize ML.

Table 1-6. *ML Monetization Approaches*

Strategy	Type	Description
AIaaS	Direct	AI as a Service, such as Salesforce Einstein or IBM Watson.
MLaaS	Direct	ML as a Service, such as the Google, Amazon, or Microsoft examples in Table 1-5.
Model API	Indirect	You can create models and then publish an API that will allow others to use your model to make their own predictions, for example.
NLPaaS	Direct	NLP as a Service. Chatbots such as Apple Siri, Microsoft Cortana, or Amazon Echo/Alexa. Companies such as Nuance Communications, Speechamatics, and Vocapia.
Integrated ML	Indirect	You can create a model that helps solve your problem and integrate that model into your project or app.

Many of the direct strategies employ DL approaches. In this book, the focus is mainly on the indirect ML strategies. You will implement several integrated ML apps later in the book. This strategy is indirect because the ML functionality is not visible to your end user.

Customers are not going to pay more just because you include ML in your application. However, if you can solve a new problem or provide them capability that was not previously available, you greatly improve your chances to monetize.

There is not much debate about the rapid growth of AI and ML. Table 1-7 shows estimates from Bank of America Merrill Lynch and Transparency Market Research. Both firms show a double-digit cumulative annual growth rate, or CAGR. This impressive CAGR is consistent with all the hype previously discussed.

Table 1-7. *AI and ML Explosive Growth*

Firm	Domain	Growth	CAGR
Bank of America Merrill Lynch	AI	US$58 bn in 2015 toUS$153 bn in 2020	27%
Transparency Market Research	ML	US$1.07 bn in 2106 toUS$19.86 bn in 2025	38%

These CAGRs represent impressive growth. Some of the growth is attributed to DL; however, you should not discount the possible opportunities available to you with CML, especially for mobile devices.

The Case for Classic Machine Learning on Mobile

Classic machine learning is not a very commonly used term. I will use the term to indicate that we are excluding deep learning. Figure 1-3 shows the relationship. These two approaches employ different algorithms, and I will discuss them in Chapter 4.

This book is about implementing CML for widely available computing devices using Java. In a sense, we are going after the "low-hanging fruit." CML is much easier to implement than DL, but many of the functions we can achieve are no less astounding.

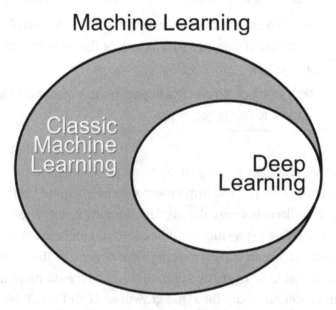

Figure 1-3. *Classic machine learning relationship diagram*

There is a case for mastering the tools of CML before attempting to create DL solutions. Table 1-8 highlights some of the key differences between development and deployment of CML and DL solutions.

Table 1-8. *Comparison of Classic Machine Learning and Deep Learning*

Classic machine learning	Deep learning
Algorithms	
Algorithms are mostly commoditized. You do not need to spend a lot of time choosing the best algorithm or tweaking algorithms. Algorithms are easier to interpret and understand.	There is a lot of new research behind neural network algorithms. A lot of theory is involved and a lot of tweaking is required to find the best algorithm for your application.
Data requirements	
Modest amounts of data are required. You can generate your own data in certain applications.	Huge amounts of data are required to train DL models. Most entities lack sufficient data to create their own DL models.
Performance	
Sufficient performance for many mobile, web app, or embedded device environments.	The recent growth in deep learning neural network algorithms is largely due to their ability to outperform CML algorithms.
Language	
Many Java tools are available, both open source and commercial.	Most DL libraries and tools are Python or C++ based, with the exception of Java-based DL4J. There are often Java wrappers available for some of the popular C++ DL engines.
Model creation	
Model size can be modest. Possible to create models on desktop environments. Easy to embed in mobile devices or embedded devices.	Model size can be huge. Difficult to embed models into mobile apps. Large CPU/GPU resources required to create models.

(continued)

Table 1-8. (*continued*)

Classic machine learning	Deep learning
Typical use cases	
Regression	Image classification
Clustering	Speech
Classification	Computer vision
Specific use cases for your data	Playing games
	Self-driving cars
	Pattern recognition
	Sound synthesis
	Art creation
	Photo classification
	Anomaly (fraud) detection
	Behavior analysis
	Recommendation engine
	Translation
	Natural language processing
	Facial recognition
Monetization	
Indirect ML	Model APIsMLaaS

For mobile devices and embedded devices, CML makes a lot of sense. CML outperforms DL for smaller data sets, as shown on the left side of the chart in Figure 1-7.

It is possible to create CML models with a single modern CPU in a reasonable amount of time. CML started on the desktop. It does not require huge compute resources such as multiple CPU/GPU, which is often the case when building DL solutions.

The interesting opportunity arises when you build your models on the desktop and then deploy them to the mobile device either directly or through API interface. Figure 1-4 shows a breakdown of funding by AI category according to Venture Scanning.

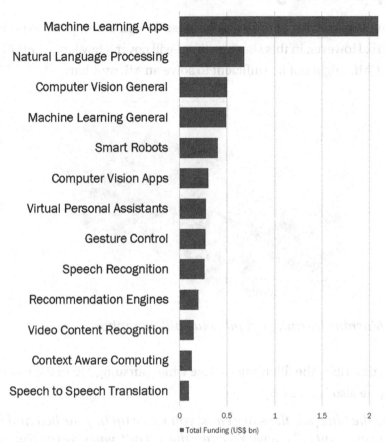

Figure 1-4. *Funding by AI category*

The data show that ML for mobile apps has approximately triple the funding of the next closest area, NLP. The categories included show that many of the common DL fields, such as computer vision, NLP, speech, and video recognition, have been included as a specific category. This allows us to assume that a significant portion of the ML apps category is classic machine learning.

1.4 Deep Learning

I will not cover deep learning in this book because we can accomplish so much more easily with CML. However, in this short section I will cover a few key points of DL to help identify when CML might not be sufficient to solve an ML problem.

Figure 1-5. *Machine learning red pill/blue pill metaphor*

Morpheus described the dilemma we face when pursuing ML in the motion picture "The Matrix" (see also Figure 1-5):

> *"You take the blue pill, the story ends; you wake up in your bed and believe whatever you want to believe. You take the red pill, you stay in Wonderland, and I show you how deep the rabbit hole goes."*

Deep learning is a sort of Wonderland. It is responsible for all of the hype we have in the field today. However, it has achieved that hype for a very good reason.

You will often hear it stated the DL operates at scale. What does this mean exactly? It is a performance argument, and performance is obviously very important. Figure 1-6 shows a relationship between performance and data set size for CML and DL.

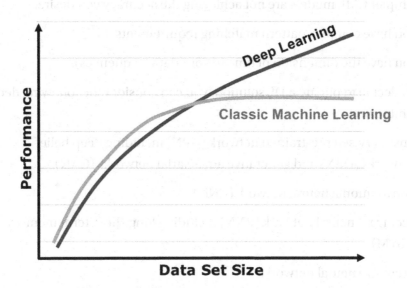

Figure 1-6. *Deep learning operating at scale*

The chart shows that CML slightly outperforms DL for smaller data set sizes. The question is, how small is small? When we design ML apps, we need to consider which side of the point of inflection the data set size resides. There is no easy answer. If there were, we would place the actual numbers on the x-axis scale. It depends on your specific situation and you will need to make the decision about which approach to use when you design the solution.

Fortunately, we have tools that enable us to define the performance of our CML models. In Chapters 4 and 5, you will look at how to employ the Weka workbench to show you if increasing your data set size actually leads to increased performance of the model.

Identifying DL Applications

Deep learning has demonstrated superior results versus CML in many specific areas including speech, natural language processing, computer vision, playing games, self-driving cars, pattern recognition, sound synthesis, art creation, photo classification, irregularity (fraud) detection, recommendation engine, behavior analysis, translation, just to name a few.

As you gain experience with ML, you begin to develop a feel for when a project is a good candidate for DL.

Deep networks work well when

- Simpler CML models are not achieving the accuracy you desire.

- You have complex pattern matching requirements.

- You have the dimension of time in your data (sequences).

If you do decide to pursue a DL solution, you can consider the following deep network architectures:

- Unsupervised pre-trained network (UPN) including deep belief networks (DBN) and generative adversarial networks (GAN)

- Convolutional neural network (CNN)

- Recurrent neural network (RNN) including long short-term memory (LSTM)

- Recursive neural networks

I will talk more about algorithms in Chapter 4. When designing CML solutions, you can start by identifying the algorithm class of CML you are pursuing, such as classification or clustering. Then you can easily experiment with algorithms within the class to find the best solution. In DL, it is not as simple. You need to match your data to specific network architectures, a topic that is beyond the scope of this book.

While building deep networks is more complicated and resource intensive, as described in Table 1-8, tuning deep networks is equally challenging. This is because, regardless of the DL architecture you choose, you define deep learning networks using neural networks that are comprised of a large number of parameters, layers, and weights. There are many methods used to tune these networks including the methods in Table 1-9.

Table 1-9. *Tuning Methods for DL Networks*

Tuning methods for DL neural networks	
Back propagation	Stochastic gradient descent
Learning rate decay	Dropout
Max pooling	Batch normalization
Long short-term memory	Skipgram
Continuous bag of words	Transfer learning

As the table suggests, DL is complicated. The AI engines available for DL try to simplify the process. Table 1-10 shows many of the popular AI engines that include DL libraries. In this book, you will focus on CML solutions for Java developers.

When you create DL solutions there are not as many Java tools and libraries available. DL4J and Spark ML are the two most common Java-based packages that can handle DL. DL4J is built from the ground up with DL in mind, whereas the popular Spark open source project has recently added some basic DL capabilities. Some of the excellent C++ libraries do provide Java wrappers, such as Apache MXNet and OpenCV.

Table 1-10. *AI Engines with Deep Learning Libraries*

Package	Description	Language
Theano	Powerful general-purpose tool for mathematical programming. Developed to facilitate deep learning. High-level language and compiler for GPU.	Python
Tensor Flow	Library for all types of numerical computation associated with deep learning. Heavily inspired by Theano. Data flow graphs represent the ways multi-dimensional arrays (tensors) communicate. (Google)	C++ and Python
CNTK	Computational Network Toolkit. Release by Microsoft Research under a permissive license.	C++
Caffe	Clean and extensible design. Based on the AlexNet that won the 2012 ImageNet challenge. (Facebook support)	C++ and Python
DL4J	Java-based open source deep learning library (Apache 2.0 license). Uses a multi-dimensional array class with linear algebra and matrix manipulation. (Skymind)	Java
Torch	Open source, scientific computing framework optimized for use with GPUs.	C
Spark MLlib	A fast and general engine for large-scale distributed data processing. MLlib is the machine learning library. Huge user base. DL support is growing.	Java
Apache MXNet	Open source Apache project. Used by AWS. State of the art models: CNN and LSTM. Scalable. Founded by University of Washington and Carnegie Mellon University.	C++Java Wrapper
Keras	Powerful, easy-to-use library for developing and evaluating DL models. Best of Theano and Tensor flow.	Python
OpenCV	Open source computer vision library that can be integrated for Android.	C++Java Wrapper

While it is entirely possibly that DL can solve your unique problem, this book wants to encourage you to think about solving your problem, at least initially, by using CML. The bottom line before we move onto ML methodology and some of the technical setup topics is the following:

> *Deep learning is amazing, but in this book, we resist the temptation and favor classic machine learning, simply because there are so many equally amazing things it can accomplish with far less trouble.*

In the rest of the book, we will choose the blue pill and stay in the comfortable simulated reality of the matrix with CML.

1.5 ML-Gates Methodology

Perhaps the biggest challenge of producing ML applications is training yourself to think differently about the design and architecture of the project. You need a new data-driven methodology. Figure 1-7 introduces the ML-Gates. The methodology uses these six gates to help organize CML and DL development projects. Each project begins with ML-Gate 6 and proceeds to completion at ML-Gate 0. The ML-Gates proceed in a decreasing order. Think of them as leading to the eventual launch or deployment of the ML project.

Machine Learning
ML-Gates Methodology

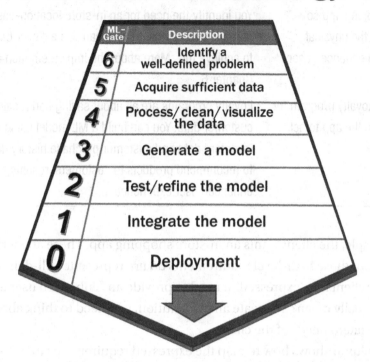

ML-Gate	Description
6	Identify a well-defined problem
5	Acquire sufficient data
4	Process/clean/visualize the data
3	Generate a model
2	Test/refine the model
1	Integrate the model
0	Deployment

Figure 1-7. *ML-Gates, a machine learning development methodology*

As developers, we write a lot of code. When we take on new projects, we typically just start coding until we reach the deliverable product. With this approach, we typically end up with heavily coded apps.

With ML, we want to flip that methodology on its head. We instead are trying to achieve data-heavy apps with minimal code. Minimally coded apps are much easier to support.

ML-Gate 6: Identify the Well-Defined Problem

It all starts with a well-defined problem. You need to think a bit more narrowly in this phase than you do when undertaking traditional non-ML projects. This can result in creating ML modules that you integrate into the larger system.

To illustrate this, let's consider an example project with client requirements.

For the project, you map the client requirements to well-defined ML solutions. Table 1-11 shows the original client requirements mapped to the ML models.

Table 1-11. *Mapping Requirements to ML Solution*

Initial client requirement	Well-defined ML solution
R1: Create a shopping app so customers inside the physical store will have an enhanced user experience.	You identify the need for an in-store location-based solution to make this app useful. You can use a clever CML approach to achieve this. More about the implementation at the end of Chapter 6.
R2: Implement a loyalty program for shoppers who use the app to help increase sales.	Loyalty programs are all about saving and recalling customer data. You can build a ML model using product inventory data and customer purchase history data to recommend products to customers, resulting in an enhanced user experience.

In this example, the client wants an in-store shopping app. These are perfectly valid requirements, but these high-level requirements do not represent well-defined ML problems. Your client has "expressed" a need to provide an "enhanced user experience." What does that really mean? To create an ML solution, you need to think about the unexpressed or latent needs of the client.

The right column shows how to map the expressed requirements to well-defined ML solutions. In this case, you are going to build two separate ML models. You are going to need data for these models, and that leads you to ML-Gate 5.

ML-Gate 5: Acquire Sufficient Data

Data is the key to any successful ML app. In MLG5, you need to acquire the data. Notice this is happening well before you write any code. There are several approaches for acquiring data. You have several options and I will discuss the following in detail in Chapter 2:

- Purchase the data from a third party.

- Use publicly available data sets.

- Use your own data set.

- Generate new static data yourself.

- Stream data from a real-time source.

ML-Gate 4: Process/Clean/Visualize the Data

Once you have a well-defined problem and sufficient data, it is time to architect your solution. The next three gates cover this activity. In MLG4, you need to process, clean, and then visualize your data.

MLG4 is all about preparing your data for the model construction. You need to consider techniques such as missing values, normalization, relevance, format, data types, and data quantity.

Visualization is an important aspect because you strive to be accountable for your data. Data that is not properly preprocessed can lead to errors when you apply CML or DL algorithms to the data. For this reason, MLG4 is very important. The old saying about garbage in, garbage out is something you must avoid.

ML-Gate 3: Generate a Model

With your data prepared, MLG3 is where you actually create the model. At MLG3, you will make the initial decision on which algorithm to use.

In Chapter 4, I will cover the Java-based CML environments that can generate models. I will cover how to create models and how to measure the performance of your models.

One of the powerful design patterns you will use to build models offline for later use in Java projects. Chapter 5 will cover the import and export of "pre-built" models.

At MLG3, you also must consider version control and updating approaches for your models. This aspect of managing models is just as important as managing code updates in non-ML software development.

ML-Gate 2: Test/Refine the Model

With the initial model created, MLG2 allows you to test and refine the model. It is here that you are checking the performance of the model to confirm that it will meet your prediction requirements.

Inference is the process of using the model to make predictions. During this process, you may find that you need to tweak or optimize the chosen algorithm. You may find that you need to change your initial algorithm of choice. You might even discover that CML is not providing the desired results and you need to consider a DL approach.

Passing ML-Gate 2 indicates that the model is ready, and it is time to move on to MLG1 to integrate the model.

ML-Gate 1: Integrate the Model

At MLG1, it is time to write actual production code. Notice how far back in the methodology you have pushed the actual code writing. The good news is that you will not have to write as much code as you normally do because the trained model you have created will accomplish much of the heavy lifting.

Much of the code you need to write at MLG1 handles the "packaging" of the model. Later in this chapter, I will discuss potential target environments that can also affect how the model needs to be packaged.

Typically, you create CML models at MLG3/4 with training data and then utilize the model to make predictions. At MLG1, you might write additional code to acquire new real-time data to feed into the model to output a prediction. In Chapter 6, you will see how to gather sensor data from devices to feed into the model.

MLG1 is where you recognize the coding time savings. It usually only take a few lines of code to open a prebuilt model and make a new prediction.

This phase of the methodology also includes system testing of the solution.

ML-Gate 0: Deployment

At MLG0, it is time for deployment of the completed ML solution. You have several options to deploy your solution because of the cross-platform nature of Java, including

- Release a mobile app though an app store such as Google Play.

- Ship a standalone software package to your clients.

- Provide the software online through web browser access.

- Provide API access to your solution.

Regardless of how you deploy your ML solutions, the important thing to remember at MLG0 is that "ship it and forget it" is wrong.

When we create models, we have to recognize that they should not become static entities that never change. We need a mechanism to update them and keep them relevant. ML models help us to avoid the downside of code-heavy apps, but instead we must effectively manage the models we create so they do not become outdated.

Methodology Summary

You now have covered the necessary background on CML, and you have a methodology you can use for creating CML applications.

You have probably heard that saying "When you are a hammer, everything looks like a nail." After becoming proficient in CML and adopting a data-driven methodology, you soon discover that most problems have an elegant ML solution for at least for some aspect of the problem.

Next, you will look at the setup required for Java projects in the book, as well as one final key ingredient for ML success: creative thinking.

1.6 The Case for Java

There is always a raging debate about which programming language is the best, which language you should learn, what's the best language for kids to start coding in, which languages are dying, which new languages represent the future or programming, etc.

Java is certainly a big part of these debates. There are many who question the ability of Java to meet the requirements of a modern developer. Each programming language has its own strengths and weaknesses.

Exercises in Programming Style by Christina Videira Lopes is interesting because the author solves a common programming problem in a huge variety of languages while highlighting the strengths and weaknesses of each style. The book illustrates that we can use any language to solve a given problem. As programmers, we need to find the best approach given the constraints of the chosen language. Java certainly has its pro and cons, and next I will review some reasons why Java works well for CML solutions.

Java Market

Java has been around since 1995 when it was first released by Sun Microsystems, which was later acquired by Oracle. One of the benefits of this longevity is the market penetration it has achieved. The Java market share (Figure 1-8) is the single biggest reason to target the Java language for CML applications.

Figure 1-8. *Java market*

Java applications compile to bytecode and can run on any Java virtual machine (JVM) regardless of computer architecture. It is one of the most popular languages with many millions of developers, particularly for client-server web applications.

When you install Java, Oracle is quick to point out that three billion devices run Java. It is an impressive claim. If we drill down deeper into the numbers, they do seem to be justified. Table 1-12 shows some more granular detail of the device breakdown.

Table 1-12. *Devices Running Java*

Device	Count
Desktops running Java	1.1 billion
JRE downloads each year	930 million
Mobile phones running Java	3 billion
Blue-ray players	100% run Java
Java cards	1.4 billion manufactured each year
Proprietary boxes	Unknown number of devices which include set-top boxes, printers, web cams, game consoles, car navigation systems, lottery terminals, parking meters, VOIP phone, utility meters, industrial controls, etc.

The explosion of Android development and the release of Java 8 helped Java to gain some of its market dominance.

Java's massive scale is the main reason I prefer it as the language of choice for CML solutions. Developers only need to master one language to produce working CML solutions and deploy them to a huge target audience.

For your target environments, the focus will be on the following three areas that make up the majority of installed Java devices:

- **Desktops running Java**: This category includes personal computers that can run standalone Java programs or browsers on those computers that can run Java applets.

- **Mobile phones running Java**: Android mobile devices make up a large part of this category, which also includes low-cost feature phones. One of the key findings of ML is the importance of data, and the mobile phone is arguably the greatest data collection device ever created.

- **Java cards**: This category represents the smallest of the Java platforms. Java cards allow Java applets to run on embedded devices. Device manufacturers are responsible for integrating embedded Java and it is not available for download or installation by consumers.

Java Versions

Oracle supplies the Java programming language for end users and for developers:

- JRE (Java Runtime Environment) is for end users who wish to install Java so they can run Java applications.

- JDK (Java SE Developer Kit) Includes the JRE plus additional tools for developing, debugging, and monitoring Java applications.

There are four platforms of the Java programming language:

- Java Platform, Standard Edition (Java SE)

- Java Platform, Enterprise Edition (Java EE), is built on top of Java SE and includes tools for building network applications such as JSON, Java Servlet, JavaMail, and WebSocket. Java EE is developed and released under the Java Community Process.

- Java Platform, Micro Edition (Java ME), is a small footprint virtual machine for running applications on small devices.

- Java FX is for creating rich internet applications using a lightweight API.

All of the Java platforms consist of a Java Virtual Machine (JVM) and an application programming interface (API).

Table 1-13 summarizes the current Java releases.

Table 1-13. *Latest Supported Java Releases*

Release	Description
Java 8 SE build 171	Currently supported long-term-support (LTS) version. Introduces lambda expressions
Java 10 SE 10.0.1	Currently supported rapid release version. Released March 20 2018. Includes 12 new major features. Latest update was 171.
Android SDK	Alternative Java software platform used for developing Android apps. Includes its own GUI extensive system and mobile device libraries. Android does not provide the full Java SE standard library. Android SDK supports Java 6 and some Java 7 features.

The most recent versions of Java have addressed some of the areas where the language was lagging behind some of the newer, more trendy languages. Notably, Java 8 includes the far-reaching feature known as the ***lambda expression*** along with a new operator (->) and a new syntax element. Lambda expressions add functional programming features and can help to simplify and reduce the amount of code required to create certain constructs.

In the book, you will not be using lambda expression, nor will you use any of the many new features added to the language in Java 10. Nonetheless, it is best to run with the latest updates on either the long-term support release of Java 8 or the currently supported rapid release of Java 10.

If you are looking for a comprehensive Java book, ***Java, The Complete Reference*** Tenth Edition from Oracle, which weighs in at over 1,300 pages, is an excellent choice. It covers all things Java. When it comes to Java performance tuning, ***Java Performance*** by Charlie Hunt and John Binu is the 720-page definitive guide for getting the most out of Java performance.

Installing Java

Before installing Java, you should first uninstall all older versions of Java from your system. Keeping old versions of Java on your system is a security risk. Uninstalling older versions ensures that Java applications will run with the latest security and performance environment.

The main Java page and links for all the platform downloads are available at the following URLs:

```
https://java.com/en/
https://java.com/en/download/manual.jsp
```

Java is available for any platform you require. Once you decide which load you need, proceed to download and install. For the projects in this book, it is recommended to install the latest stable release of Java 8 SE. For the Android projects, allow Android Studio to manage your Java release. Android Studio will typically use the latest stable release of Java 7 until the Android team adds support for Java 8.

Figure 1-9 shows the main Java download page.

Figure 1-10 shows the Java installation.

Figure 1-11 shows the completion of the installation.

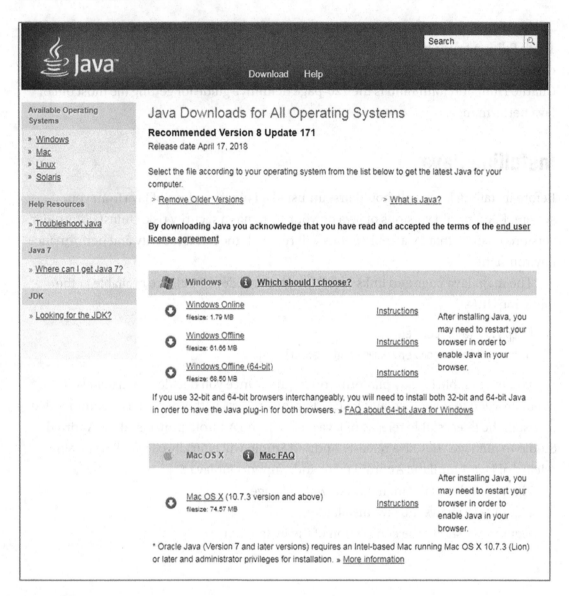

Figure 1-9. *Downloading Java*

Figure 1-10. *Installing Java*

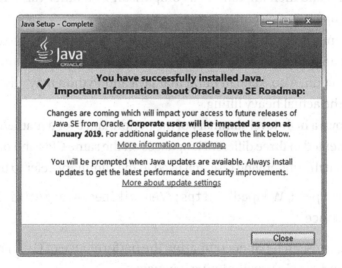

Figure 1-11. *Successful Java SE installation*

Java Performance

Steve Jobs once famously said about Java, "It's this big, heavyweight ball and chain."
Of course, Apple was never a big fan of the language. One of the results or perhaps the
reason for Java's longevity is the support and improvements added to the language over
the years. The latest versions of Java offer far more features and performance than the
early versions.

One of the reasons developers have been hesitant to choose Java for ML solutions is the concern over performance.

Asking which language is "faster" or offers better performance is not really a useful question. It all depends, of course. The performance of a language depends on its runtime, the OS, and the actual code. When developers ask, "Which language offers the best performance for machine learning?" we really should be asking, "Which platform should I use to accomplish the training and building of machine learning models the most quickly and easily?"

Creating ML models using algorithms is CPU intensive, especially for DL applications. This book is about Java, but if you research ML, you know that Python and C++ are also very popular languages for ML. Creating a fair comparison of the three languages for ML is not easy, but many researchers have tried to do this and you can learn from their findings. Since ML is algorithm-based, they often try to choose a standard algorithm and then implement a comparison with other variables being equal, such as CPU and operating system.

Java performance is the hardest of the languages to measure because of several factors including unoptimized code, Java's JIT compilation approach, and the famous Java garbage collection. Also, keep in mind that Java and Python may rely on wrappers to C++ libraries for the actual heavy lifting.

Table 1-14 shows a high-level summary of the performance for a mathematical algorithm implemented in three different languages on the same CPU and operating system. To learn more about the underlying research used in the summary, refer to these sources:

- Program Speed, Wikipedia, `https://en.wikipedia.org/wiki/Java_performance`

- A Google research paper comparing the performance of C++, Java, Scala, and the Go programming language:

  `https://days2011.scala-lang.org/sites/days2011/files/ws3-1-Hundt.pdf`

- Comparative Study of Six Programming Languages:

  `https://arxiv.org/ftp/arxiv/papers/1504/1504.00693.pdf`

- Ivan Zahariev's blog:

  `https://blog.famzah.net/2016/02/09/cpp-vs-python-vs-perl-vs-php-performance-benchmark-2016/`

Table 1-14. Language Performance Comparison - Mathematical Algorithms

Language	% Slower than C++	Note
C++	-	C++ compiles to native, so it is first.
Java 8	15%	Java produces bytecode for platform independence. Java's "kryptonite" has been its garbage collection (GC) overhead. There have been many improvements made to the Java GC algorithms over the years.
Kotlin	15+%	Kotlin also produces Java Virtual Machine (JVM) bytecode. Typically, Kotlin is as fast as Java.
Python	55%	Python has high-level data types and dynamic typing, so the runtime has to work harder than Java.

Table 1-14 is certainly not an exhaustive performance benchmark, but does provide some insight to relative performance with possible explanation for the differences.

When you create prebuilt models for your ML solutions, it is more important to focus on the data quality and algorithm selection than programming language. You should use the programming language that most easily and accurately allows you to express the problem you are trying to solve.

Java skeptics frequently ask, "Is Java a suitable programming language for implementing deep learning?" The short answer: absolutely! It has sufficient performance, and all the required math and statistical libraries are available. Earlier in the chapter, I listed DL4J as the main Java package written entirely in Java. DL4J is a fantastic package and its capabilities rival all of the large players in DL. Bottom line: With multi-node computing available to us in the cloud, we have the option to easily add more resources to computationally intensive operations. Scalability is one of the great advantages provided by cloud-based platforms I will discuss in Chapter 2.

1.7 Development Environments

There are many IDEs available to Java developers. Table 1-15 shows the most popular choices for running Java on the desktop or device. There are also some online browser-based cloud Java IDEs such as Codenvy, Eclipse Che, and Koding, which I will not cover.

Table 1-15. *Java IDE Summary*

IDE Name	Features
Android Studio	Android-specific development environment from Google. It has become the de facto IDE for Android. Offers a huge number of useful development and debugging tools.
IntelliJ IDEA	Full featured, professional IDE. Annual fee. Many developers love IntelliJ. Android Studio was based on IntelliJ.
Eclipse	Free open source IDE. Eclipse public license. Supports Git. Huge number of plugins available.
BlueJ	Lightweight development environment. Comes packaged with Raspberry Pi.
NetBeans	Free open source IDE, alternative to Eclipse. The open source project is moving to Apache, which should increase its popularity.

The book uses two development environments for the projects depending on the target platform:

- Google's **Android Studio** helps developers create apps for mobile devices running Android.

- The **Eclipse** IDE for Java projects that do not target Android mobile devices. This includes Java programs that target the desktop, the browser, or non-Android devices such as the Raspberry Pi.

Android Studio

Google makes it easy to get started with Android Studio. The latest stable release build is version 3.1.2 available April 2018. The download page is `https://developer.android.com/studio/`.

Figure 1-12 shows the available platforms. Note that the files and disk requirements are large. The download for 64-bit Windows is over 700MB.

Android Studio downloads

Platform	Android Studio package	Size	SHA-256 checksum
Windows (64-bit)	android-studio-ide-173.4720617-windows.exe Recommended	758 MB	e2695b73300ec398325cc5f242c6ecfd6e84db190b7d48e6e78a8b0115d49b0d
	android-studio-ide-173.4720617-windows.zip No .exe installer	854 MB	e8903b443dd73ec120c5a967b2c7d9db82d8ffb4735a39d3b979d22c61e882ad
Windows (32-bit)	android-studio-ide-173.4720617-windows32.zip No .exe installer	854 MB	c238f54f795db03f9d4a4077464bd9303113504327d5878b27c9e965676c6473
Mac	android-studio-ide-173.4720617-mac.dmg	848 MB	4665cb18c838a3695a417cebc7751cbe658a297a9d6c01cbd9e9a1979b8b167e
Linux	android-studio-ide-173.4720617-linux.zip	853 MB	13f290279790df570bb6592f72a979a495f7591960a378abea7876ece7252ec1

See the **Android Studio release notes**.

Command line tools only

If you do not need Android Studio, you can download the basic Android command line tools below. You can use the included `sdkmanager` to download other SDK

These tools are included in Android Studio.

Platform	SDK tools package	Size	SHA-256 checksum
Windows	sdk-tools-windows-3859397.zip	132 MB	7f6037d3a7d6789b4fdc06ee7af041e071e9860c51f66f7a4eb5913df9871fd2
Mac	sdk-tools-darwin-3859397.zip	82 MB	4a81754a760fce88cba74d69c364b05b31c53d57b26f9f82355c61d5fe4b9df9
Linux	sdk-tools-linux-3859397.zip	131 MB	444e22ce8ca0f67353bda4b85175ed3731cae3ffa695ca18119cbacef1c1bea0

Figure 1-12. *Android Studio downloads*

Android Studio has really been improving the last couple of years. The full featured development environment for Android includes

- Kotlin version 1.2.30

- Performance tools

- Real-time network profiler

- Visual GUI layout editor

- Instant run

- Fast emulator

- Flexible Gradle build system

- Intelligent code editor

Figure 1-13 shows the show the Android Studio installation setup.

Figure 1-13. *Android Studio install*

Figure 1-14 shows the shows the Android Studio opening banner including the current version 3.1.2.

Figure 1-14. *Android Studio Version 3.1.2*

Android Studio uses the ***SDK Manager*** to manage SDK packages. SDK packages are available for download. The SDK packages are required to compile and release your app for a specific Android version. The most recent SDK release is Android 8.1 (API level 27), also known as Oreo. Figure 1-15 shows the Android SDK Manager.

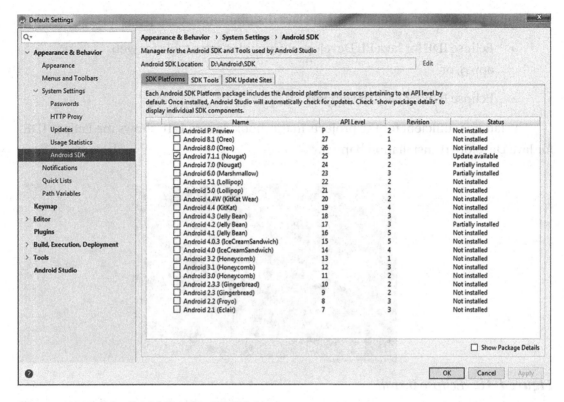

Figure 1-15. *Android Studio SDK Manager*

> *Always keep an eye out for updates to both Android Studio and the SDK platforms you use. Google frequently releases updates, and you want your development environment to stay current.*

This is especially important for mobile development when end users are constantly buying the latest devices.

Eclipse

Android mobile apps are a big part of our CML strategy, but not the only target audience we have available to us. For non-Android projects, we need a more appropriate development environment.

Eclipse is the versatile IDE available from the Eclipse foundation. The download page is https://eclipse.org/downloads. Eclipse is available for all platforms. The most recent version is Oxygen.3a and the version is 4.7.3a. Similar to Android, Eclipse uses proceeds through the alphabet and, like Android, is also currently at "O."

Similar to the options available for the Java distributions, developers can choose either

- Eclipse IDE for Java EE Developers (includes extra tools for web apps), or

- Eclipse IDE for Java Developers

The latter is sufficient for the projects in this book. Figure 1-16 shows the Eclipse IDE for Java Developers installation banner.

Figure 1-16. *Eclipse install*

Eclipse makes it easy to get started with your Java projects. Once installed, you will have the option to

- Create new projects.

- Import projects from existing source code.

- Check out or clone projects from the Git source code control system.

The Git checkout feature is very useful, and you can use that option to get started quickly with the book projects. Figure 1-17 shows the Eclipse IDE for Java Developers startup page with the various options.

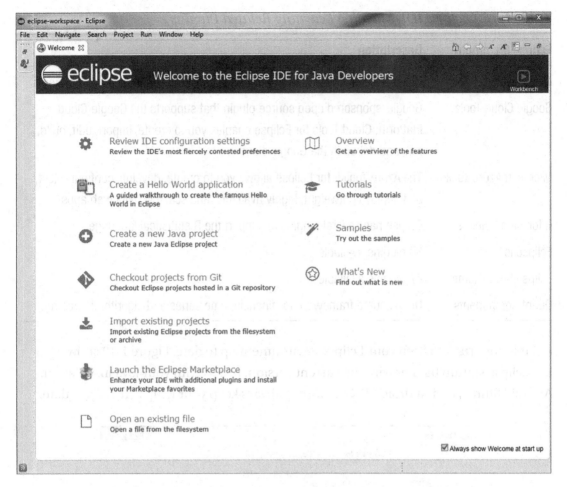

Figure 1-17. *Eclipse IDE for Java developers*

One of the big advantages of Eclipse is the huge number of plugins available. There are plugins for almost every imaginable integration. Machine learning is no exception. Once you get a feel for the types of ML projects you are producing, you may find the Eclipse plugins in Table 1-16 to be useful. For the book projects, you will use a basic Eclipse installation without plugins.

Table 1-16. *Eclipse IDE Machine Learning Related Plugins*

Eclipse ML plugin	Description
AWS Toolkit	Helps Java developers integrate to the AWS services to their Java projects.
Google Cloud Tools	Google-sponsored open source plugin that supports the Google Cloud Platform. Cloud Tools for Eclipse enables you to create, import, edit, build, run, and debug in the Google cloud.
Microsoft Azure Toolkit	The Azure Toolkit for Eclipse allows you to create, develop, configure, test, and deploy lightweight, highly available, and scalable Java web apps.
R for Data Science	Eclipse has several plugins to support the R statistical language.
Eclipse IoT	80 plugins available.
Eclipse SmartHome	47 plugins available.
Quant Components	Open source framework for financial time series and algorithmic trading.

It is important to keep your Eclipse environment up to date. Figure 1-18 shows the Eclipse startup banner with the current version. Just as with your Java installation, Android Studio, and Android SDK platforms, always keep your Eclipse IDE up to date.

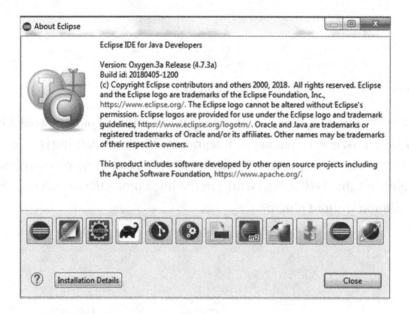

Figure 1-18. *Eclipse IDE for Java developers*

Net Beans IDE

The *Net Beans* IDE is an alternative for Java developers who do not want to use Eclipse. The download page is `https://netbeans.org.downloads`.

Eclipse has gained more users over the years, but NetBeans still has its supporters. Recently, Oracle announced that it would turn over NetBeans to the Apache Foundation for future support. Fans of NetBeans see this as a positive development because now the long-time supporters of NetBeans will be able to continue its development.

I will not be using NetBeans in the book, but you are free to do so. The projects should import easily. It is an IDE worth keeping an eye on in the future. Figure 1-19 shows the NetBeans main page.

Figure 1-19. *NetBeans IDE*

1.8 Competitive Advantage

Earlier in this chapter, you developed a strategy to deploy CML apps for Java-based devices. You also established a methodology, the ML-Gates for data-driven development. The goal is to create a competitive advantage and monetize your ML solutions. Achieving this goal takes more than just using the development tools that are readily available to everyone.

This section will discuss two additional ingredients needed to help create a competitive advantage when designing ML solutions:

- Creative thinking

- Bridging domains

One of the key success factors when trying to create ML solutions is creativity. You need to think out of the box. It is a cliché, but it often takes a slightly different perspective to discover a unique ML solution.

Standing on the Shoulders of Giants

If you visit the mathematics, computer science, or physics departments of your local college or university, you will find academic research papers plastered on the corridor walls. Upon closer look, you will find that many of these works focus on machine learning. If you search online, you will also find many of these papers.

PhD students in mathematics or statistics usually author these papers. They typically spend months or even years on the particular topic they are exploring. These papers are often difficult for developers to understand. Sometimes we may only grasp a fraction of the content. However, these papers are a very useful resource in our search for creative ideas.

Academic research papers can provide valuable ideas for content and approaches we can utilize in our machine learning apps.

Leveraging the findings of these researchers could potentially help you identify a solution, or save you a lot of time. If you find a relevant research paper, do not be afraid to reach out to the author. In most cases, they are not software developers, and you could form an interesting partnership.

Bridging Domains

Everybody has access to the technologies in this book. How can we differentiate ourselves? Recall from Table 1-1 in the beginning of this chapter, ML terminology originates from different domains. Figure 1-20 shows a graphical view of the domains. As developers, we approach the problem from the technology domain. With our toolkits, we occupy a unique position, allowing us to produce Java ML solutions that lie at the intersection of the domains.

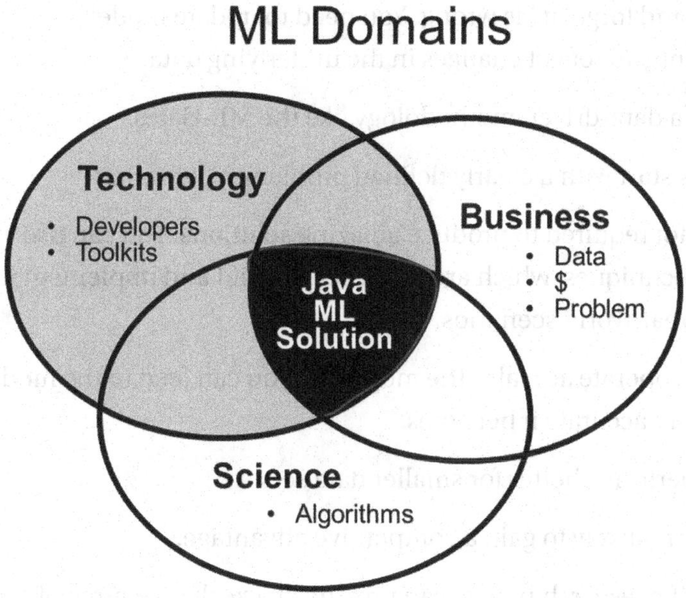

ML Domains

Technology
- Developers
- Toolkits

Business
- Data
- $
- Problem

Java ML Solution

Science
- Algorithms

Figure 1-20. *Domain relationships*

Businesses have the data, the capital ($) to deploy, and many problems they need to solve. The scientists have the algorithms. As Java developers, we can position ourselves at the intersection and produce ML solutions. Developers who can best understand the business problem, connect the problem to the available data, and apply the most appropriate algorithm will be in the best position for monetization.

1.9 Chapter Summary

I have covered quite a few broad topic areas in this chapter. A quick review of the key findings follows. Keep them in mind as you proceed through the rest of the book.

Key Findings

1. Adopt a data-driven methodology.

2. "Set it and forget it" is wrong. You need to update models frequently to reflect changes in the underlying data.

3. Adopt a data-driven methodology like the ML-Gates.

4. Always start with a clearly defined problem.

5. DL is not required to produce amazing solutions. You can use CML techniques, which are far easier to build and implement for many real-world scenarios.

6. DL can operate at scale. The more data you can feed to the model, the more accurate it becomes.

7. CML performs better for smaller data sets.

8. Think creatively to gain a competitive advantage.

9. Scientific research papers can provide an excellent source of ideas.

10. Think across domains. Bridge the gap between the technology, business, and science domains.

CHAPTER 2

Data: The Fuel
for Machine Learning

Machine learning is all about data. This chapter will explore the many aspects of data with the goal of meeting the following objectives:

- Review the data explosion and three megatrends that are making this machine learning revolution possible.

- Introduce the importance of data and reprogramming yourself to think like a data scientist.

- Review different categories of data.

- Review various formats of unstructured data, including CSV, ARFF, and JSON.

- Use the OpenOffice Calc program to prepare CSV data.

- Find and use publicly available data.

- Introduce techniques for creating your own data.

- Introduce preprocessing techniques to enhance the quality of your data.

- Visualize data with JavaScript (Project).

- Implement data visualization for Android (Project).

© Mark Wickham 2018
M. Wickham, *Practical Java Machine Learning*, https://doi.org/10.1007/978-1-4842-3951-3_2

2.1 Megatrends

Why is the ML revolution happening now? It is not the first time. In Chapter 1, I reviewed the previous AI booms and subsequent winter periods. How do we know if this time it is for real? Three transformational megatrends are responsible for the movement.

Three megatrends have paved the way for the machine learning revolution we are now experiencing:

1) Explosion of data

2) Access to highly scalable computing resources

3) Advancement in algorithms

It is worth diving a little deeper into each of these megatrends.

Explosion of Data

You have probably seen those crazy statistics about the amount of data created on a daily basis. There is a widely quoted statistic from IBM that states that 90% of all data on the Internet today was created since 2016. Large amounts of data certainly existed prior to 2016, so the study confirms what we already knew: people and devices today are pumping out huge amounts of data at an unprecedented rate. IBM stated that more than 2.5 exabytes (2.5 billion gigabytes) of data is generated every day.

How much data is actually out there, and what are the sources of the data? It is hard to know with any degree of certainty. The data can be broken down into the following categories:

- Internet social media

- Internet non-social media

- Mobile device data

- Sensor data

- Public data

- Government data

- Private data

- Synthetic data

Table 2-1 attempts to provide some insight into each category.

Table 2-1. *Data Categories*

Data Category	Observation
Internet data	There are 3.8 billion desktop global Internet users.
	In 2017, users watched 4 million YouTube videos per minute.
	There were 5 billion daily Google searches in 2017.
Social media data	There are 655 million tweets per day.
	There are 1 million new social media accounts per day.
	There are 2 billion active Facebook users.
	67 million Instagram posts are added each day
Mobile device data	22 billion text messages were sent each day in 2017.
	There are 3.5 billion mobile device Internet users.
	40 million wearable devices sold in 2017.
	91% of people own a mobile device.
Sensor data	56% of people own a smart device.
	There will be 25 billion connected things by 2020.
	Individual sensors could top 1 trillion by 2020.
	The Internet of Things (IoT) market is all about sensors. IoT market projected growth from US$ 3 trillion in 2014 to US$ 9 trillion in 2020, a 20% CAGR.

(*continued*)

Table 2-1. (*continued*)

Data Category	Observation
Public data	Research institutions make available large datasets. For example, University of California Irvine (UCI) has many useful datasets: ***http://archive.ics.uci.edu/ml/index.php*** Awesome public datasets on GitHub: ***https://github.com/awesomedata/awesome-public-datasets*** CIA World Factbook offers information on the history, population, economy, government, infrastructure, and military of 267 countries: ***www.cia.gov/library/publications/the-world-factbook/*** AWS public datasets is a huge resource of public data, including the 1000 Genome Project and NASA's database of satellite imagery of Earth: ***https://aws.amazon.com/datasets***
Government data	Census data. Debt and financing data. Election commission data. The US Government pledged to make all government public data freely available online: ***https://data.gov***
Private data	Individuals increasingly are collecting their own data due to availability of low cost sensor devices and smartphones with accelerometers and GPS capability.
Synthetic data	Computer-generated data that mimics real data.

As Table 2-1 suggests, there are many types of data. If you require a specific type of data for your ML project, a quick Google search will probably identify a dataset that can at least get you started on a proof of concept.

We can digitize practically anything today. Once digitized, the data becomes eligible for machine learning.

You have heard the term "big data." Similar to the terminology used in ML, the usage of this term is also inconsistent. Table 2-2 shows some guidelines for relative data sizes and the related architectures.

Table 2-2. *Relative Data Sizes*

Name	Size	Database	Architecture
Normal data	< 1GB	Flat/SQL	Local
Small data	1GB - 100GB	NoSQL	Local
Medium data	100GB - 1TB	NoSQL	Distributed
Big data	> 1TB	HadoopSpark	Distributed multiple clusters

Typically, big data refers to datasets larger than one terabyte (TB).

You may not be working with data at big data scale on your projects, but it is important to consider data scalability when designing ML projects. Much of the data existing today is unstructured. This means that it is not labelled or classified. It is often text-based and does not really follow a predefined structure. I will discuss unstructured data in Chapter 3.

Both Chapters 2 and 3 present tools to help tame the data explosion.

Highly Scalable Computing Resources

The explosion in data would not be possible if not for the ability to store and process the data. The second megatrend is the highly scalable computing resources we have available to us today.

Cloud service providers have changed the game for practitioners of ML. They give us on-demand highly scalable access to storage and computing resources. These resources are useful for many ML functions, such as the following:

- Storage: We can use cloud services as a repository for our ML data.

- CPU resources: We can create ML models more quickly by configuring highly available distributed compute clusters with a large CPU capacity.

- Hosting: We can provide hosted access to our data or ML models using API or other interface methods.

- Tools: All of the cloud providers have a full suite of tools that we can use to create ML solutions.

Chapter 3 will take a closer look at the potential ML use cases with cloud providers.

Advancement in Algorithms

The third megatrend is the advancement in ML algorithms. ML algorithms have been around for quite some time. However, once the explosion in data and IaaS providers began to emerge, a renewed effort to optimize their performance began to take place.

Advancements for DL neural network algorithms were the most significant. However, CML algorithm advancements also took place. Chapter 4 will explain the algorithms in detail.

2.2 Think Like a Data Scientist

Data is the single most important ingredient for a successful ML project. You need high quality data, and you need lots of it.

DM is all about working with your data to identify hidden patterns. ML takes the additional step of applying algorithms to process the data. Data is the essential ingredient for each discipline. In both DM and ML, you are often working with large, loosely structured data sets.

You need a good understanding of your data before you can construct ML models that effectively process your data. In *The Signal and the Noise* by Nate Silver, the author encourages us to take ownership for our data. This is really the essence of thinking like a data scientist.

As software engineers, we are used to thinking about the code. It has always been all about the code for us. Recall from Chapter 1, I flipped the development methodology on its head, placing the data up front in the ML-Gates and holding the coding phase until the very end.

Mr. Silver summed it up perfectly:

"The numbers have no way of speaking for themselves. We speak for them. Data-driven predictions can succeed, and they can fail. It is when we deny our role in the process that the odds of failure rise. Before we demand more of our data, we need to demand more of ourselves."

In today's ML world, you must start by considering how data can influence your solution, decide what data you have, how you can organize it, and then let the data drive your software architecture.

Data Nomenclature

A first step in taking ownership for your data is classifying the type of data itself. Before you can understand which algorithm is best suited for your well-defined ML problem, you need to understand the nature and type of the data you possess. Table 2-3 shows the two broad types of data.

Table 2-3. *Summary of General Data Types*

Data Type	Description	Example
Qualitative data	Observations fall into separate distinct categories. Data is discrete because there is a finite number of possible categories into which each observation may fall.	Favorite color: blue, green, brown
Quantitative data	Quantitative or numerical data arise when the observations are counts or measurements.	Height of a person

Qualitative data, classified as

- Nominal if there is no natural order between the categories (such as eye color).

- Ordinal if an ordering exists (such as test scores or class rankings).

Quantitative data, classified as

- Discrete, if the measurements are integers (such as population of a city or country).

- Continuous, if the measurements can take on any value, usually within some range (such as a person's height or weight).

Defining Data

Recall from Chapter 1, MLG5 requires you to identify and define your data. Next, you will perform this task for a dataset that you will use for a project later in the book, the Android Activity Tracker application.

The data shown in Table 2-4 is from the PAMAP2_Dataset, available from the University of California Irvine (UCI) machine learning repository mentioned in Chapter 1. It is freely available data and there are no constraints when using it for research purposes. You can download the dataset via the link below. The dataset is not included in the book resources due to its size. The files are large so the download can take a bit of time.

http://archive.ics.uci.edu/ml/datasets/pamap2+physical+activity+monitoring

To collect this data, the researchers asked subjects to wear sensors while performing various activities. The table shows each of the fields together with a data type assigned.

Table 2-4. *Defining Your Data*

Field (column)	Units	Example	Data type
Timestamp	Seconds	3.38	Quantitative Continuous
Activity ID	1 lying 2 sitting 3 standing 4 walking 5 running 6 cycling 7 nordic	2	Qualitative Nominal
Heart rate	BPM	104	Quantitative Discrete
Sensor 1: Temperature	Degrees C	30	Quantitative Discrete
Sensor 1: 3D acceleration	ms^{-2}	2.37223	Quantitative Continuous
Sensor 1: 3D acceleration	ms^{-2}	8.60074	Quantitative Continuous
Sensor 1: 3D gyroscope	rad/s	3.51058	Quantitative Continuous
Sensor 1: 3D magnetometer	uT	2.43954	Quantitative Continuous
Sensor 1: Orientation	rad	8.76165	Quantitative Continuous

Recognizing what type of data you have is the first step in demanding more of yourself when it comes to your data. You will take a closer look at the PAMAP2_Dataset in Chapter 7 when you build a classifier for the data.

2.3 Data Formats

Data format is a key consideration when building ML models. Table 2-5 shows the important file formats and their common file extensions.

Table 2-5. *Common Data File Types*

File format	Filename extension
Text files	.txt
	.dat
Comma-separated value (CSV) Supported by all spreadsheet packages including MS Excel and OpenOffice Calc	.csv
Attribute-relation file format Supported by Weka	.arff
JavaScript Object Notation (JSON) Standard interchange format widely used on the Internet	.json
	.txt

When you locate data for your ML project, it could potentially be in any format. Plain text files are common. The data files are often .txt or .dat files, both of which are text files. Many of the data files in the University of California-Irvine repository referenced in Table 2-1 are .dat text files.

The first step in using text data files for ML is to open them and understand how they are structured. You can use any text editor. Figure 2-1 shows the ***subject101.dat*** file from the PAMAP2_Dataset.

Figure 2-1. *File subject101.dat from the PAMAP2_Dataset opened in a text editor*

You can see that spaces separate the data fields. Each row contains 54 values or columns separated by a single space character. Note that Figure 2-1 does not show all of the columns. The easiest way to work with datasets for ML is to convert them to CSV. The first step is to make a copy of the .dat file and then rename it as .csv. Figure 2-2 shows the list of all files in the PAMAP2_Dataset, with the newly created .csv copy file.

Name	Date modified	Type	Size
subject101.dat	1/10/2012 1:33 PM	DAT File	138,378 KB
subject102.dat	1/10/2012 1:34 PM	DAT File	202,490 KB
subject103.dat	1/10/2012 1:35 PM	DAT File	115,101 KB
subject104.dat	1/10/2012 1:37 PM	DAT File	149,637 KB
subject105.dat	1/10/2012 1:37 PM	DAT File	169,701 KB
subject106.dat	1/10/2012 1:38 PM	DAT File	164,320 KB
subject107.dat	1/10/2012 1:39 PM	DAT File	142,406 KB
subject108.dat	1/10/2012 1:40 PM	DAT File	185,567 KB
subject109.dat	1/10/2012 1:41 PM	DAT File	3,800 KB
subject101.csv	1/10/2012 1:33 PM	Microsoft Excel C...	138,378 KB

Figure 2-2. *PAMAP2_Dataset after copying the .dat file to .csv*

Just because you renamed the file as a .csv does not make it so. You must convert it. It is possible to perform the conversion with your text editor by performing a global search and replace of the spaces to commas, but there is a better way. You will use a spreadsheet program.

CSV Files and Apache OpenOffice

Spreadsheet programs have the advantage of allowing you to do some basic editing to our data. They also allow you to import or export CSV files easily.

Microsoft Excel can get the job done, but the Apache open source program OpenOffice is a better choice. OpenOffice contains a spreadsheet, word processor, presentation package, database, vector graphic editor, and math equation editor. You are interested in Calc, the spreadsheet program. You are required to download the entire suite.

Calc has several advantages over Excel, including

- Calc is free and open source, licensed under the Apache 2.0 software license. It is part of the OpenOffice suite.

- Calc is better at importing and exporting CSV files. There are more options available, such as escaping text fields in quotation marks ("").

- Calc supports UTF-8 encoding of data fields. This is important, especially if you have projects that use international or multi-byte character sets.

- Calc supports BOM handling. BOM stands for Byte Order Marker. Windows systems use the BOM as the first character in every file to inform applications of the byte order. Files created in Windows that contain the BOM can be problematic on other platforms, such as Unix. When you save files in Calc, Calc lets you specify how you want the BOM handled (very thoughtful; thank you, Apache).

Figure 2-3 shows the installation screen for Apache OpenOffice. The OpenOffice download link is **www.openoffice.org/download/**.

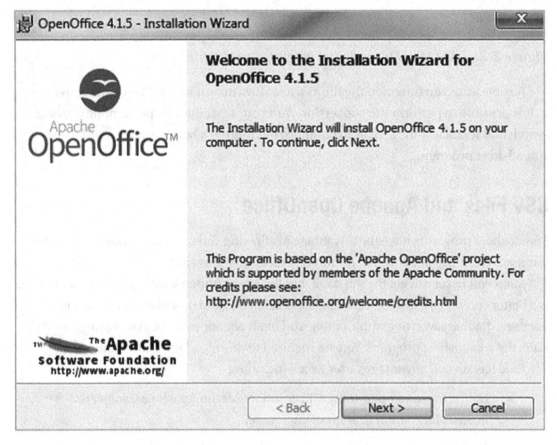

Figure 2-3. *Installing Apache OpenOffice*

Once you have installed OpenOffice, launch Calc. If you are familiar with the Microsoft Office suite, you will notice that Calc looks similar. Open the **subject101.csv** file you copied earlier. Figure 2-4 shows that Calc recognizes it as a text file and give you some import options on the text import window.

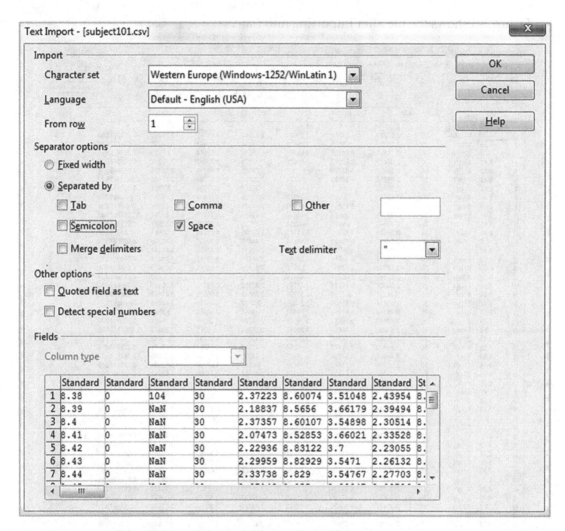

Figure 2-4. *OpenOffice Calc importing a CSV file*

Calc allows you to select the character set, the field delimiter, and even the column type for each of the detected fields. The most important setting for this data is to select the space as the separator. Once you have the space checked, you will see the data populated correctly in the fields shown at the bottom of the text import window.

After you click OK, Calc will import the data.

The PAMAP2_Dataset you will be using is large. Just the single file **subject101.dat** *contains 54 columns and 376,417 rows. It is a large spreadsheet, so give Calc some time to import or export the file.*

Figure 2-5 shows the file after importing into Calc.

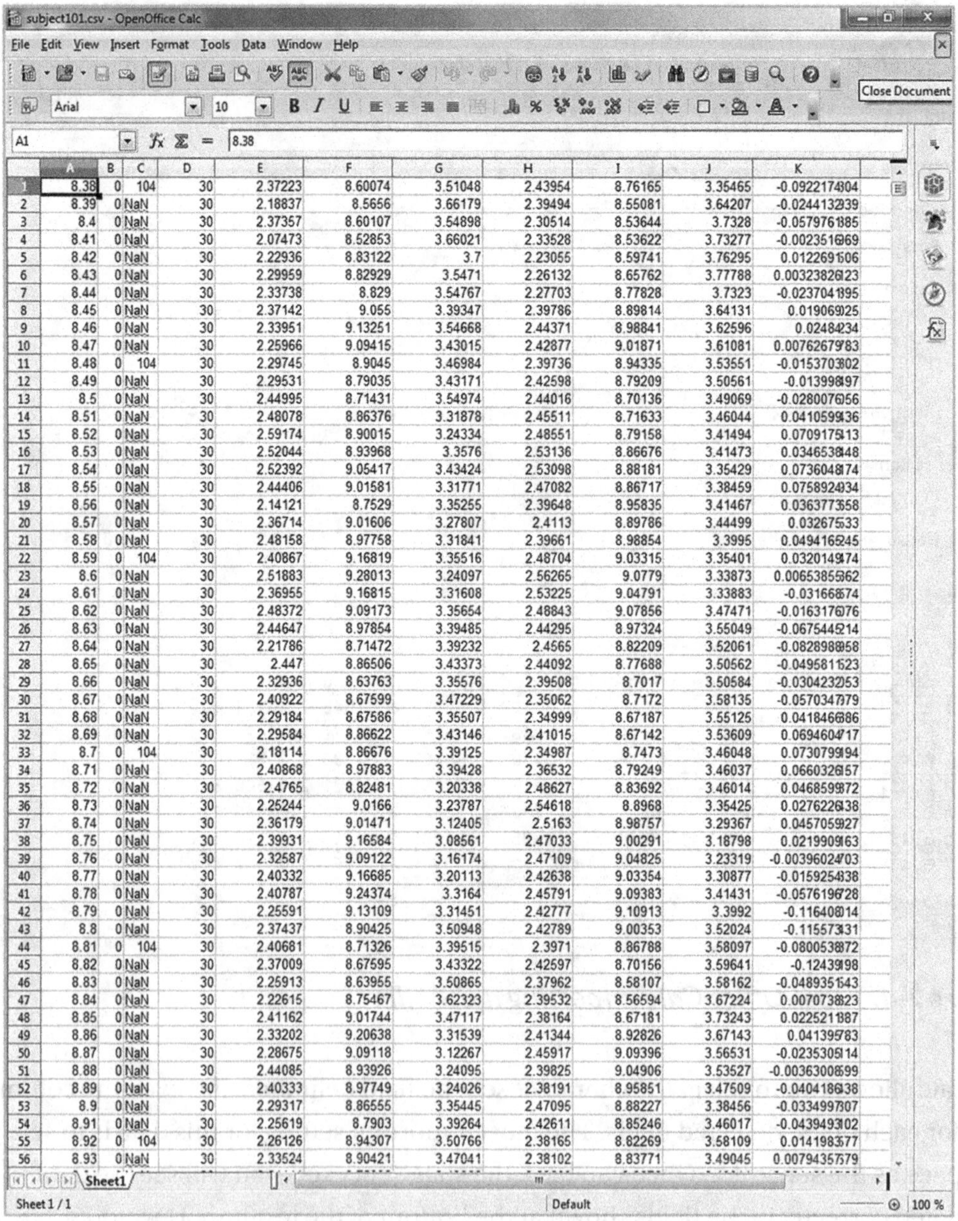

Figure 2-5. subject101.dat file imported into OpenOffice Calc

The advantage of using Calc over a text editor is that once Calc completes the import, it is easy to view and manipulate the data. Some common operations for manipulating ML data in Calc are as follows:

- You can search for missing values. The data in this file is relatively clean. The abbreviation "NaN" stands for "Not a Number" and represents missing values. Column C contains mostly NaN values.

- It's easy to add or delete columns. If you wish to remove a column(s), just highlight the column, right-click, and delete. Removing unneeded columns reduces the size and therefor reduces the time and storage space required to import, export, and train the ML model.

- Macros can remove rows or columns based on a condition, such as the value of a cell. This is useful if, for example, you want to remove all of the missing value rows in the data. Calc can use Excel macros. It also allows you to record keystrokes.

- You can export a file in true CSV format using "," as the separator character.

Figure 2-6 shows the save dialog box for the CSV file export. Click the "Keep Current Format" box to save a CSV file.

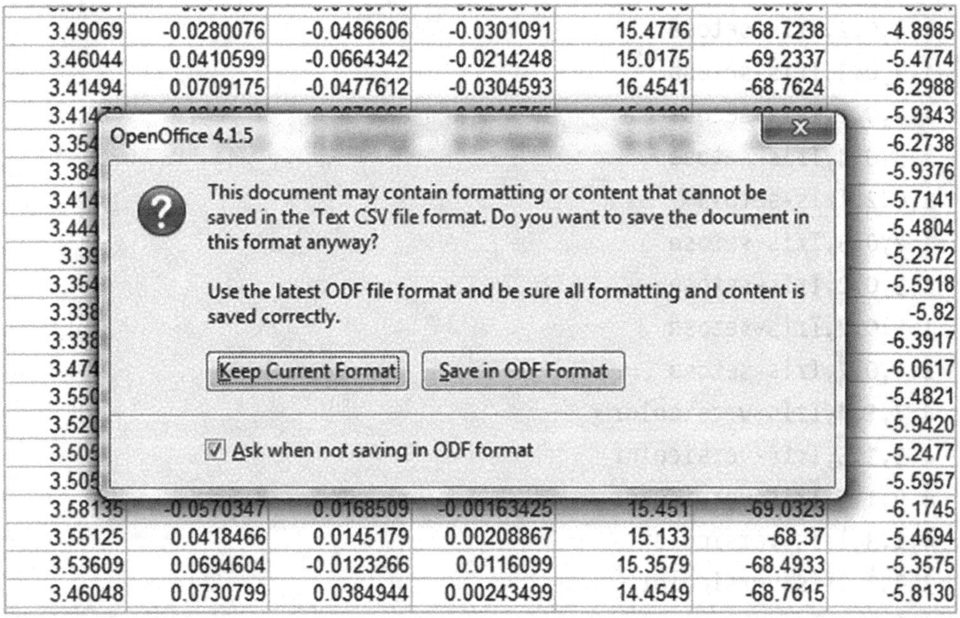

Figure 2-6. *Saving the CSV file*

Most ML environments allow the direct import of CSV files, and Apache OpenOffice Calc is the best way to prepare such files. CSV is the simplest data format you can use for ML. Next, you will look at additional approaches that are more sophisticated.

ARFF Files

ARFF is an abbreviation for Attribute-Relation File Format. It is an extension of the CSV file format. The Weka machine learning environment uses ARFF files to load data. Weka comes with many sample datasets. The iris flower dataset is one of the most famous in machine learning. The following code block shows a partial view of the iris.arff dataset included with the environment:

```
001    @relation iris-weka.filters.unsupervised.attribute.Remove-R1-2
002    % Iris.arff file available with the Weka distribution (partial file)
003
004    @attribute petallength numeric
005    @attribute petalwidth numeric
006    @attribute class {Iris-setosa,Iris-versicolor,Iris-virginica}
007
008    @data
009    1.4,0.2,Iris-setosa
010    1.4,0.2,Iris-setosa
011    1.3,0.2,Iris-setosa
012    1.7,0.2,Iris-setosa
013    1.5,0.4,Iris-setosa
014    1,0.2,Iris-setosa
015    1.7,0.5,Iris-setosa
016    1.9,0.2,Iris-setosa
017    1.5,0.2,Iris-setosa
018    1.4,0.2,Iris-setosa
019    4.7,1.4,Iris-versicolor
020    4.5,1.5,Iris-versicolor
021    4.9,1.5,Iris-versicolor
022    4,1.3,Iris-versicolor
023    3.3,1,Iris-versicolor
024    4.2,1.3,Iris-versicolor
```

```
025   6.6,2.1,Iris-virginica
026   5.4,2.3,Iris-virginica
027   5.1,1.8,Iris-virginica
```

Note that the familiar CSV data follows the **@data** directive at the bottom of the file. In ARFF files, an additional header at the top provides metadata about the data and labels. The following describes the differences between CSV and ARFF file formats:

- Comments start by preceding the comment line with the percentage sign, %.

- The **@relation** directive starts the file and allows you to specify the name of the dataset.

- The **@attribute** directive defines the name and data type of each attribute in the dataset.

- The header section of ARFF files (above the **@data** directive) can contain blanks lines.

- Nominal data, such as the **@attribute class**, are followed by the set of values they can take on, enclosed in curly braces.

- CSV data follows the **@data** directive.

- Unknown or missing values in the dataset are specified with the question mark, ?.

Weka includes conversion tools to convert CSV data to ARFF format. Once you generate the initial ARFF file, there is no need to convert it again.

JSON

CSV and ARFF files are very useful. However, the flat structure of the CSV data does not provide much flexibility. You need an additional tool in your toolbox to help you represent more complex data structures.

As Java or Android developers, you are probably familiar with JSON. JSON stands for JavaScript Object Notation. It is a very lightweight, text-based, flexible exchange format. JSON is a data exchange format that is widely used between servers and client devices.

You can learn more about how JSON works and find downloads for all of the platforms at https://json.org.

JSON has several important properties that have helped to make it hugely popular across the Internet and especially for mobile app development:

- JSON is easy for us to read and write and is easy for machines to parse and generate.

- There is a JSON library available for almost every platform and language.

- JSON is based on a subset of the JavaScript programming language, hence its name.

- JSON is a text format and is language independent.

- JSON uses conventions that are familiar to programmers of the C-family of languages.

JSON uses a simple but powerful collection of ***arrays*** and ***objects*** to represent data. Name/value pairs often represent the data within an object. This has made JSON very popular throughout the Internet. The flexible structure of JSON enables it to represent very complex data relationships.

In JSON, the placement of parenthesis and brackets to represent arrays and objects is very important. Figure 2-7 shows valid construction rules for JSON structures.

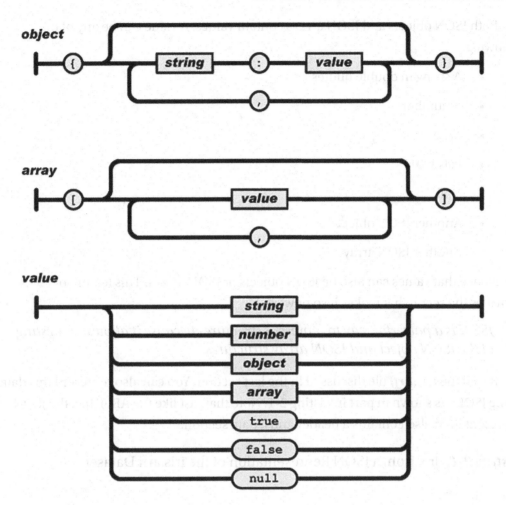

Figure 2-7. *JSON structure definition*

Notice the usage of the [(left bracket) and] (right bracket) and { (left brace) and } (right brace) as identifiers in JSON.

JSON consists of two primitives, objects and arrays, and values that can be strings, numbers, objects, arrays, or Booleans. JSON is surprisingly simple, as Figure 2-7 shows.

Using only the following two primitives, you can construct complex structures to represent almost any type of data relationship:

- JSONObject: An unordered set or collection of name/value pairs

- JSONArray: An ordered list of values

Both JSON objects and JSON arrays contain values. A value can be any of the following:

- A string in double quotes

- A number

- True

- False

- Null

- Another JSON object

- Another JSON array

Notice that values can also be JSON objects or JSON arrays. This feature of JSON provides the secret that makes it so powerful:

> *JSON is a powerful way to represent structures because it allows for nesting of the JSON object and JSON array structures.*

Recall the *iris.arff* file discussed in the last section. You can also represent this data using JSON, as shown in part in Listing 2-1. Note that just like the ARFF file, the JSON representation also contains a header and a data section.

Listing 2-1. iris.json, a JSON Representation of the iris.arff Dataset

```
001    {
002         "header" : {
003              "relation" : "iris",
004              "attributes" : [
005                   {
006                        "name" : "sepallength",
007                        "type" : "numeric",
008                        "class" : false,
009                        "weight" : 1.0
010                   },
011                   {
012                        "name" : "sepalwidth",
013                        "type" : "numeric",
014                        "class" : false,
```

```
015                        "weight" : 1.0
016                    },
017                    {
018                        "name" : "petallength",
019                        "type" : "numeric",
020                        "class" : false,
021                        "weight" : 1.0
022                    },
023                    {
024                        "name" : "petalwidth",
025                        "type" : "numeric",
026                        "class" : false,
027                        "weight" : 1.0
028                    },
029                    {
030                        "name" : "class",
031                        "type" : "nominal",
032                        "class" : true,
033                        "weight" : 1.0,
034                        "labels" : [
035                            "Iris-setosa",
036                            "Iris-versicolor",
037                            "Iris-virginica"
038                        ]
039                    }
040                ]
041            },
042            "data" : [
043                {
044                    "sparse" : false,
045                    "weight" : 1.0,
046                    "values" : [
047                        "5.1",
048                        "3.5",
049                        "1.4",
050                        "0.2",
```

```
051                      "Iris-setosa"
052                 ]
053            },
054            {
055                 "sparse" : false,
056                 "weight" : 1.0,
057                 "values" : [
058                      "4.9",
059                      "3",
060                      "1.4",
061                      "0.2",
062                      "Iris-setosa"
063                 ]
064            },
065            {
066                 "sparse" : false,
067                 "weight" : 1.0,
068                 "values" : [
069                      "5.9",
070                      "3",
071                      "5.1",
072                      "1.8",
073                      "Iris-virginica"
074                 ]
075            }
076        ]
077    }
```

The file *iris.json* is available in the book resources if you would like to experiment with the iris dataset in JSON format.

You might be asking why we need JSON for data files when we already have CSV and ARFF that are perfectly capable of representing data for ML. There are two reasons you may want to consider using JSON:

- JSON is ideal for data interchange over the network. If you need to send data to a networked device, it is a trivial task with JSON and HTTP, but it is not as simple to accomplish with CSV and ARFF.

- Many NoSQL databases use JSON files as the object store for their data. I will discuss these databases further in Chapter 3. This database architecture solves the scalability problem presented by large amounts of data.

JSON files are always larger than the CSV or ARFF versions because they contain structure and spaces for indenting. The increased file size is a fair trade-off for the additional flexibility JSON provides.

The Weka desktop environment makes it easy to convert between ARFF and JSON. You will explore Weka in Chapter 4.

2.4 JSON Integration

JSON is an important part of ML solutions. One of the JSON advantages is that libraries exist for almost every development platform. It is truly cross-platform. Because your focus is on Java, you will next examine how to integrate JSON for Android and the Java JDK.

JSON with Android SDK

JSON has been included in Android since the earliest release of the SDK. Table 2-6 shows a list of the Android JSON classes including the exception handler.

Table 2-6. *JSON Classes Included in the Android SDK*

Classes	Description
JSONArray	A dense indexed sequence of values
JSONObject	A modifiable set of name/value mappings
JSONStringer	Implements *JSONObject.toString()* and *JSONArray.toString()*
JSONTokener	Parses a JSON-encoded string into the corresponding object
JSONException	Thrown to indicate a problem with the JSON API

The **_JSONArray_** and **_JSONObject_** objects are all you need to manage your JSON encoding and decoding. The following code shows how to define JSON objects and JSON arrays in Android:

```
001    // Define a new JSON Object
002    // Remember that JSON Objects start with { (left brace) and end with
       } (right brace)
003
004    JSONObject jsonObject = new JSONObject(myJsonDataString);
005
006    // Define a new JSON Array
007    // Remember that JSON Arrays start with [ (left bracket) and end with ]
       (right bracket)
008
009    JSONArray jsonArray = new JSONArray(myJsonDataString);
```

The trick to using JSON effectively lies in defining a JSON data structure using the JSON object and JSON array primitives to represent your data. You will explore how to achieve this later in the chapter.

JSON with Java JDK

While JSON classes have been included in the Android SDK since the very beginning, this is not the case for the Java JDK. To use JSON with Java, you must include the JSON library.

There are many JSON libraries available for Java. Table 2-7 shows two common sources for Java JDK JSON libraries.

Table 2-7. _JSON Libraries for the Java JDK_

JSON Source	Link
Google JSON Simple	**_https://code.google.com/archive/p/json-simple/_**
Maven JSON Repository	**_https://mvnrepository.com/artifact/org.json/json_**

The Maven Repository is useful because it allows you to download the jar file for Eclipse. There are many version of JSON available at the Maven Repository. The 20171018 version works well and is available at the following link:

https://mvnrepository.com/artifact/org.json/json/20171018

Figure 2-8 shows the download page for this version of Java JSON. The page contains instructions for many different types of build environments, including Maven, Gradle, SBT, Ivy, and others. The Java build environment you use will determine how you include the JSON library.

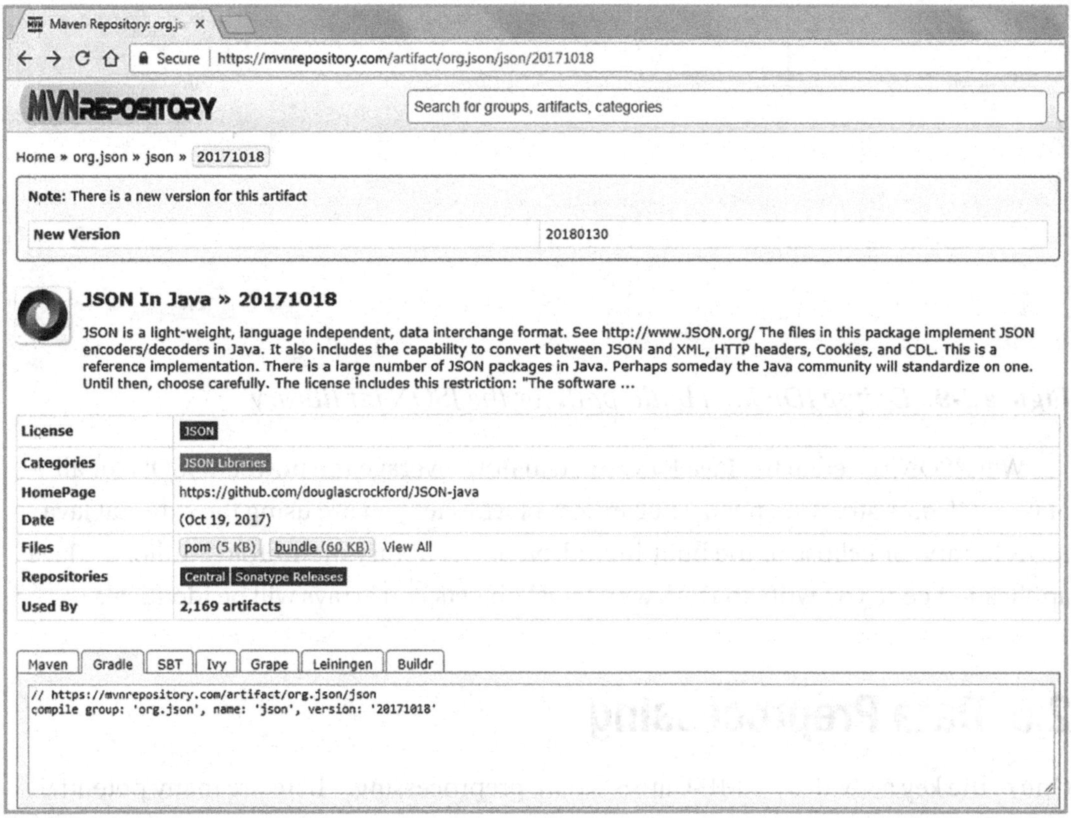

Figure 2-8. *Maven Repository for Java JSON*

If you wish to download the jar file for Eclipse, select "JSON Libraries" and download the jar zip file. You can then directly add the jar file library to the Eclipse Java build Path.

Figure 2-9 shows the *json-20171018.jar* file added to the Eclipse Java build path.

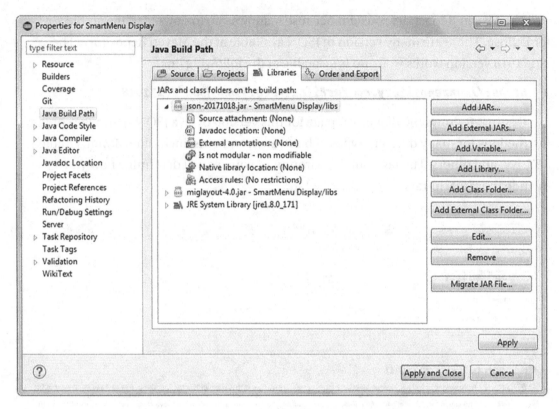

Figure 2-9. *Eclipse IDE Java build path for the JSON jar library*

With JSON added to the Java JDK, you can now leverage the power of JSON for all of your ML data structure needs. Regardless of whether you are using the external Java JSON library for Eclipse or the built-in Android JSON library in Android Studio, the Java application code you write to work with JSON objects and arrays will be identical.

2.5 Data Preprocessing

One of the key activities for ML-Gate 5 is data preprocessing. There are many potential actions you can take in this area to improve the quality of your data. This section does not include an exhaustive list. Nor does it provide a deep dive into the mathematical or statistical principles behind each technique.

> *There is no substitute for getting to know your data. It is a time-intensive manual exercise. Investing the time up front to analyze your data to improve its quality and integrity always pays dividends in the latter phases of the ML project.*

Think of the following sections as a checklist. You can use the checklist to explore the various aspects of your data before selecting the ML algorithm, building the ML model, or writing any code. Data cleaning pays off over time.

Instances, Attributes, Labels, and Features

At the top of the checklist is the identification of instances, attributes, labels, and features. ML-Gate 6 requires you to have a well-defined problem. This directly relates to understanding the structure of your data. Some important definitions:

- **Instances**: A row of data. Instances are the inputs to a machine learning scheme. CSV files can express instances as independent lists, while JSON can represent relationships within the data.

- **Attributes**: A column of data. Attributes can have different data types, such as real, integer, nominal, or string. With supervised learning, there are type types of attributes, features and labels.

- **Features**: The descriptive attributes.

- **Labels**: What you are attempting to predict or forecast.

For example, if you look back at the data in Table 2-3, the table shows the attributes (or columns) of the PAMAP2 dataset. Recall in this dataset there are 54 attributes (or columns). In this dataset, the *Activity Id* is the label and the remaining attributes are features.

Checklist questions to ask:

1. Are all the instances consistent in their structure?

2. How many instances are there?

3. How many attributes are there?

4. What is the format and raw file size of the dataset?

5. Do attributes contain a label(s) or are all of the attributes features?

6. Do all label(s) contain a compliant value?

7. Can you add new attributes later?

8. If you add a new attribute, how would you update existing instances for the new attribute?

The last two questions are particularly important because datasets can grow and evolve over time. When you add new attributes, you essentially have missing values for that attribute in each of the instances that predate the change. In the next section on missing values and duplicates, I will discuss some techniques to handle this situation.

Data Type Identification

Table 2-2 summarized the data types for ML datasets. Define the data type of each attribute in your dataset. The data types can be either

- Qualitative data (nominal or ordinal)

- Quantitative data (discrete or continuous)

Some companies maintain a data dictionary for all of their software projects. The data dictionary represents a formal record of all of the data assets, including the data type of each attribute. This is a best practice. Maintaining the data dictionary creates overhead, but just as data cleaning pays off over time, so too does data organizational knowledge.

Checklist questions to ask:

1. Does each attribute in the dataset have a defined data type?

2. During the project lifecycle, when changes are made that affect data design, are the data types updated?

Missing Values and Duplicates

Missing values and duplicates are an important aspect of data preprocessing.

Missing values can take the form of blanks, dashes, or NaN, as you saw in the PAMAP2_Dataset.

Missing values are not hard to find. The difficulty lies with what action you should take when you find them. Missing values tend to fall into two categories:

- MCAR (Missing Completely At Random)

- Systematically missing: The values are missing for a good reason.

Just because the value is missing does not tell you why the value is missing. When you find missing values, you have to think carefully about the resolution. Most ML algorithms do not place significance on missing values. Replacing a missing value with a generated value can sometimes improve the overall data integrity. It all depends on the context of the data.

There are multiple approaches you can consider when handling missing values. When you have familiarity with the data and the collection methodology, you can make an informed judgement and select one of the following approaches:

- Take no action. Preserve the value as missing.

- Replace the value with a "Not Tested" or "Not Applicable" indicator. In such cases, you are adding detail and improving data integrity because you actively know that a value should not be present.

- If a label contains a missing value, you should consider deleting the entire instance because it does not add value to a model you train.

- Assign a lower range or upper range value for a missing value if the data type is quantitative and range bound. Sometimes you have normalized values within a range, and assigning a value minimum or maximum value can make the algorithm more efficient.

- Impute a value for the missing value. Impute means to replace the value with a new value based on study of other attributes.

Duplicates are not always easy to find. Once located, they are relatively easy to handle. They can be deleted, or if practical, they can be combined with other instances if not all attributes are duplicated.

Checklist questions to ask:

1. Does the dataset have duplicate values? How do you find the duplicate values? When duplicates exist, delete the instance if dataset integrity is increased.

2. Does the dataset have missing values? How will missing values be resolved to maximize dataset integrity?

Erroneous Values and Outliers

Finding errors and outliers in the data is more difficult than identifying missing values and duplicates.

Let's start with an example. The dataset shown in Figure 2-10 is a time series containing 24 data points. The graph shows data released by the Belgium Ministry of Economy. It represents international phone calls made during a 23-year period.

Figure 2-10. *Time series dataset of 24 points*

It is obvious that the data contains several outliers during a seven-year period. Knowing the context of this data, something does not make sense. We could imagine a scenario where such a dataset could make sense. For example, what if we looked at manufacturing output of a steel plant, and we knew there was a multi-year period where a war caused a surge in demand? Such a chart might make sense.

However, in this case, the data does not make sense. Should we disregard the outliers?

It turns out this data was erroneous. During the period from 1963 to 1970, the ministry used a different recording methodology. During the affected period, the data represents the ***total number of minutes*** instead of the ***total number of calls***. Oops.

Even if we did not know what caused the mistake, we should still delete the outliers because they do not make sense in the context of the data. We might not notice the minor impact at years 1963, 1970, but retaining them would not have a drastic impact.

The chart includes two regression lines. Regression is a simple way to make predictions. The Least Squares method is not very accurate in this case because it is highly susceptible to outliers. The Least Median Squares regression method does a much better job at ignoring the outliers.

The lesson learned in this case is that we need to assess outliers and then select an ML method to minimize outlier impact if possible.

Ironically, machine learning can detect outliers. One-class learning is the special class of ML used for this task.

Checklist questions to ask:

1. Does a visualization of the data show outliers?

2. Do the outliers make sense in the context of the data? If so, consider deleting the outliers.

3. If outliers persist, consider a method that can reasonably tolerate noisy data.

Macro Processing with OpenOffice Calc

In Chapter 3, I will introduce the Weka ML environment. Weka has many capabilities for preprocessing data using its Java-based tools. However, you can also use the macro processing capabilities of OpenOffice Calc to preprocess your data.

Learning to use Calc spreadsheet macros is a very powerful ML tool. Macros allow you to make bulk changes to data files based on certain conditions. They allow you to automate a repetitious task. With large data sets, this can save you a lot of time and effort. Calc, just like Microsoft Excel, uses Visual Basic to handle macros.

Like Microsoft Excel, Calc uses the Visual Basic programming language for macros. It is not difficult to master. Calc macros can automate any spreadsheet operation you can perform manually. Calc allows you to record keystrokes to build macros. Calc also allows you to manually enter macro code.

Chapter 12 of the OpenOffice documentation contains an excellent introduction to Calc macros:

www.openoffice.org/documentation/manuals/userguide3/0312CG3-CalcMacros.pdf

Additional documentation for Calc macros is available on the OpenOffice wiki page:

**https://wiki.openoffice.org/wiki/Documentation/OOoAuthors_User_Manual/
Getting_Started/Creating_a_simple_macro**

The following code shows a useful macro for iterating through all rows in a Calc spreadsheet and displaying non-empty cells. Calc and the Visual Basic language contain a huge library of functions and the possibilities are endless.

```
001    Sub TraverseRows
002        Dim oRange 'The primary range
003        Dim oSheet 'Sheet object
004        Dim oRows 'Rows object
005        Dim oRow 'A single row
006        Dim oRowEnum 'Enumerator for the rows
007        Dim s As String 'General String Variable
008
009        oSheet = ThisComponent.Sheets(3)
010        oRange = oSheet.getCellRangeByName("B6:C9")
011
012        oRows = oRange.getRows()
013
014        oRowEnum = oRows.createEnumeration()
015        Do While oRowEnum.hasMoreElements()
016            oRow = oRowEnum.nextElement()
017            s = s & NonEmptyCellsInRange(oRow, " ") & CHR$(10)
018        Loop
019        MsgBox s, 0, "Non-Empty Cells In Rows"
020    End Sub
```

If you are struggling to find a way to make a necessary cleanup of your data, Calc macros are a good solution, especially for CSV data.

If you have huge spreadsheets, Calc macros might not offer the best performance for data cleaning and manipulation. The limitations of Apache OpenOffice Calc are

- Maximum number of rows: 1,048,576

- Maximum number of columns: 1,024

- Maximum number of sheets: 256

JSON Validation

If you use JSON as a data format, you need to validate your JSON after creation. There are many online tools that can perform JSON validation. Many of them are open source or created with scripting languages, so you can run the validation locally if you wish.

Figure 2-11 shows the JSON validation of the file you created earlier in the chapter by the online tool available at ***https://jsonlint.com***.

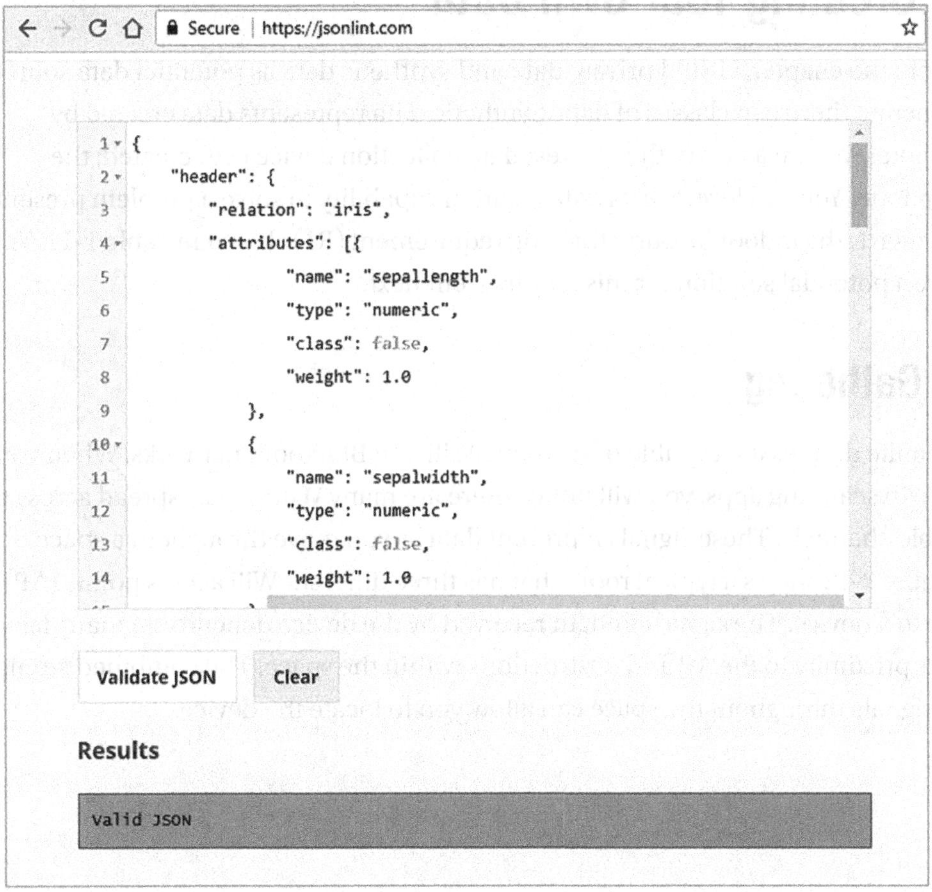

Figure 2-11. *JSON validation*

It is always a good idea to run any JSON you create, especially if you create it manually, through a JSON validation.

Checklist question to ask:

1. Do you represent data with JSON? Validate all JSON files prior to model building.

2.6 Creating Your Own Data

Earlier in the chapter, I listed private data and synthetic data as potential data sources. We generate these two classes of data. Synthetic data represents data created by a computer. We are all carry the greatest data collection device ever created: the smartphone. You can leverage its data creation capability to solve a problem presented in Chapter 1, the indoor location tracking requirement (R1) shown in Table 1-11. You will explore a potential solution for this requirement next.

Wifi Gathering

Our mobile devices are capable of scanning Wifi and Bluetooth networks. When you use those Wifi scanning apps, you will notice there are many Wifi signals spread across the available channels. These signals represent data as you move throughout a space.

Figure 2-12 shows a typical room that has three different Wifi access points (AP) visible to a device. The signal strength received by the device depends on many factors, such as proximity to the AP and obstructions within the space. The combined strength of these signals throughout the space can allow you to locate the device.

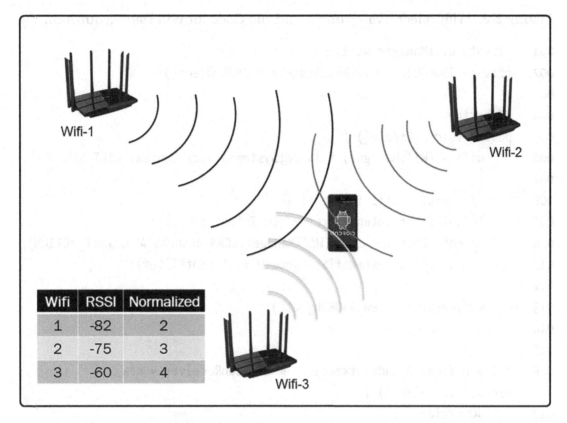

Figure 2-12. *Indoor location using Wifi signal strength*

Two units of measure, dBm and RSSI, represent signal strength. RSSI is a relative index, while dBm is an absolute number. For dBm, the closer to 0 dBm, the better the signal is. Android devices return relevant RSSI in the range between -100 (weakest) to -55 (strongest).

You'll use the Android *WifiManager* to gather signal strength information from all the visible Wifi access points (AP). Mobile phone owners are familiar with the four bar Wifi signal strength icon shown in the status bar of the device. Android provides a static method called *WifiManager.calculateSignalLevel* that computes the signal level in a range of 0-4. Android uses this value to generate the signal strength icon. This method also can provide the *normalized* value shown in Figure 2-12.

As an example, let's consider the simple code required to gather the Wifi signal strength data and save it in JSON format as the Android device moves around a room. Listing 2-2 shows the key Android code. This code is not a complete Android project, but the code excerpt file, *WifiCollect.java* is available in the book resources if you wish to leverage it when building your own project.

Listing 2-2. WifiCollect.java - Sample Android Code for Wifi Data Acquisition

```
001   private WifiManager wifi;
002   private JSONObject wifiResults = new JSONObject();
003
004   @Override
005   public void onCreate() {
006       wifi = (WifiManager) this.getSystemService(Context.WIFI_SERVICE);
007
008       // register wifi intent filter
009       IntentFilter intentFilter = new IntentFilter();
010       intentFilter.addAction(WifiManager.SCAN_RESULTS_AVAILABLE_ACTION);
011       registerReceiver(mWifiScanReceiver, intentFilter);
012
013       wifiResults = new JSONObject();
014   }
015
016   private final BroadcastReceiver mWifiScanReceiver = new
      BroadcastReceiver() {
017       @Override
018       public void onReceive(Context c, Intent intent) {
019           if (intent.getAction().equals(WifiManager.SCAN_RESULTS_
              AVAILABLE_ACTION)) {
020               List<ScanResult> wifiScanList = wifi.getScanResults();
021               for (int i = 0; i < wifiScanList.size(); i++) {
022                   String name = wifiScanList.get(i).BSSID.
                      toLowerCase();
023                   int rssi = wifiScanList.get(i).level;
024                   Log.v(TAG, "wifi-ssid: " + name + " => " + rssi +
                      "dBm");
025                   try {
026                       wifiResults.put(name, rssi);
027                   } catch (Exception e) {
028                       Log.e(TAG, e.toString());
029                   }
030               }
```

```
031                    saveData();
032             }
033        }
034    };
```

To summarize the key code in Listing 2-2:

- You define a *JSONObject* in line 002. This object will hold the names (SSID) and the signal strengths of all the Wifi networks the device identifies during the scan.

- In the *onCreate()* method, you use the Android *WifiManager* to create an intent and register a *BroadcastReceiver*.

- Because you are using Wifi, remember to include permissions for *SCAN_WIFI_NETWORKS* and *ACCESS_WIFI_STATE* in the manifest file.

- You define the *BroadcastReceiver* in line 016. Android notifies the *BroadcastReceiver* when it detects new Wifi networks.

- Lines 022 and 023 show the network name and the signal level retrieved from the Wifi scan. These values are stored in the JSON object in line 026. The JSON object grows in size as the *BroadcastReceiver* receives new networks.

- Line 031 shows a call to a *saveData()* function. This function will save the JSON object for processing. You may wish to send it over the network to a server, add it to a NoSQL database, or use it internally to build a model on the device.

This approach to determining indoor location is very accurate and can operate with very low latency. To achieve the result requires a two-step process:

1. Map out your space and collect the Wifi data samples using code such as shown in Listing 2-2. For each sample you capture, assign it to a label identifying the device location within the space. For example, you may wish to divide your target space into a square grid and assign numbers to the grid locations.

2. Once you have collected all the data for the space, use it to build the ML model. You can then use the model to make predictions about where you are located in the room.

Indoor location using ML is a powerful example of creating your own data to solve a problem with ML. To make the solution even more robust, you can implement the same approach for Bluetooth signals.

While this example illustrates the gathering and usage of RF data in the device vicinity, there is another type of data the smartphone excels at producing: sensor data. I will discuss sensor data in detail in the last chapter, including ML sensor data implementations for Java devices and Android smartphones.

2.7 Visualization

Being able to visualize your data is important. Visualization allows you to gain insights into your data easily. Data visualization is one of the best tools you can add to your toolkit on the journey to demanding more from yourself with respect to your data.

One of the best approaches to implement data visualization is to use third-party open source graphic libraries in conjunction with the web browser or Android WebView. Applying this approach, you can generate amazing visualizations with minimal coding.

JavaScript Visualization Libraries

Table 2-8 shows a partial list of visualization libraries available. JavaScript is the language of choice for most of these libraries because it provides the following benefits:

- All modern browsers support JavaScript, including Android's WebView control. This means any visualizations you create will be widely available across platforms.

- JavaScript excels at interactive functionality. This makes your visualizations more compelling than static images.

Table 2-8. *JavaScript Visualization Libraries*

Library/Link	Description
D3 Plus d3plus.org	D3 Plus version 2.0. Amazing set of examples and visualizations.
Leaflet leafletjs.com	An open-source JavaScript library for mobile-friendly interactive maps.
Timeline JS timeline.knightlab.com	Open-source tool that enables anyone to build visually rich, interactive timelines.
Highcharts highcharts.com	Widely used library. Simple and powerful charting API. License required.
FusionCharts fusioncharts.com	JavaScript charts for web and mobile. Includes 90+ charts and 1000+ maps. Free.
Dygraphs dygraphs.com	Fast, flexible, open source JavaScript charting library. Allows users to explore and interpret dense data sets.
Plotly plot.ly	Compose, edit, and share interactive data visualization via the Web.
Raw rawgraphs.io	The missing link between spreadsheets and data visualization.
Chart.js chartjs.org	Simple, flexible JavaScript charting. Open source. Nice transitions and animations.
Datawrapper datawrapper.de	From data to beautiful charts. Used by many journalists. Monthly subscription model.
ChartBlocks chartblocks.com	Online chart building tool. Monthly subscription model.
Google Charts developers.google.com/chart	Simple to use, rich gallery of interactive charts. Free.
Tableau tableau.com	Large-scale commercial solution with many large clients. NYSE listed.
Infogram infogr.am	Large corporate vendor with complete offering.

The libraries in Table 2-8 are all highly capable of helping you to visualize your data. When you explore them, you may find that one of them matches your requirements best. Highcharts and D3 Plus are two of the most popular libraries.

D3 Plus

D3 stands for data-driven documents. D3 is a JavaScript visualization package. It is lightweight. D3 Plus is an extension to D3. The current supported version of D3 Plus is version 2.0.

You will explore D3 Plus in more detail for the following reasons:

- D3 is a based on JavaScript, which provides a smooth interactive user experience.

- All of the modern browsers can render JavaScript, so it's a good solution for Java as well as Android apps.

- D3 Plus makes it very simple to create and display CSV and JSON visualizations.

- Free and open source.

Download links for the D3 library, D3 Plus, and a comprehensive gallery of charts are located at

https://d3js.org
https://d3plus.org
github.com/d3/d3/wiki/Gallery

Next, you will use the dendogram class of charts for the D3 visualization project. A dendogram is a tree diagram useful to display hierarchy. The D3 gallery page links to dendogram examples at `https://bl.ocks.org/mbostock/4063570`.

2.8 Project: D3 Visualization

You saw earlier in this chapter that CSV and JSON are useful data formats for ML. In this project, you will implement D3 visualization for the desktop browser.

Dendograms are useful for showing hierarchy. The project will explore a variety of dendograms to visualize both CSV and JSON data.

Table 2-9 shows the project file summary. The book resources contain the zip file, *d3_visualization.zip*, which includes all the project files.

Table 2-9. *D3Visualization Project File Summary*

Project Name: D3 Visualization

Source: *d3_visualization.zip*

Type: Desktop browser

File	Description
d3.min.js	D3 library
flare.csv	CSV data file
flare.json	JSON data file
dendo-csv.html	Dendogram example using CSV data
tree-dendo-csv.html	Tree dendogram example using CSV data
radial-dendo-csv.html	Radial tree dendogram example using CSV data
collapse-tree-json.html	Collapsible tree dendogram example using JSON data
cluster-dendo-json.html	Cluster dendogram example using JSON data

Visualization is all about choosing the best graphical style to represent your data. Dendogram charts work well for JSON visualization because they show hierarchy.

In this project, you have two data file sources, ***flare.csv*** and ***flare.json***. They represent different file formats of the same data. D3 is capable of rendering each version into several interesting dendograms. If you wish to render another chart type, the code will likely be very similar to the examples; just check the D3 gallery for a code example of the chart you desire.

To view the visualization in a browser, you must set up a web server to host the files shown in Table 2-9. If you wish to view them locally on your desktop, you can install a local web server, depending on your desktop platform.

If you need to install a web server, refer to the following platform-specific instructions:

- Windows: IIS is the most popular web server on Windows but is not enabled by default. To enable it, follow these instructions:

  https://msdn.microsoft.com/en-us/library/ms181052 (v=vs.80).aspx

- Windows: You may also install WAMP software on windows. WAMP stands for Windows, Apache web server, MySQL, PHP. To install WAMP for Windows, follow these instructions:

  www.wampserver.com/en/

- Mac: Apache web server comes preinstalled on Apple computers.

Once you have your web server set up, just point your browser at one of the five HTML files. Each file renders a slightly different dendogram for the chosen data format type.

D3 visualizations require a minimal amount of JavaScript code. The JavaScript code is included within the HTML file. Listing 2-3 shows an example of the *dendo-csv.html* file that renders a dendogram from CSV data.

There are two key parts in the structure of any D3 based visualizations:

- A reference to the D3 library file needs to be included. You can use either a local copy of the library or an online repository. Include the library reference within *<script>* tags (line 014).

- Specify the CSV file to be loaded for the visualization using the *d3.csv* assignment statement (line 025).

Note that Listing 2-3 includes the JavaScript code (lines 016-053) and the CSS style code (lines 004-010) used to format the visualization.

Listing 2-3. dendo-csv.html

```
001    <!DOCTYPE html>
002    <meta charset="utf-8">
003
004    <style>
005    .node circle {fill: #999;}
006    .node text {font: 10px sans-serif;}
007    .node--internal circle {fill: #555;}
008    .node--internal text {text-shadow: 0 1px 0 #fff, 0 -1px 0 #fff, 1px 0
       0 #fff, -1px 0 0 #fff;}
009    .link {fill: none; stroke: #555; stroke-opacity: 0.4; stroke-width:
       1.5px;}
010    </style>
011
012    <svg width="1200" height="800"></svg>
```

```
013
014    <script src="./d3.js"></script>
015
016    <script>
017    var svg = d3.select("svg"),
018        width = +svg.attr("width"),
019        height = +svg.attr("height"),
020        g = svg.append("g").attr("transform", "translate(40,0)");
021    var cluster = d3.cluster()
022        .size([height, width - 160]);
023    var stratify = d3.stratify()
024        .parentId(function(d) { return d.id.substring(0, d.id.
           lastIndexOf(".")); });
025    d3.csv("flare.csv", function(error, data) {
026      if (error) throw error;
027      var root = stratify(data)
028          .sort(function(a, b) { return (a.height - b.height) || a.id.
             localeCompare(b.id); });
029      cluster(root);
030      var link = g.selectAll(".link")
031          .data(root.descendants().slice(1))
032        .enter().append("path")
033          .attr("class", "link")
034          .attr("d", function(d) {
035            return "M" + d.y + "," + d.x
036                + "C" + (d.parent.y + 100) + "," + d.x
037                + " " + (d.parent.y + 100) + "," + d.parent.x
038                + " " + d.parent.y + "," + d.parent.x;
039          });
040      var node = g.selectAll(".node")
041          .data(root.descendants())
042        .enter().append("g")
043          .attr("class", function(d) { return "node" + (d.children ? "
             node--internal" : " node--leaf"); })
044          .attr("transform", function(d) { return "translate(" + d.y +
             "," + d.x + ")"; })
```

```
045    node.append("circle")
046        .attr("r", 2.5);
047    node.append("text")
048        .attr("dy", 3)
049        .attr("x", function(d) { return d.children ? -8 : 8; })
050        .style("text-anchor", function(d) { return d.children ? "end" :
           "start"; })
051        .text(function(d) { return d.id.substring(d.id.lastIndexOf(".")
           + 1); });
052    });
053    </script>
```

A dendogram aligns each of the lower-level leaf nodes, so the visualization appears right justified. Figure 2-13 shows the dendogram visualization of the CSV file that D3 generates when you open the ***dendo-csv.html*** file in your browser.

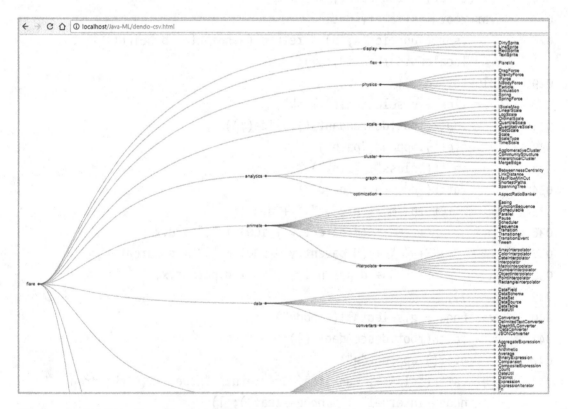

Figure 2-13. *Dendogram visualization generated by dendo-csv.html*

The dendogram visualization is obviously much easier to read than the raw CSV file.

If you wish to change styling of the dendogram, you can modify the CSS elements in the HTML file in lines 004-010. CSS stands for cascading style sheet. It is a common language for webpage layout design and styling. It can control all aspects of a layout such as font, font size, margins, padding, spacing, alignment, etc.

If you wish to change the layout structure of the rendered dendogram, you can modify the JavaScript code that constructs the dendogram. For example, lines 045-046 control the radius of the circles drawn to represent each node.

There are many other related visualizations useful for depicting ML data. The tree visualization is a variation on the dendogram. Think of it as a left-justified dendogram, where the nodes extend to the right as the tree depth increases.

Figure 2-14 shows the *flare.csv* data file visualized as a tree. The tree display differs from the dendogram because of the way the JavaScript code renders the nodes. The *tree-dendo-csv.html* file actually gives you the choice to select whether you want the CSV data rendered as a dendogram or a tree.

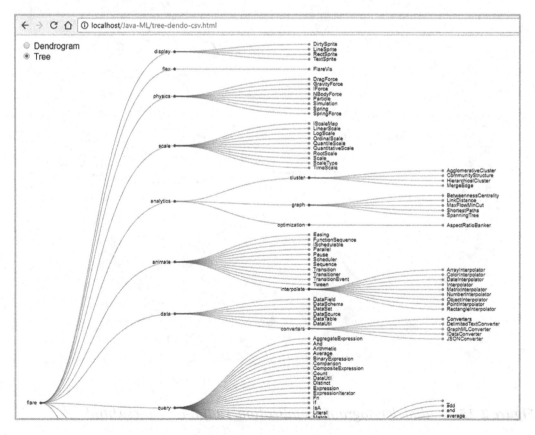

Figure 2-14. *Tree visualization rendered, tree-dendo-csv.html*

The final CSV visualization you will produce with D3 is the radial dendogram. A picture is worth a thousand words, and the radial dendogram is possibly the most artistic and useful visualization. For large datasets, the dendogram and tree can become lengthy and require scrolling to view the entire visualization. The radial dendogram fills a circle, so it tends to be more compact and easily visible.

Figure 2-15 shows a radial dendogram produced by ***radial-dendo-csv.html***. Even though the font may be small and there are many labels in the dataset, the radial dendogram gives you a good feel for the structure of your data. With practice, you can take a quick glance at a radial dendogram of your data and identify problems or irregularities.

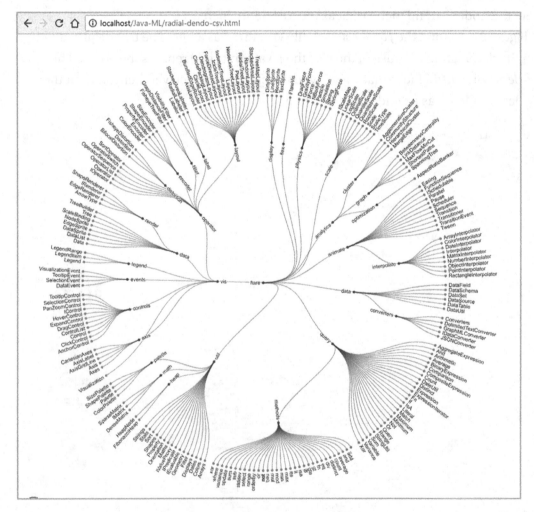

Figure 2-15. *Radial dendogram visualization, radial-dendo-csv.html*

The final two visualizations in the project will use JSON data as their source. The file *flare.json* is a JSON version of the *flare.csv* file used in the prior three visualizations.

The *cluster-dendo-json.html* file structure is similar to the approach used with CSV data. The following code block assigns the JSON file in D3 at line 008:

```
001    <!DOCTYPE html>
002    <meta charset="utf-8">
003    <body>
004    <script src="./d3.v3.min.js"></script><script>
005
006    ...
007
008    d3.json("flare.json", function(error, root) {
009      if (error) throw error;
010
011    ...
012
013    });
014    d3.select(self.frameElement).style("height", height + "px");
015...</script>
```

Note that when loading JSON into D3, there are some requirements for the JSON structure. The JSON needs to be compatible with D3's hierarchy rules. If you examine the *flare.json* file, you will see that it is comprised of "name" and "children" nodes.

```
001    {
002      "name": "flare",
003      "children": [
004      {
005        "name": "analytics",
006        "children": [
007        {
008          "name": "cluster",
009          "children": [
010
011          ...
```

If your JSON data does not comply with this structure, you may need to convert it so D3 can parse and display it properly. There are tools available to handle this conversion. D3 includes a function called ***d3.nest()*** and there is also an external function called ***underscore.nest()***. Documentation and download links for these functions can be found at

https://github.com/d3/d3-collection

https://github.com/iros/underscore.nest

Once you have your JSON data in the proper format, D3 can render it.

Figure 2-16 shows the cluster dendogram visualization of the JSON file as rendered by ***cluster-dendo-json.html***.

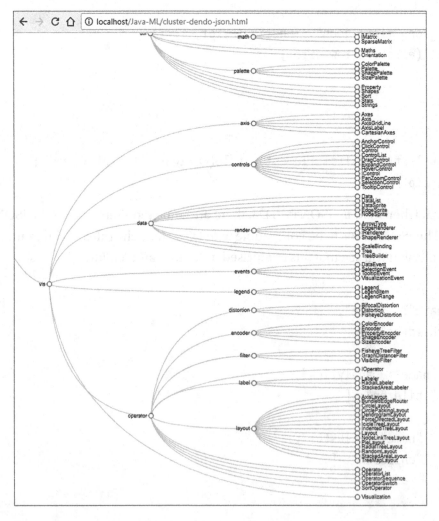

Figure 2-16. *Cluster dendogram visualization, cluster-dendo-json.html*

Flare.json is a large file with many nodes. D3 uses this file for many of its visualization examples. If you look inside the HTML file, you will see the following line of code:

```
<svg width="1200" height="2200"></svg>
```

This sets the height of the render window to 2200 pixels. That is probably larger than your monitor, which means you will have to scroll to see the whole visualization. If you reduced the height to match your display size, for example 1200 pixels, you will see that the visualization becomes so compressed that is no longer readable.

A solution to this problem is the collapsible tree. Remember, JavaScript is interactive. The collapsible tree visualization allows you to click on nodes to expand or contract them. Figure 2-17 shows the much cleaner collapsible tree visualization as rendered by ***collapse-tree-json.html***.

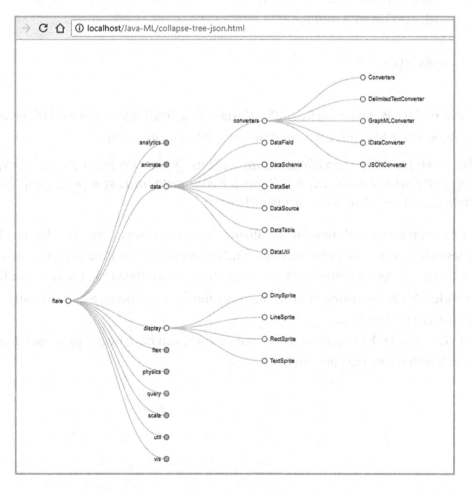

Figure 2-17. *Collapsible tree, collapse-tree-json.html*

The collapsible tree is useful because it allows you to click on individual node to expand them. It does not leave your entire screen cluttered with the whole visualization. It is a much easier way to explore the data interactively. The ***collapse-tree-json.html*** file is larger than the other versions because it contains JavaScript code, such as the following function, to manage the interactive node navigation:

```
001    // Toggle children on click.
002    function click(d) {
003      if (d.children) {
004        d._children = d.children;
005        d.children = null;
006      } else {
007        d.children = d._children;
008        d._children = null;
009      }
010      update(d);
011    }
```

In this project, you covered five different data visualizations from the dendogram family: three with CSV source data and two with JSON source data.

> *JavaScript produces excellent visualizations. If you browse the D3 gallery, you will find a visualization suitable for your data and example JavaScript code to help implement your visualization.*

Having a JavaScript solution for visualizing data allows you to see what the data looks like. These visualizations can be beautiful, and the power of visualization is obvious. Visualizations give you a better feel for the structure of your data than the raw data files can provide. This is a first step in understanding the data and being able to identify hidden patterns in the data.

With CSV and JSON visualization in your toolbox, you have begun to ***demand more of yourself*** with respect to your data.

2.9 Project: Android Data Visualization

This project will extend the work you with did with D3 visualizations on the desktop to Android mobile devices. Displaying visualization may not be a core function of your Android app, but there may be times when it is very helpful for your users.

Table 2-10 shows the project file summary.

Table 2-10. *Project File Summary - Android Data Visualization*

Project Name: Android Data Visualization
Source: *android_data_vis.zip*
Type: Android

File	Description
app->src->main *AndroidManifest.xml*	Configuration file.
app->src->main->res->layout *activity_main.xml*	Layout file for display of the WebView.
app->src->main->assets *d3.min.js* *flare.csv* *radial-dendo-csv.html*	Assets if you decide to build the app with local copy of the assets. Not required if you load the assets from web server.
app->src->main->javaMainActivity. *java*	Main Java source to load and display the D3 visualization.

You saw D3 visualization working on the desktop browser, so setting it up for Android is straightforward.

Rather than importing a visualization or charting library into your app, you will take a shortcut and use Android's ***WebView*** class to display the D3 visualization. ***WebView*** is a system component powered by Chrome that allows Android apps to display content from the web directly inside an application. The class provides a clean, integrated user experience for your app. Like any good web browser, ***WebView*** supports JavaScript, so it works well for D3 content.

Figure 2-18 shows the Android Data Visualization project in Android Studio.

Figure 2-18. *Project Android Data Visualization in Android Studio*

There are two methods to handle the D3 integration with **WebView**, depending on how you decide to manage access to the required files:

- Internal: Place the required files inside the app assets folder.

- External: Load the assets from a remote web server.

The following code from **MainActivity.java** shows how to set up a full screen **WebView** layout. A **progressDialog** provides an indication to the user that network content is loading, which is especially useful if the resources are loaded from external server. Lines 067-068 show the **radial-dendo-csv.html** file reference, depending on whether you choose the internal or external approach.

```
001    package android.wickham.com.datavis;
002
003    import android.annotation.SuppressLint;
004    import android.app.Activity;
005    import android.app.ProgressDialog;
006    import android.content.DialogInterface;
```

```
007    import android.graphics.Color;
008    import android.os.Bundle;
009    import android.webkit.WebChromeClient;
010    import android.webkit.WebView;
011
012    public class MainActivity extends Activity {
013
014        private WebView webView;
015
016        @SuppressLint("SetJavaScriptEnabled")
017        @Override
018        protected void onCreate(Bundle savedInstanceState) {
019            super.onCreate(savedInstanceState);
020            setContentView(R.layout.activity_main);
021
022            webView = (WebView) findViewById(R.id.wb_webview);
023
024            //Scroll bars should not be hidden
025            webView.setScrollbarFadingEnabled(false);
026            webView.setHorizontalScrollBarEnabled(true);
027            webView.setVerticalScrollBarEnabled(true);
028            webView.setFitsSystemWindows(true);
029
030            //Enable JavaScript
031            webView.getSettings().setJavaScriptEnabled(true);
032
033            //Set the user agent
034            webView.getSettings().setUserAgentString("AndroidWebView");
035
036            //Clear the cache
037            webView.clearCache(true);
038            webView.setBackgroundColor(Color.parseColor("#FFFFFF"));
039            webView.setFadingEdgeLength(10);
040            webView.getSettings().setBuiltInZoomControls(true);
041            webView.getSettings().setDisplayZoomControls(false);
042
```

```
043        final Activity activity = this;
044        final ProgressDialog progressDialog = new
           ProgressDialog(activity);
045        progressDialog.setProgressStyle(ProgressDialog.STYLE_SPINNER);
046        progressDialog.setProgressStyle(ProgressDialog.THEME_HOLO_LIGHT);
047        progressDialog.setCancelable(true);
048
049        webView.setWebChromeClient(new WebChromeClient() {
050            public void onProgressChanged(WebView view, int progress) {
051                progressDialog.setCanceledOnTouchOutside(true);
052                progressDialog.setTitle("Loading visualization ...");
053                progressDialog.setButton("Cancel", new
                   DialogInterface.OnClickListener() {
054                    public void onClick(DialogInterface dialog, int
                       which) {
055                        webView.destroy();
056                        finish();
057                    } });
058                progressDialog.show();
059                progressDialog.setProgress(0);
060                activity.setProgress(progress * 1000);
061                progressDialog.incrementProgressBy(progress);
062                if(progress == 100 && progressDialog.isShowing())
063                    progressDialog.dismiss();
064            }
065        });
066        // Uncomment one of the following two lines based on Internal
           or External loading
067        //webView.loadUrl("file:///android_asset/radial-dendo-csv.html");
068        webView.loadUrl("https://www.yourwebserver.com/radial-dendo-
           csv.html");
069    }
070 }
```

The following code shows the layout file, *fullscreen.xml*. It includes the Android *WebView* control that is contained within a *FrameLayout*.

```
001    <FrameLayout xmlns:android="http://schemas.android.com/apk/res/
       android"
002        xmlns:tools="http://schemas.android.com/tools"
001        android:layout_width="match_parent"
002        android:layout_height="match_parent"
003        tools:context="android.wickham.com.datavis.MainActivity">
004
005        <WebView
006            android:id="@+id/wb_webview"
007            android:layout_width="fill_parent"
008            android:layout_height="fill_parent" />
009
010    </FrameLayout>
```

This Android app, when executed, downloads the HTML/JavaScript file and then displays the visualization on your device, as shown in Figure 2-19.

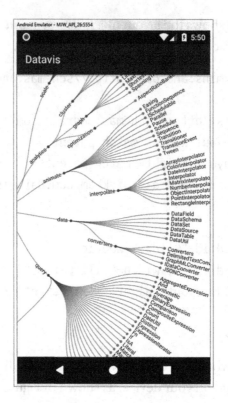

Figure 2-19. *Android Data Visualization app screenshot*

WebView contains many configuration parameters that control how the visualization will appear, such as zooming, scrolling, etc. Keep in mind that this approach can display any D3 visualization, not just the dendograms you have focused on for their usefulness with ML data files such as CSV and JSON files.

2.10 Summary

This chapter was all about data. It certainly is the fuel for machine learning. In the subsequent chapters, you will be selecting algorithms, building models, and finally integrating those models. Without careful attention to the data in this early phase, you will not be able to achieve the desired results. Figure 2-20 shows how the data topics you learned in this chapter fit into the overall ML-Gates methodology introduced in Chapter 1.

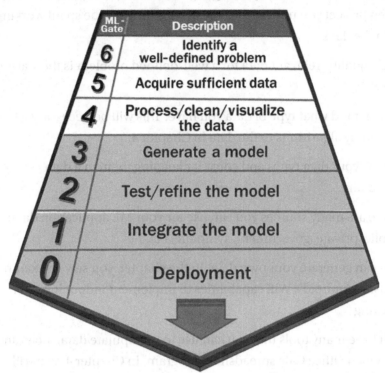

**Machine Learning
ML-Gates 6/5/4**

ML-Gate	Description
6	Identify a well-defined problem
5	Acquire sufficient data
4	Process/clean/visualize the data
3	Generate a model
2	Test/refine the model
1	Integrate the model
0	Deployment

Figure 2-20. *The initial three gates of the ML-Gates methodology are data driven*

It should come as no surprise that the initial three gates of your methodology all center on the data.

Failure to invest adequate time working with your data at ML-Gates 6/5/4 will usually lead to poor results when you get to ML-Gates 3 and 2. At that time, it becomes expensive to go back to resolve data issues.

The next section offers a quick review the key chapter findings before moving on to cloud-based ML implementations.

Key Data Findings

You are on the path to becoming data scientist when you follow these best practices:

- To develop ML applications, you must adopt a data-driven methodology.

- To develop successful ML applications, you must demand more of yourself with respect to your data.

- Most of your code is data wrangling. The 80/20 rule applies: for any given project you undertake, 80% of your time will be spent working with the data.

- High-quality, relevant data for a well-defined problem is the starting point.

- Understand what type of data you have. This will be necessary when you apply algorithms to the data in Chapter 4.

- Define your data types and consider keeping them in a data dictionary.

- There are many sources you can use for your ML application data: public, private, government, synthetic, etc.

- You can generate your own data. In the chapter, you saw an example of using Android's Wifi capabilities to implement indoor location tracking.

- You have many tools that you can use to manipulate data, including the Open Office Calc spreadsheet program. In Chapter 4, you will explore additional data filtering tools available in ML environments.

- The JSON, CSV, and ARFF formats are popular data formats for ML. Get comfortable with them all.

- Most entities do not have enough high-quality data for DL, while CML applications only require a reasonable amount of data to succeed.

- The smartphone is the best data collection device ever invented.

- Visualization is a key aspect of ML and understanding your data.

- To help you visualize your data, you can leverage third-party packages that make it easy to visualize data in the browser and on Android devices.

CHAPTER 3

Leveraging Cloud Platforms

Cloud platforms can be very helpful for deploying ML. This chapter will explore the cloud provider offerings with the following objectives:

- A review of the cloud providers who offer IaaS solutions

- An overview of Google Cloud Platform (GCP) and Amazon Web Services (AWS) cloud offerings, including data storage, data preprocessing, model creation, and model deployment capabilities

- How to implement Weka in the cloud

- An overview of ML cloud provider API offerings

- Project: Implement GCP ML using the Cloud Speech API for Android

- An overview of cloud data tools for ML

- A review of cloud data strategies for ML, including the use of NoSQL databases

3.1 Introduction

The availability of highly scalable computing resources is one of the three megatrends driving the AI explosion. In this chapter, you will analyze the cloud service providers. You are specifically looking for ways they can assist you in delivering ML solutions.

M. Wickham, *Practical Java Machine Learning*, https://doi.org/10.1007/978-1-4842-3951-3_3

The big four cloud providers that offer Infrastructure as a Service (IaaS) solutions are the drivers behind this megatrend. Table 3-1 shows a summary of the big four service providers.

Table 3-1. *Big Four US-Based Cloud Service Providers*

IaaS Provider	Website	Note
Google Cloud Platform	*cloud.google.com*	Easy integration with all of the useful Google tools, including Android for mobile.
Amazon Web Services	*aws.amazon.com*	The largest cloud provider. Full service offering for ML.
Microsoft Azure	*azure.microsoft.com*	Fastest growing IaaS provider.
IBM Cloud	*ibm.com/cloud*	Pioneer in cloud ML with Watson.

IaaS solutions allow you to scale your compute environment to match your demands in terms of CPU, memory, and storage requirements. You only need to pay for resources required. The also give you the ability to easily distribute your resources across geographic regions.

This approach is much easier and affordable than building your own servers and upgrading them when they became too slow.

In this chapter, you will investigate the cloud offerings from the major players to see how they can help you create and deploy ML solutions.

Commercial Cloud Providers

One of the advantages of creating CML solutions compared to DL is that they require for less data and CPU resources. This generally enables you to create solutions entirely on the desktop. However, you should not overlook the cloud. The cloud providers continuously improve their ML offerings. Today they provide an amazing array of services and APIs that make it easier than ever for developers who do not have prior ML experience to create and deploy ML solutions.

Cloud ML services are not free. Regardless of the type of container or virtu-alization technology they use, dedicated or shared hardware (CPU, mem-ory, storage) is required at some point. Each provider typically has a free trial so you can experiment with the service before buying.

Pricing is proportional to the computing and storage resources you consume.

With your focus on Java, you will next investigate the ML cloud potential of the four large US-based cloud providers. In the next sections, you will review the following ML-related services for each of the providers:

- **Data storage**: The IaaS providers have excellent data storage offerings for ML solutions. They include flat file storage, traditional relational databases, NoSQL databases, and others.

- **Data preprocessing**: What tools does the platform provide to help you prepare your data (ML-Gate 4)?

- **Model creation**: What tools and ML frameworks does the cloud platform provide to help you create your model (ML-Gate 3)?

- **Model deployment**: What methods are available to deploy your ML model for predictions, such as API creation or direct hosting access?

The key considerations outlined in Table 3-2 can help you decide if cloud services are a good fit for your ML project.

Table 3-2. *Cloud Provider Considerations*

Category	Consideration
Local resource availability	Do you have a local desktop machine or server that can process large datasets and build ML models? Local processing allows you to retain control of your data and avoid cloud usage fees.
Deep learning?	Deep learning projects tend to favor cloud-based architectures because of their reliance on larger datasets and high computational requirements for model creation.
Geographic diversity	The cloud providers can allow you to spin up resources in a variety of countries and regions globally. It is advantageous to place resources as close as possible to users.
Data size	Do you have a dataset size that is manageable on the desktop, as if often the case for CML projects?
Scalability	Do you anticipate your data or storage requirements will grow in the future? Cloud providers offer much better scalability. Adding cloud resources is much easier than upgrading or purchasing a more powerful desktop/server.
Time constraints	Is model creation time important? Even for CML projects with modest to large datasets, creating the model on the desktop or server single CPU could take minutes to hours. Moving these computation-intensive operations to the cloud could drastically cut your model creation times. If you need real-time or near real-time creation times, the cloud is your only option.
Availability	Do you require high availability? Your project can benefit from the distributed, multi-node architectures provided by all of the cloud providers.
Security considerations	If you operate your own Internet-connected server, you know what a challenge security is. Cloud providers simplify security because you can leverage their massive infrastructure.
Privacy considerations	Your clients might not want their data on a public cloud network managed by one of the big four providers. In this case, you can implement a private cloud solution and charge a premium.

Even if you decide against using a cloud provider for your project, it is important to keep an eye on their product offerings. The services are constantly being updated, and your decision may change based on those updates.

Competitive Positioning

Everybody wants to know which cloud provider is the best for machine learning. Of course, there is no easy answer.

The incumbent advantage plays a large role in any decision. If you already have an established relationship with a cloud provider for non-ML services, you would more likely choose the same provider for its ML offerings. The downside is that you may find yourself locked into a certain provider. The ML landscape changes rapidly and there are some significant differences in the ML product offerings. Keep a watchful eye on how all the services are evolving.

Choosing a framework-agnostic cloud provider has advantages. You will see in the upcoming section that Google Cloud Platform has limited framework selection, mainly relying on the powerful TensorFlow framework. GCP does have the advantage of aligning well with your focus on mobile devices and Android.

The various cloud providers all have their strengths and weaknesses. Figure 3-1 shows a cloud provider summary for some of the largest cloud providers. The chart plots market share along the X-axis with growth rate along the Y-axis. Publicly available corporate earnings reports provided the data. Growth rates represent quarter-by-quarter revenue comparisons. Market share represents reported active users for each of the providers. The cloud providers shown offer pay-as-you-go services that help you deploy ML solutions. The big four US-based players have a combined market share near 70%. Most observers would agree that Amazon Web Services is the market share leader. However, there is fierce competition amongst all the providers. Outside North America, particularly in Asia, Alibaba cloud, also known as Aliyun, is a very strong player.

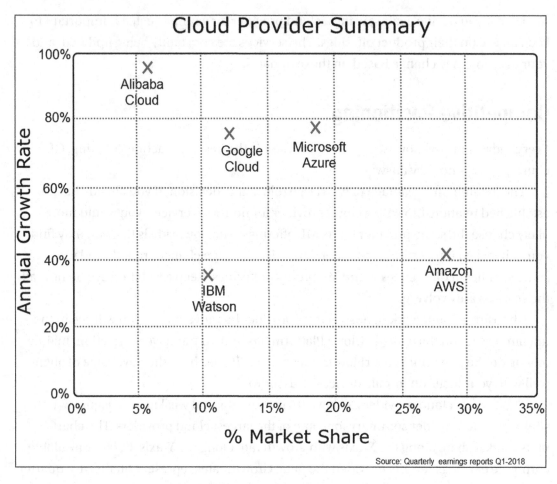

Figure 3-1. *Cloud provider competitive position*

Pricing

If you decide to deploy with cloud services, pricing is important. It represents a direct expense, sitting on the opposite side of the balance sheet as the monetization discussed in Chapter 1.

Fierce market competition between the big four players in recent years has driven down the price of cloud services. Today, there is essentially no pricing arbitrage opportunity available.

> *Due to fierce competition among the largest cloud providers, the cost of cloud resources today is largely identical across platforms. The big four are keenly aware of their competitor's offerings, and pricing arbitrage opportunities no longer exist.*

The cloud providers make it easy to estimate your potential costs. Each provider gives you access to pricing calculators that can give you an accurate idea of your potential costs. Figure 3-2 shows GCP pricing calculator. These interactive tools allow you to specify many parameters including cloud service type, CPU(s), storage, operating system, availability, region, etc. Once you complete the required fields, the tool shows you a calculated monthly and hourly cost.

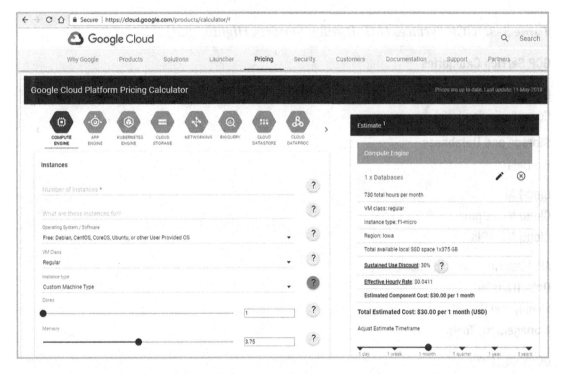

Figure 3-2. *GCP pricing calculator*

Figure 3-2 shows a specified minimum configuration for Google Compute Engine service. The results show a cost of $30 per month or $.04 per hour. If you run a similar calculation on AWS, Azure, or Watson, you will find that pricing is comparable.

Keep in mind when using the pricing tools that the free trial period often offered by the services is not included in the pricing estimates. In many cases, you can receive a one-year free trial to test the provider's services.

3.2 Google Cloud Platform (GCP)

GCP gives you access to a large and growing set of hardware and software resources, known as services. The GCP services offered are vast. Google distributes the GCP services into the higher-level categories shown in Table 3-3. There are many services in each category. Only the specific services you need for ML and DL are highlighted.

Table 3-3. *GCP Services (ML-Related Services Highlighted)*

GCP Service Categories
Compute
Compute Engine
Storage and Databases
Big Data
Cloud AI
Cloud ML Engine
Cloud ML APIs
API Platforms and Ecosystems
Data Transfer
Identity and Security
Management Tools
Developer Tools
Cloud SDK
Cloud Tools for Eclipse
Internet of Things
Professional Services
Productivity Tools
Android
Networking

Next, you will explore the highlighted ML-related services. The first step is to sign up for GCP or sign into your existing account. Figure 3-3 shows the GCP dashboard. The GCP dashboard address is ***https://console.cloud.google.com/***.

The GCP dashboard shows Compute Engine midway down the left panel. Compute Engine lets you use virtual machines that run on Google's infrastructure. When you click Compute Engine, you will be able to create your first virtual machine instance.

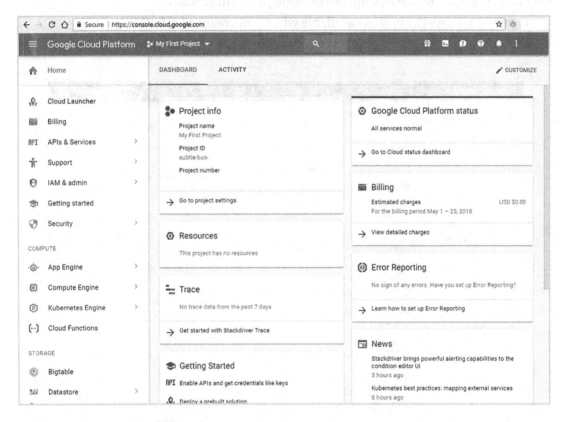

Figure 3-3. *GCP dashboard*

Google Compute Engine (GCE) Virtual Machines (VM)

Even though the GCP ML services focus on DL, the GCE VM gives you the flexibility to deploy any open source package. You can deploy virtual machines to run Java, the open source Weka ML environment, and a Java-based data repository such as the Cassandra NoSQL database. Running these packages on GCE virtual machines is typically easier than configuring them for a local desktop environment because Google provides ready-to-go images for many of the popular packages, and if your project needs to scale at a later date, you have all the advantages of cloud platform scalability.

Figure 3-4 shows the options available when you create a GCE VM.

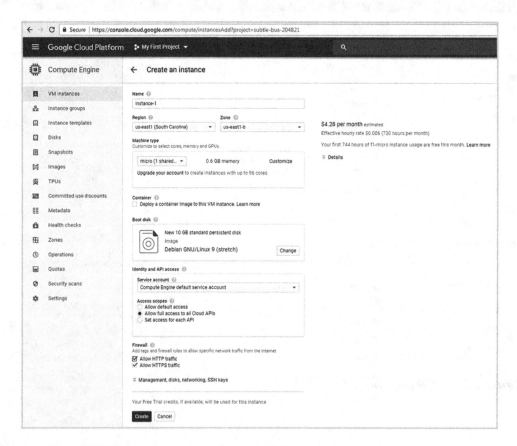

Figure 3-4. *GCE VM instance creation options*

When creating a VM you can choose an instance name and a region for the VM. Of particular interest are the machine type and the boot disk. The machine type specifies the CPU/memory capacity. The pricing information show in the right panel directly relates to the machine capacity you select. For initial testing, you can choose the micro instance. Figure 3-5 shows the boot disk options available. Many Unix configurations are available.

Figure 3-5. *GCE VM instance operating system options*

After you create the instance, CGE will process the request. It will take a few seconds while the instance spins up and becomes available. Figure 3-6 shows the new micro VM instance. If you click the SSH drop-down dialog box, you will be able to immediately connect to the instance, as also shown in Figure 3-6.

Each VM instance you create has an internal and external IP address. If you wish to access the VM from the Internet, you should use the external IP address. You can use FTP clients that support SSH, such as FileZilla, to transfer files to/from your VM. You can also use third-party SSH shell programs such as Putty on Windows. For more information about connection to you VM instance, refer to this Google page:

https://cloud.google.com/compute/docs/instances/connecting-advanced

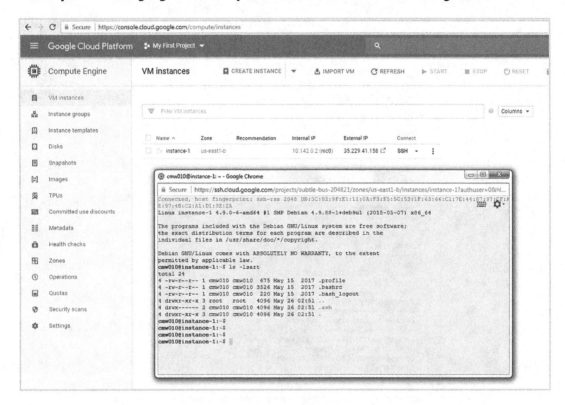

Figure 3-6.   *SSH connection to GCE VM from the GCP dashboard*

If you prefer to use a command-line interface to manage your CGE VMs, Google provides the Google Cloud SDK.

Google Cloud SDK

Google Cloud SDK is a command-line interface for Google Cloud Platform products and services. Cloud SDK is a set of tools:

- gcloud tool: Manages authentication, local configuration, developer workflow, and interactions with the Cloud Platform APIs.

- gsutil tool: gsutil provides command line access to manage Cloud Storage buckets and objects.

- bq tool: Allows you to run queries, manipulate datasets, tables, and entities in BigQuery through the command line.

- kubectl tool: Orchestrates the deployment and management of Kubernetes container clusters on gcloud.

You can run each of these tools interactively or in your automated scripts. Figure 3-7 shows the Cloud SDK download page.

Figure 3-7.   *Google Cloud SDK download page*

Cloud SDK is available for all platforms. Figure 3-8 shows the Cloud SDK after successful installation.

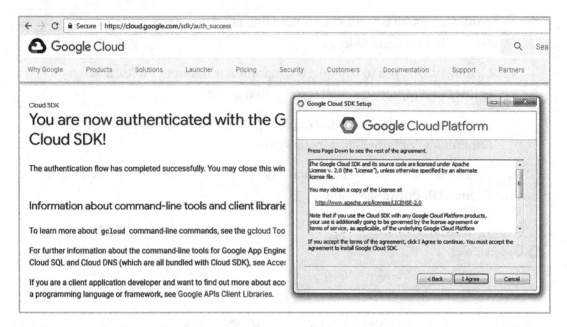

Figure 3-8. *Cloud SDK installation*

Once you have installed Cloud SDK, you can manage any of the GCP services from the command line. This includes the Google Compute Engine (GCE) and Machine Learning Engine (MLE).

The ***gcloud compute*** command-line tool lets you manage your Google Compute Engine resources in a friendlier format than using the Compute Engine API. The ***gcloud init*** command shown in Figure 3-9 allows you to update the parameters of the VM if you decide to change them later.

Figure 3-9. *Configuring GCE VM with gcloud init*

For installing packages such as Java, Weka, or Casssandra, SSH access is the best method. You launched this earlier from the dashboard (Figure 3-6). If you wish to do this from the command line, you can use the following:

```
001    gcloud compute --project "subtle-bus-204821" ssh --zone "us-east1-b" "instance-1"
```

The command line possibilities are endless with Cloud SDK. Check the GCP *gcloud* reference page shown below for all of the available *gcloud* commands:

https://cloud.google.com/sdk/gcloud/reference/

Google Cloud Client Libraries

Google makes it easy for you to use Java with all of the GCP services. The GCP Java client library is available on GitHub:

https://github.com/GoogleCloudPlatform/google-cloud-java

Google recommends the client libraries for calling Google Cloud APIs. According to Google, they provide an optimized developer experience by using each supported language's natural conventions and styles.

The Java client library is also useful for Android developers who wish to integrate with GCP services.

Cloud Tools for Eclipse (CT4E)

Chapter 1 covered setting up the Eclipse development environment for Java. Even though Android developers no longer use Eclipse in favor of Android Studio, Google has always been supportive of the Eclipse IDE. It is no surprise that they provide a cloud tools plugin for Eclipse (CT4E).

Figure 3-10 shows the CT4E documentation page. The plugin is available at

https://github.com/GoogleCloudPlatform/google-cloud-eclipse.

The CT4E wiki page also contains a lot of useful information:

https://github.com/GoogleCloudPlatform/google-cloud-eclipse/wiki/Cloud-Tools-for-Eclipse-Technical-Design

Figure 3-10. *Cloud Tools for Eclipse Quickstart and documentation*

CT4E supports development of Java applications on GCP inside the Eclipse IDE version 4.5 and later. With CT4E, you can build web applications that run on top of GCE.

GCP Cloud Machine Learning Engine (ML Engine)

You have been exploring the Google cloud platform and Cloud SDK. Now you will look at the Cloud ML Engine, the Google Machine Learning Engine API.

Figure 3-11 shows the GCP Cloud ML Engine setup page. The first step is to enable the API. It can take up to 10 minutes to enable.

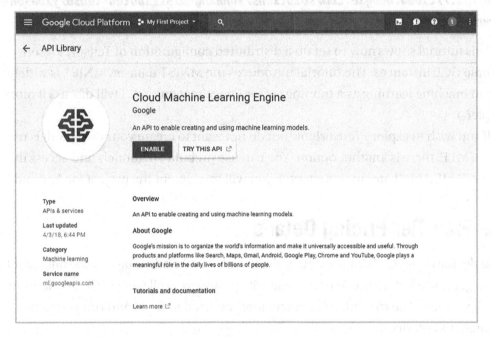

Figure 3-11. *Cloud Machine Learning Engine API*

The Cloud ML Engine API allows you to create and use machine learning models. In the prior section, you saw how to create a VM instance that could host any software package, such as the Weka ML Environment. The Cloud ML Engine simplifies the process by letting you directly interface to specific Google ML tools via API.

The downside is that you are restricted to the ML frameworks that Google MLE supports. Google Cloud MLE currently supports the following frameworks:

- Cloud ML Engine for TensorFlow

- Cloud ML Engine for scikit-learn and XGBoost

- Cloud ML Engine for Keras

Note that none of the Google ML Engine options are Java-based.

The GCP ML services excel for developers who wish to create and deploy DL models based on the TensorFlow framework. Recently, Google added support for additional frameworks including scikit-learn and XGBoost and Keras. Google states that Python-based scikit-learn is for developers who wish to deploy classic ML models.

If you do wish to experiment with Tensorflow on GCE, Google provides an excellent tutorial:

https://cloud.google.com/solutions/running-distributed-tensorflow-on-compute-engine

This tutorial shows how to set up a distributed configuration of TensorFlow on multiple GCE instances. The tutorial introduces the MNIST dataset. MNIST is widely used in machine learning as a training set for image recognition. I will discuss it more in Chapter 4.

If you wish to explore TensorFlow but do not want to create your own models using Google MLE, there is another option. You can use prebuilt DL models and access them with GCP ML APIs. Later in this chapter, you will implement the project for Android.

GCP Free Tier Pricing Details

If you decide to use GCP for you ML project, you can take advantage of the one-year free trial to get started. With the free trial, you will get access to all Google Cloud Platform (GCP) products. The trial includes everything you need to build and run your apps, websites, and services.

The free trial has some limitations:

- Service Level Agreements (SLAs) do not apply. This is reasonable for a free tier offering. You have no recourse if the service(s) become unavailable for any reason.

- Compute engines are limited to eight cores.

- Not all services are available.

- Crypto currency mining not allowed.

- Duration of the free trial is 12 months or $300 usage.

- Does not auto-renew. There is no auto-charge after the free trial ends.

The GCP free trial is a very good deal and certainly can help you identify if the services are suitable for your project.

While you use your GCP free trial, keep in mind that if you go over the trial usage limits shown below, charges will apply:

- 1 f1-micro VM instance per month (US regions, excluding Northern Virginia)

- 30GB of standard persistent disk storage per month

- 5GB of snapshot storage per month

- 1GB egress from North America to other destinations per month (excluding Australia and China)

3.3 Amazon AWS

AWS has a bewildering number of cloud-based services. It seems like every week they introduce a new service. In this section, you will explore the machine learning aspects of AWS.

AWS has a free one-year trial that allows you to explore many of the services, including ML.

Earlier you saw that Synergy Research Group placed AWS in a league of its own. Consistent with their research, AWS does seem to have some advantages:

- AWS has a more robust offering of services, regions, configurations, etc. It really is hard to keep track of all the AWS offerings.

- AWS has a well-developed marketplace. Third-party vendors package free and commercial solutions. These marketplace offerings simplify the setup because you don't have to worry about all of the setup steps.

- For ML, AWS is framework agnostic. AWS ML supports bring your own algorithm and bring your own framework, which provides maximum flexibility.

Table 3-4 shows a list of the AWS ML and EC2 compute services.

Table 3-4. *AWS ML Services*

Service	Description
Amazon Comprehend	Amazon's NLP solution. Amazon Comprehend can extract insights about the content of documents.
Amazon DeepLens	AWS DeepLens is a wireless video camera and API that allow you to develop computer vision applications.
Amazon Lex	A service for building conversational interfaces into any application using voice and text.
Machine Learning	The AWS core ML service for creating and deploying ML models.
Amazon Polly	A cloud service that converts text into lifelike speech. You can use Amazon Polly to develop applications that increase engagement and accessibility.
Amazon SageMaker	A fully managed machine learning service. Many algorithms are available based on the type of data and prediction. SageMaker allows users to deploy TensorFlow on AWS or Apache MXNet on AWS.
Amazon Rekognition	ML API for image and video analysis. The service can identify objects, people, text, scenes, and activities.
Amazon Transcribe	Uses ML to recognize speech in audio files and transcribe them into text.
Amazon Translate	Uses ML to translate documents between English and six other languages.
EC2 Compute Engine	EC2 is the main AWS compute engine you can use to manage VM instances for ML, including AWS Deep Learning AMIs.

Many of these services are similar to DL products available with GCP. You will focus on the two highlighted ML core services: AWS Machine Learning and SageMaker.

AWS Machine Learning

At the heart of AWS ML is the ML service. Similar to GCP, its main interface is the dashboard. Figure 3-12 shows the AWs ML dashboard. The AWS ML dashboard shows all of your AWS ML work items in a single integrated interface.

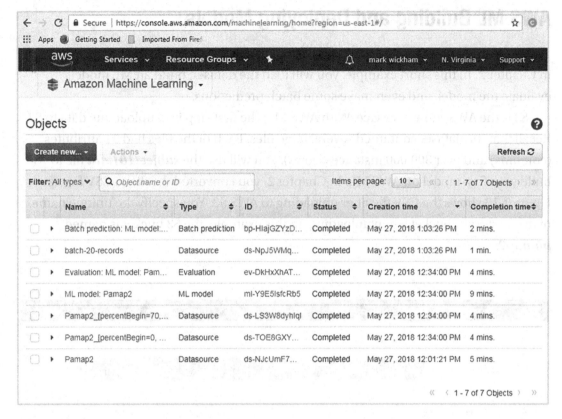

Figure 3-12. *AWS ML dashboard*

Figure 3-12 shows several types of items the AWS dashboard can manage, including

- Datasources

- Models

- Batch predictions

- Evaluations

The dashboard and intuitive AWS ML workflow make it easy to import data, build models, and evaluate the model results.

AWS ML Building and Deploying Models

To demonstrate how simple AWS ML is, let's return to the **PAMAP2_Dataset** introduced in Chapter 2. In this short example, you will load the dataset, build an ML model, evaluate the model, and even make some batch predictions.

S3 is the AWS storage service. With AWS ML, the first step is to upload the data to S3. Recall that the dataset contained several large files. Each of the files had 54 attributes (columns) and over 300,000 instances (rows). You will use the **subject101.dat** file to build your first model on AWS ML. In Chapter 2, you converted the file to CSV format. Figure 3-13 shows the CSV file after uploading to AWS S3. You specify the unique name of the S3 storage bucket when uploading. In this example, the S3 bucket is named **pamap2**.

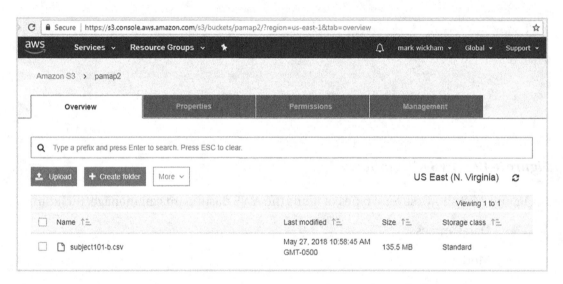

Figure 3-13. *Uploading ML data to AWS S3*

Due to the size of the file, it takes a couple of minutes for the upload to complete. AWS S3 shows the size of the data file as 135MB. Even for CML applications, data sizes can be large, and this is where cloud platforms like AWS excel.

With the data uploaded to S3, the next step is to specify the input data for AWS ML. The easiest way to accomplish this is to use S3 data access. Figure 3-14 shows the AWS ML Create Datasource - Input data screen. Specify the name of the S3 storage bucket you wish to use in the **S3 location** field.

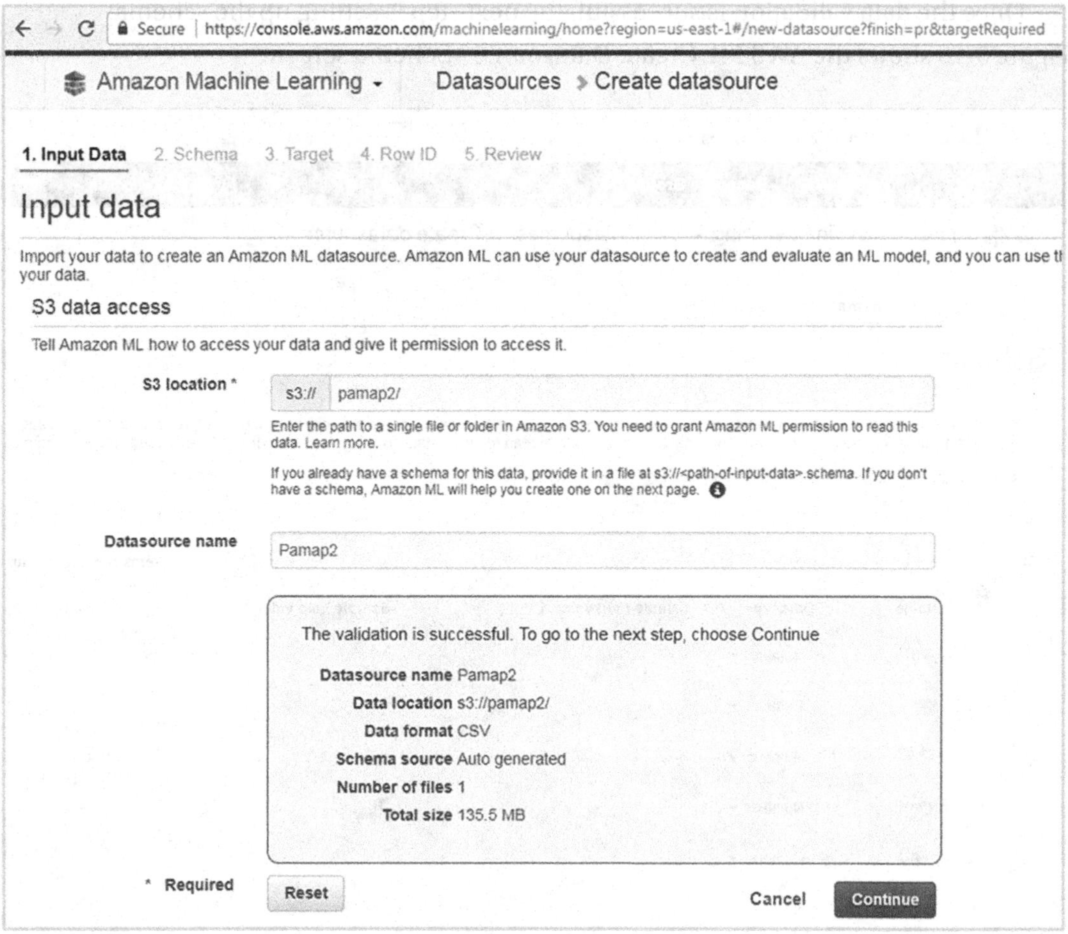

Figure 3-14. *AWS ML input data using S3 input data*

AWS ML will validate the data and let you know if the validation was successful. If unsuccessful, you will need to record the specific issue and then return to OpenOffice where you can correct the data. The three most common issues with data validation are as follows:

- Incorrect field separators are the most common validation issue. Make sure you use comma separators in your CSV files.

- Use quotation marks around text fields. Comma characters (,) inside the text will cause issues. OpenOffice can enclose all text fields in quotation marks.

- Save the file with no BOM (byte order mark) character.

Once the data validation is successful, the next step is setting up the schema. Figure 3-15 shows the AWS ML Create Datasource - Schema screen.

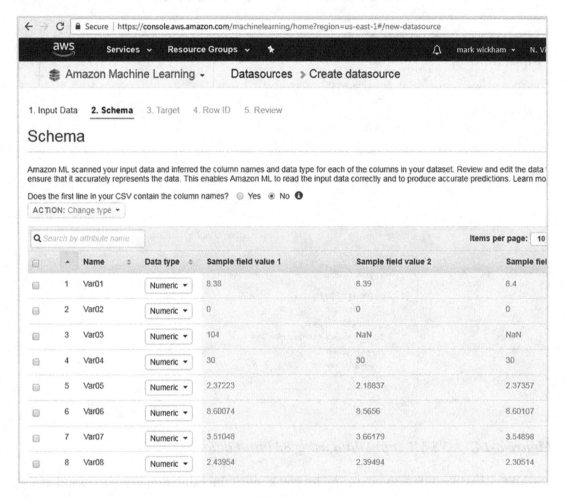

Figure 3-15. *AWS detecting data schema*

When AWS ML validated your data, it assigned a name and data type to each of the attributes (columns). In this step, you want to scan through each attribute and confirm that these assignments were correct. It is also a good time to check that the number of attributes is correct; in this case, there are 54 attributes. This confirms that your CSV value parsing is correct.

Step 3 in the AWS ML Create Datasource sequence is to specify the ***target***. In Chapter 2, you defined this important attribute as the ***label***. In classification, the ***label*** is the value you are trying to predict.

In the **PAMAP2_Dataset**, the label is located in column 2 and identified by assigned name of **Var02**. This label represents the **Activity ID**, as described earlier in Table 2-4. After you specify the label, press Continue, and proceed to the AWS ML model settings. It is now time to create the model.

Figure 3-16 shows the AWS ML model settings screen. This is where the magic happens.

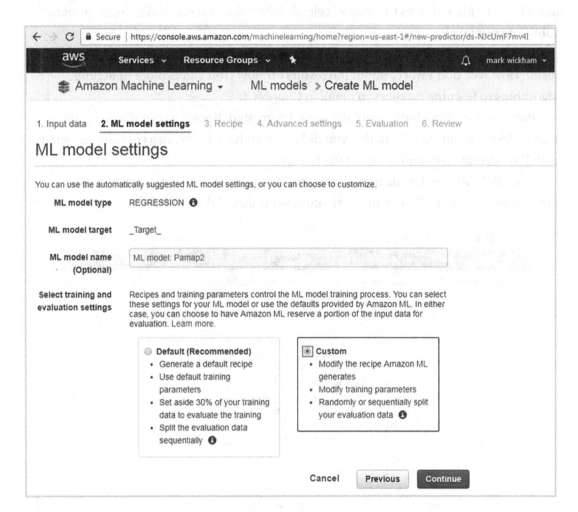

Figure 3-16. *AWS ML model settings*

In the AWS ML model settings, you have two options. You can choose default or custom model training methods.

Spoiler alert: You are not going to get a good result with this model, regardless of which method you choose.

The custom option allows you to specify several items such as division of training data, random or sequential split of evaluation data, and a few other training parameters.

The problem is, even though you have a large dataset, AWS ML is going to choose a regression algorithm for you, regardless of whether you choose custom or go with the defaults. AWS ML enforces this model selection because you entered a single numeric value for your label.

Performing a regression on the **PAMAP2_Dataset** is not going to produce a great result. However, don't worry about the results for now. You will explore matching algorithms to learning category in detail in Chapter 4.

Press the Continue button and the model is created. Because your dataset is large, it can take a few minutes. Note that you did not even have to create a compute resource with VM (virtual machine) to create the model.

After AWS ML creates the model, you can evaluate the model and make batch predictions. Figure 3-17 show the evaluation summary of the model.

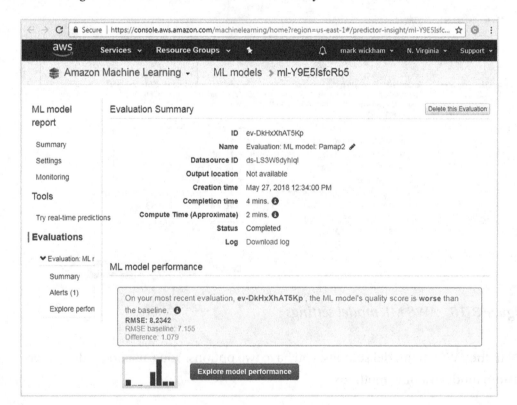

Figure 3-17. *AWS ML model evaluation*

The evaluation summary provides useful information. As you can see, the model creation time was four minutes including two minutes of compute time, which is not bad considering how large the dataset is.

The model performance shows disappointing results: the regression algorithm yielded a quality score worse than the baseline. For regression tasks, AWS uses the standard RMSE (Root Mean Square Error) metric for the baseline. For RMSE baselines, the closer the value is to zero, the better. One of the goals for this book is to avoid math equations, but if you would like to learn more about the RMSE baseline, AWS has an excellent page on measuring regression model accuracy:

https://docs.aws.amazon.com/machine-learning/latest/dg/regression-model-insights.html

The goal of building a model is to utilize it to make predictions. AWS ML allows for real-time, single, or batch predictions. Batch predictions are particularly useful, allowing you to load many instances to classify as a batch. AWS ML accomplishes this by letting you load the batch predictions into an S3 storage bucket, in exactly the same way you loaded the original dataset. You then just need to specify the S3 location of the batch predictions and then the model will produce the results. Making batch predictions does have an incremental cost and I will discuss that at the end of the section.

AWS ML is a really well-designed service. All of the assets created during the process of loading data through to making predictions are available at the dashboard. It is easy to make changes at any phase of the process and experiment with the results.

> *In just a few short minutes, the AWS ML service allows you to load and validate data, define your schema, build a model, evaluate the model, and make batch prediction, all controlled by the centralized AWS ML dashboard. It is ridiculously simple.*

For those cases where you require more control over the selection of the ML algorithm, as with the complex *PAMAP2_Dataset*, let's next explore using AWS compute resources to build your own ML environment.

AWS EC2 AMI

EC2 is the AWS compute engine service. The abbreviation stands for Elastic Compute Cloud. EC2 uses the AMI (Amazon Machine Interface) to define its virtual instances.

EC2 supports many types of AMIs. The first step in building your own ML environment on AWS EC2 is selecting an AMI type to support the application software you intend to deploy.

131

Figure 3-18 shows just a few of the AMI types available. The AMI types span the entire range of operating systems, including Amazon Linux, Ubuntu, Red Hat, CentOS, Windows, etc.

If you look closely at Figure 3-18, you will see several AMIs that are deep learning-based. This is just another example of how easy AWS makes it to deploy ML solutions. In this example, you will select the Deep Learning AMI (Amazon Linux) version 13.0.

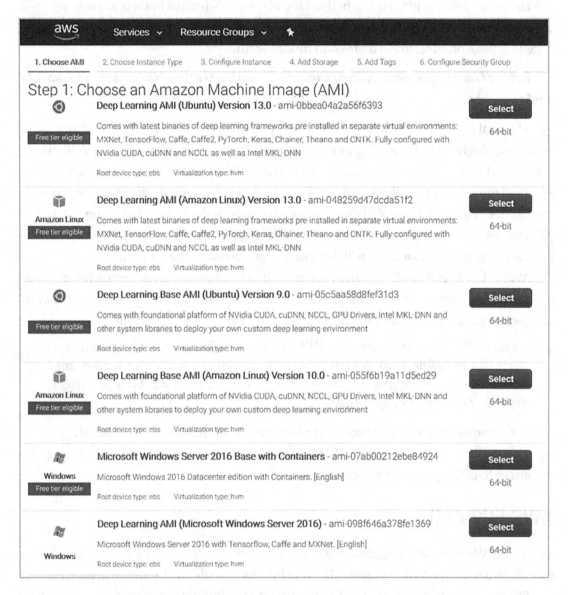

Figure 3-18. *AWS AMI selection*

The AWS ML is framework agnostic. You saw that Google GCP has a strong focus on TensorFlow; in contrast, AWS ML provides you many framework options. When you create a new instance based on the Deep Learning Base AMIs, AWS packages popular ML frameworks with the instance. These special AMIs contain various combinations of Apache MXNet, TensorFlow, Caffe, Caffe2, PyTech, Keras, Theano, CNTK, Nvidia, CUDA, etc. If you look back at Table 1-10 in Chapter 1, you will see that the AWS Deep Learning Base AMIs include almost all of the ML frameworks shown. This eliminates the need to download and install all of the ML framework packages, a real time saver.

After you select your AMI, the next step allows you to choose an instance type. Figure 3-19 shows the AWS instance type selection.

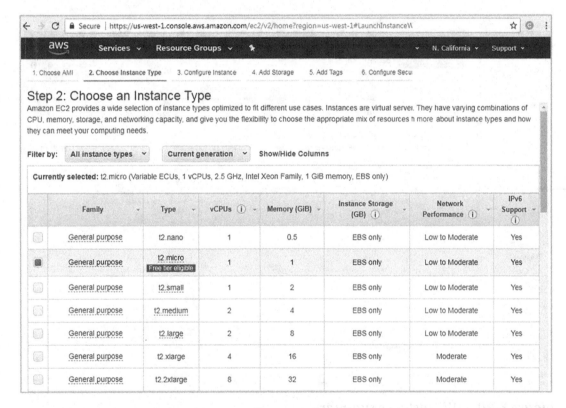

Figure 3-19. *AWS instance type configuration*

For this example, you will choose the *t2.micro* instance type. This is the only instance type that is available for the one-year free tier trial. It is capable of handling many applications, including your goal to host the Weka ML environment in the cloud. Sometimes AWS will warn you that your selected instance is not available for the free tier.

This is often due to the storage settings. If you receive this warning, double check that your storage does not exceed 30GB before you launch the instance. You can edit the storage in the *Storage* section of the *Review* stage.

The t2.micro instance is fine for getting to know AWS ML, but Amazon recommends higher-level configurations for ML training and predictions. Amazon recommends the ml.m4, ml.c4, and ml.c5 instance families for training and the ml.c5.xl instance type for predictions.

Before you can access the instance, you must configure its security. Proceed through the steps, including assigning keys for the secure shell access.

Figure 3-20 shows the instance once it is up and running.

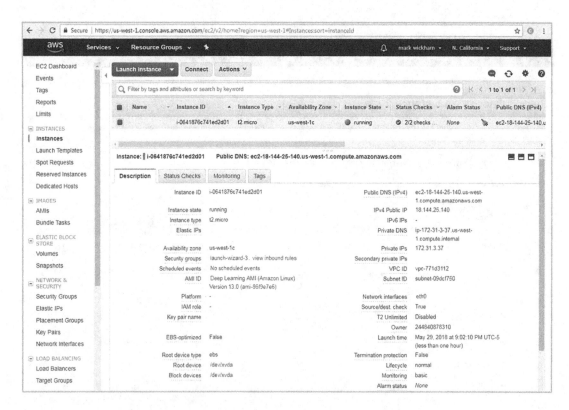

Figure 3-20. *AWS instance summary*

Notice in Figure 3-20 that the instance has a public IP and DNS name. This is how you will access the instance from the outside world. You will use secure shell (SSH) with the keys you set up during the instance security configuration.

With the instance running, you are ready to install and run Weka in the AWS cloud.

Running Weka ML in the AWS Cloud

Connect to the public IP of the instance using a secure SSH client, or Putty if you are on Windows. When connecting, note that the user name is ec2-user and the credentials are the key that you created at the completion of the setup process. Figure 3-21 shows the initial connection.

```
Using username "ec2-user".
Authenticating with public key "imported-openssh-key"
Passphrase for key "imported-openssh-key":

===================================================================
       _|  _|_  )
      _|  (     /    Deep Learning AMI (Amazon Linux)
     __|\___|__|
===================================================================

Official Conda User Guide: https://conda.io/docs/user-guide/index.html
AWS Deep Learning AMI Homepage: https://aws.amazon.com/machine-learning/amis/
Developer Guide and Release Notes: https://docs.aws.amazon.com/dlami/latest/devg
uide/what-is-dlami.html
Support: https://forums.aws.amazon.com/forum.jspa?forumID=263

Amazon Linux version 2018.03 is available.
[ec2-user@ip-172-31-3-37 ~]$
```

Figure 3-21. *Connection to the AWS EC2 instance*

When you first connect to the instance, you can change into the ***/usr/local*** directory and see the preinstalled deep learning packages included with the AMI:

```
001   [ec2-user@ip-172-31-3-37 local]$ pwd
002   /usr/local
003   [ec2-user@ip-172-31-3-37 local]$ ls -lsart
004   total 50096
005       4 drwxr-xr-x  2 root root     4096 Jan  6  2012 src
006       4 drwxr-xr-x  2 root root     4096 Jan  6  2012 sbin
007       4 drwxr-xr-x  2 root root     4096 Jan  6  2012 libexec
008       4 drwxr-xr-x  2 root root     4096 Jan  6  2012 games
009       4 drwxr-xr-x  2 root root     4096 Jan  6  2012 etc
010       4 drwxr-xr-x 13 root root     4096 Jan 15 18:42 ..
011       4 drwxr-xr-x  8 root root     4096 May  8 21:12 share
012       4 drwxr-xr-x 18 root root     4096 May  8 21:13 cuda-8.0
013       4 drwxr-xr-x 19 root root     4096 May  8 21:15 cuda-9.0
014       4 drwxr-xr-x 19 root root     4096 May 10 21:17 cuda-9.1
```

```
015        4 drwxr-xr-x 19 root root      4096 May 10 21:19 cuda-9.2
016        4 drwxr-xr-x  7 root root      4096 May 10 08:18 mpi
017        4 drwxr-xr-x  7 root root      4096 May 10 09:39 lib64
018        4 drwxr-xr-x  9 root root      4096 May 10 09:39 include
019        4 drwxr-xr-x  7 root root      4096 May 10 09:39 lib
020        4 drwxr-xr-x  2 root root      4096 May 10 09:39 test
021        4 drwxr-xr-x 22 root root      4096 May 10 09:39 caffe2
022        4 drwxr-xr-x  3 root root      4096 May 10 09:39 caffe
023        4 drwxr-xr-x  2 root root      4096 May 10 09:39 bin
024        0 lrwxrwxrwx  1 root root        20 May 10 09:51 cuda -> /usr/
                                                            local/cuda-9.0/
025        4 drwxr-xr-x 18 root root      4096 May 30 02:35 .
```

Note the above code shows the packages available for Deep Learning AMI (Amazon Linux) version 13.0. The packages are constantly being updated by AWS, so you may see slightly different contents after launching your AMI.

Weka is not included so you need to add it yourself.

Note: You will prepend **sudo** to each of the following Unix commands to avoid permission issues.

Weka requires Java, so you first need to check if Java was included, and if so, which version:

```
001    [ec2-user@ip-172-31-3-37 local]$ java -version
002    openjdk version "1.8.0_121"
003    OpenJDK Runtime Environment (Zulu 8.20.0.5-linux64) (build 1.8.0_
       121-b15)
004    OpenJDK 64-Bit Server VM (Zulu 8.20.0.5-linux64) (build 25.121-b15,
       mixed mode)
```

As is often the case with VM instances from the cloud providers, they come preinstalled with the OpenJDK Java distribution. OpenJDK is fine for most applications. However, for Weka installations, using the Oracle Java JDK is required because Weka requires some of the Swing GUI libraries not packaged in OpenJDK. If you try to run Weka with OpenJDK, you will see the following exception, indicating a Sun launcher class was not able to load:

```
001    [ec2-user@ip-172-31-3-37 local]$ sudo java -cp weka.jar weka.
       classifiers.trees.J48 -t /usr/local/weka-3-8-2/data/iris.arff
```

```
002     Exception in thread "main" java.lang.UnsupportedClassVersionError:
        weka/classifiers/trees/J48 : Unsupported major.minor version 52.0
003             at java.lang.ClassLoader.defineClass1(Native Method)
004             at java.lang.ClassLoader.defineClass(ClassLoader.java:803)
005             at java.security.SecureClassLoader.
                defineClass(SecureClassLoader.java:142)
006             at sun.misc.Launcher$AppClassLoader.loadClass(Launcher.
                java:312)
007             at java.lang.ClassLoader.loadClass(ClassLoader.java:358)
008             at sun.launcher.LauncherHelper.
                checkAndLoadMain(LauncherHelper.java:482)
```

The solution is to download the Oracle JDK with the following **wget** command. Lines 001-006 set up the environment variables. Line 008 executes the **wget**. Line 010 installs the Oracle JDK package you downloaded.

```
001     [ec2-user@ip-172-31-3-37 local]$ java_base_version="8"
002     [ec2-user@ip-172-31-3-37 local]$ java_sub_version="141"
003     [ec2-user@ip-172-31-3-37 local]$ java_base_build="15"
004     [ec2-user@ip-172-31-3-37 local]$ java_version="${java_base_version}
                                        u${java_sub_version}"
005     [ec2-user@ip-172-31-3-37 local]$ java_build="b${java_base_build}"
006     [ec2-user@ip-172-31-3-37 local]$ java_version_with_build="${java_
        version}-${java_build}"
007
008     [ec2-user@ip-172-31-3-37 local]$ sudo wget --no-check-certificate
        --no-cookies --header "Cookie: oraclelicense=accept-securebackup-
        cookie" http://download.oracle.com/otn-pub/java/jdk/${java_version_
        with_build}/336fa29ff2bb4ef291e347e091f7f4a7/jdk-${java_version}-
        linux-x64.rpm
009
010     [ec2-user@ip-172-31-3-37 local]$ sudo yum install -y jdk-8u141-
        linux-x64.rpm
```

After the install of Oracle JDK completes, you now have multiple version of Java installed on the VM instance. The following command shows that you actually have three versions: two versions of OpenJDK and the new Oracle JDK. It also allows you to select the Oracle JDK as the current selection.

```
001  [ec2-user@ip-172-31-3-37 local]$ sudo alternatives --config java
002
003  There are 3 programs which provide 'java'.
004
005    Selection     Command
006    ------------------------------------------------
007     1            /usr/lib/jvm/jre-1.7.0-openjdk.x86_64/bin/java
008     2            /usr/lib/jvm/jre-1.8.0-openjdk.x86_64/bin/java
009  *+ 3            /usr/java/jdk1.8.0_141/jre/bin/java
010
011  Enter to keep the current selection[+], or type selection number: 3
012  [ec2-user@ip-172-31-3-37 local]$
```

Now that Java is ready to go, it is time to download and install the latest stable version of Weka:

```
001  [ec2-user@ip-172-31-3-37 local]$ sudo wget http://svwh.
     dl.sourceforge.net/project/weka/weka-3-8/3.8.2/weka-3-8-2.zip
002  --2018-05-30 02:35:43--  http://svwh.dl.sourceforge.net/project/weka/
     weka-3-8/3.8.2/weka-3-8-2.zip
003  Resolving svwh.dl.sourceforge.net (svwh.dl.sourceforge.net)...
     72.5.72.15, 2606:c680:0:b:3830:34ff:fe66:6663
004  Connecting to svwh.dl.sourceforge.net (svwh.dl.sourceforge.
     net)|72.5.72.15|:80... connected.
005  HTTP request sent, awaiting response... 200 OK
006  Length: 51223056 (49M) [application/octet-stream]
007  Saving to: 'weka-3-8-2.zip'
008
009  weka-3-8-2.zip
     100%[======================================>]  48.85M  39.8MB/s
     in 1.2s
010
011  2018-05-30 02:35:45 (39.8 MB/s) - 'weka-3-8-2.zip' saved
     [51223056/51223056]
```

When the download completes, confirm the ***weka-3-8-2.zip*** file exists in the ***/usr/ local*** directory:

```
001    [ec2-user@ip-172-31-3-37 local]$ pwd
002    /usr/local
003    [ec2-user@ip-172-31-3-37 local]$ ls -lsart weka*
004    total 50096
005    50024 -rw-r--r--  1 root root 51223056 Dec 21 21:16 weka-3-8-2.zip
006    [ec2-user@ip-172-31-3-37 local]$
```

Next, unzip Weka as shown and when complete, change into the new ***weka-3-8-2*** directory, and you will see the following contents in the new directory:

```
007    [ec2-user@ip-172-31-3-37]$ pwd
008    /usr/local/
009
010    [ec2-user@ip-172-31-3-37]$ sudo unzip weka-3-8-2.zip
011
012    [ec2-user@ip-172.31.3.37]$ cd weka-3-8-2
013
014    [ec2-user@ip-172-31-3-37 weka-3-8-2]$ ls -l
015    total 42908
016    drwxr-xr-x 2 root root     4096 Dec 22 09:30 changelogs
017    -rw-r--r-- 1 root root    35147 Dec 22 09:30 COPYING
018    drwxr-xr-x 2 root root     4096 Dec 22 09:30 data
019    drwxr-xr-x 3 root root     4096 Dec 22 09:30 doc
020    -rw-r--r-- 1 root root      510 Dec 22 09:30 documentation.css
021    -rw-r--r-- 1 root root     1863 Dec 22 09:30 documentation.html
022    -rw-r--r-- 1 root root    16170 Dec 22 09:30 README
023    -rw-r--r-- 1 root root    43377 Dec 22 09:30 remoteExperimentServer.jar
024    -rw-r--r-- 1 root root 14763219 Dec 22 09:30 wekaexamples.zip
025    -rw-r--r-- 1 root root    30414 Dec 22 09:30 weka.gif
026    -rw-r--r-- 1 root root   359270 Dec 22 09:30 weka.ico
027    -rw-r--r-- 1 root root 11111002 Dec 22 09:30 weka.jar
028    -rw-r--r-- 1 root root  6621767 Dec 22 09:30 WekaManual.pdf
029    -rw-r--r-- 1 root root 10923433 Dec 22 09:30 weka-src.jar
```

You are now ready to run Weka in the cloud. To run Weka from the command line, you instruct Java to run a classifier class on one of the datasets included with Weka. In this example, you will run the random forest classifier on the iris.arff dataset. To run a specified class instead of the main class, provide the *–cp* option. The following shows the successful Weka classification:

```
001   [ec2-user@ip-172-31-3-37 weka-3-8-2]$ sudo java -cp weka.jar weka.
      classifiers.trees.J48 -t/usr/local/weka-3-8-2/data/iris.arff
002
003   === Classifier model (full training set) ===
004
005   J48 pruned tree
006   ------------------
007   ...
008   Number of Leaves  :     5
009   Size of the tree :      9
010   Time taken to build model: 0.48 seconds
011   Time taken to test model on training data: 0.01 seconds
012
013   === Error on training data ===
014
015   Correctly Classified Instances        147             98    %
016   Incorrectly Classified Instances        3              2    %
017   Kappa statistic                       0.97
018   Mean absolute error                   0.0233
019   Root mean squared error               0.108
020   Relative absolute error               5.2482 %
021   Root relative squared error          22.9089 %
022   Total Number of Instances             150
023
024   ...
025
026   === Confusion Matrix ===
027
028    a  b  c   <-- classified as
029   50  0  0 |  a = Iris-setosa
```

```
030      0 49  1 |  b = Iris-versicolor
031      0  2 48 |  c = Iris-virginica
032
033   Time taken to perform cross-validation: 0.08 seconds
034
035   === Stratified cross-validation ===
036
037   ...
038
039   === Detailed Accuracy By Class ===
040
041   ...
042
043   === Confusion Matrix ===
044
045      a  b  c   <-- classified as
046     49  1  0 |  a = Iris-setosa
047      0 47  3 |  b = Iris-versicolor
048      0  2 48 |  c = Iris-virginica
```

I will cover Weka in detail in Chapter 4. This example shows that it is quite simple to implement Weka on the AWS cloud.

AWS SageMaker

You have seen a couple approaches to building ML on AWS, first by using the AWS ML service via the dashboard, and second by implementing your own Weka environment on AWS EC2 compute instance.

AWS SageMaker is a fully managed platform to help you build DL models. It is one of the recently added AWS services. The main idea behind SageMaker is that ML has been difficult for developers for the following reasons:

- The process of gathering data, processing data, building models, testing models, and deploying models creates excessive manual work for developers.

- Due to repetitive manual work, creating ML solutions is too time consuming.

- Creating ML solutions is too complicated because the required data and analytic skillsets have replaced traditional software development.

SageMaker tries to address these issues. It promises to remove complexity and overcome the barriers that slow down developers. Figure 3-22 shows the main AWS SageMaker page.

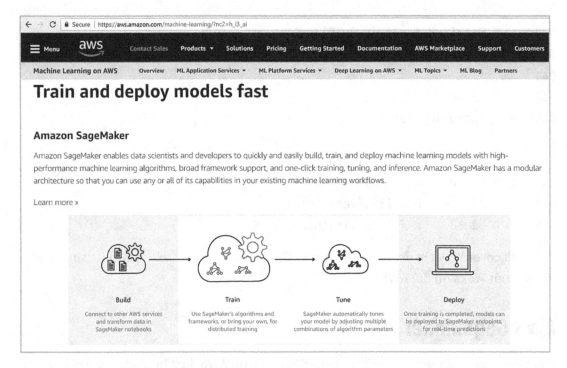

Figure 3-22. *AWS SageMaker*

Like all AWS services, there is extensive online documentation to help you understand the service. The link for the SageMaker developer guide is

https://docs.aws.amazon.com/sagemaker/latest/dg.

SageMaker has a lot of potential. Two particularly important features make it a powerful way to implement ML on AWS- notebook instances, and its flexible support for algorithms.

The SageMaker notebook instance is a compute instance running the Jupyter Notebook App. Jupyter is an open source web app that runs on Python (hence its spelling) and allows you to create and share documents that contain live code and visualizations. It is very popular in the Python and DL realms.

Hosted Jupyter notebooks make it easy to explore and visualize training data in Amazon S3 storage, similar to the JavaScript options covered in Chapter 2. There are several kernels for Jupyter, including support for Python, Apache MXNet, TensorFlow, and PySpark. Jupyter does not support a Java kernel. Notebook instances are an important part of implementing ML with SageMaker.

AWS Labs maintains some excellent examples for you to explore SageMaker on GitHub here:

https://github.com/awslabs/amazon-sagemaker-examples

The other interesting feature of SageMaker is its algorithm flexibility. SageMaker supports two classes of algorithms: built-in algorithms and bring-your-own algorithms. The list of built-in algorithms is available at

https://docs.aws.amazon.com/sagemaker/latest/dg/algos.html.

The algorithm list is very complete. AWS claims the preinstalled algorithms deliver 10 times the performance of other providers due to optimization. That's an impressive claim. However, AWS does not offer details on how they do this, or for which algorithms it applies.

User can bring their own algorithms or frameworks. The SageMaker examples on GitHub show how to do this for a variety of models and algorithms including XGBoost, k-means, R, scikit, MXNet, and TensorFlow.

AWS SageMaker provides impressive ML functionality, but unfortunately is does not integrate well with Java due to its reliance on Jupyter. Next, you will explore the AWS SDK for Java.

AWS SDK for Java

Amazon supports Java developers. To show their love for us, they release the SDK for Java to help us accelerate our development. Figure 3-23 shows the main Explore Java on the AWS page available at *https://aws.amazon.com/java/*. The page includes links for Java, Eclipse, and Android.

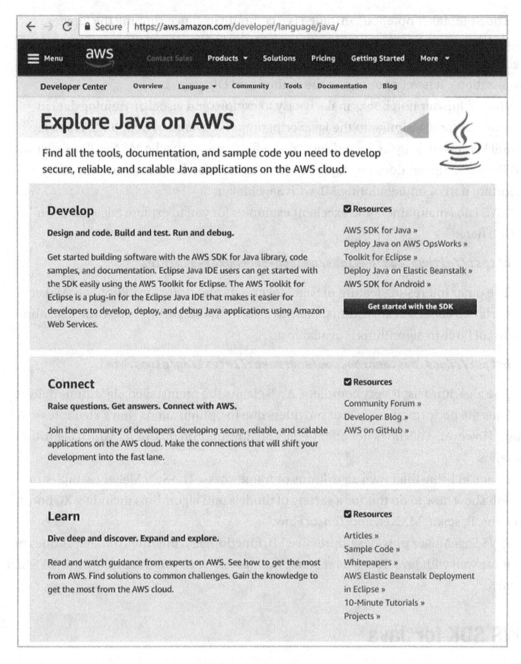

Figure 3-23. *AWS Java Developer Center*

The Java SDK is available in several formats. Table 3-5 provides a summary of the formats.

Table 3-5. *Summary of AWS Java SDK Packages*

Format	Notes
SDK for Java version 1.11	The currently supported SDK. Allows you to access all of the AWS services from Java.
Java Toolkit for Eclipse	The AWS Toolkit for Eclipse conveniently includes the AWS SDK for Java, so you can get started building Java applications on AWS infrastructure services in Eclipse, including Amazon S3, Amazon EC2, Amazon DynamoDB, and Amazon ML.
SDK for Android	Complete set of documentation, libraries, and samples to help you integrate AWS services into Android Apps.
Machine Learning SDK for Java	This is a special SDK only for AWS ML. It is only downloadable from a Maven repository. If you only need AWS ML access, this smaller library keeps your project size lean by excluding all of the other AWS services.
SDK for Java version 2.0	AWS SDK for Java 2.0 Developer Preview Build Status. Version 2.0 is currently a preview and not recommended for production use yet.

The first three formats shown in the table are available for download by directly clicking through the links provided in the AWS Java Development Center.

The SDK for Android download includes many library files, samples, and documentation for all of the AWS services. Figure 3-24 shows the ML library jar file. Note that it is only 48Kb. You can view the contents of the .jar library using the 7-Zip utility to open the archive. The link for the Maven repositories is

http://central.maven.org/maven2/com/amazonaws/aws-android-sdk-machinelearning.

```
←  →  C  ⌂  ⓘ Not secure │ central.maven.org/maven2/com/amazonaws/aws-android-sdk-machinelearning/2.6.28/

com/amazonaws/aws-android-sdk-machinelearning/2.6.28

../
aws-android-sdk-machinelearning-2.6.28-javado...   2018-08-17 00:54     153604
aws-android-sdk-machinelearning-2.6.28-javado...   2018-08-17 00:54        836
aws-android-sdk-machinelearning-2.6.28-javado...   2018-08-17 00:54         32
aws-android-sdk-machinelearning-2.6.28-javado...   2018-08-17 00:54         40
aws-android-sdk-machinelearning-2.6.28-source...   2018-08-17 00:54      54152
aws-android-sdk-machinelearning-2.6.28-source...   2018-08-17 00:54        836
aws-android-sdk-machinelearning-2.6.28-source...   2018-08-17 00:54         32
aws-android-sdk-machinelearning-2.6.28-source...   2018-08-17 00:54         40
aws-android-sdk-machinelearning-2.6.28.jar         2018-08-17 00:54      48514
aws-android-sdk-machinelearning-2.6.28.jar.as...   2018-08-17 00:54        836
aws-android-sdk-machinelearning-2.6.28.jar.md...   2018-08-17 00:54         32
aws-android-sdk-machinelearning-2.6.28.jar.sh...   2018-08-17 00:54         40
aws-android-sdk-machinelearning-2.6.28.pom         2018-08-17 00:54       1364
aws-android-sdk-machinelearning-2.6.28.pom.as...   2018-08-17 00:54        836
aws-android-sdk-machinelearning-2.6.28.pom.md...   2018-08-17 00:54         32
aws-android-sdk-machinelearning-2.6.28.pom.sh...   2018-08-17 00:54         40
```

Figure 3-24. *AWS SDK for Android Machine Learning Library*

There are two versions of the SDK for Java. Version Java 1 is the currently available version, and Java 2 is a developer preview rewrite of Java 1 with some new features. Both versions enable you to easily interface your Java projects with AWS. Java 2 includes two key new features:

- Non-blocking IO

- Pluggable HTTP protocol stacks

If you develop for Android, you probably know that Google discontinued use of the Apache *HTTPClient* stack in Android recently. The pluggable HTTP feature in Java 2 follows this trend as Java 1 only supported *HTTPClient*. With Java 2.0 you can use other stacks such as *HTTPurlConnection* or *OkHTTP*.

With the Java SDK, you can get started in minutes using Maven or any build system that supports Maven Central as an artifact source. The developer guide includes detailed setup and installation instructions, available at

https://docs.aws.amazon.com/sdk-for-java/v1/developer-guide/welcome.html.

If you are interested in the code for the Java SDK, it is available at the following sites:

https://github.com/aws/aws-sdk-java
https://github.com/aws/aws-sdk-java-v2

If you do not require all of the AWS services supported by the SDK, you can download just the SDK for Machine Learning at *https://mvnrepository.com/artifact/com.amazonaws/aws-java-sdk-machinelearning*.

Figure 3-25 shows the Maven repository for the Java machine learning library. You can download the .jar file or see the instructions for Maven or Gradle depending on your build environment.

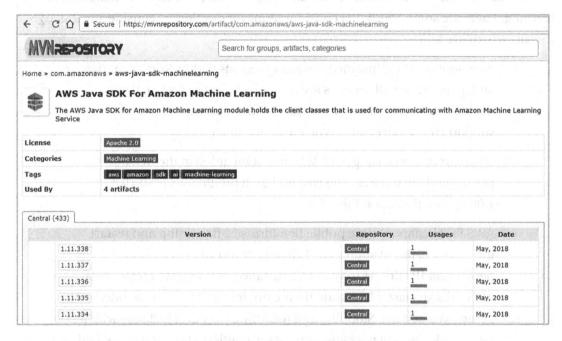

Figure 3-25. *Maven repository for AWS ML SDK for Java*

With the help of the AWS Java SDK for Machine Learning, any ML task available via the AWS ML dashboard is reproducible programmatically from your Java code.

AWS Free Tier Pricing Details

Similar to GCP, AWS offers you a 12-month introductory period. The free tier includes some free services that never expire. Other free services are available for the 12-month period. Amazon provides full details of the free-tier service coverage at

https://aws.amazon.com/free/.

The AWS free tier is quite generous. The main highlights of the free tier include

- 750 hours of EC2 t2.micro instance. You can configure the instance as you wish. You used the t2.micro instance earlier to configure Weka in the cloud.

147

- AWS provides 5GB of S3 storage in the free tier. This is adequate for exploring AWS ML.

- AWS allows 1 million API calls per month. Developers can use these API calls to explore the AWS ML APIs.

You can use the t2.micro instance for almost anything you wish, including machine learning. There are some additional considerations for developers considering the AWS free tier to explore ML:

- AWS supports EC2 instances on many regions within North America and globally. Not all services are available for every region. If you decide to use AWS ML services, you need to choose a region that supports the service before you create the instance.

- Batch predictions using AWS ML are not included in the free tier pricing and are not free. The cost for batch predictions is $0.10 per 1,000 predictions. See Table 1-5.

- AWS EC2 instances have public IP addresses. If you stop and restart the instance, the IP address will change. If you wish to assign a permanent IP address to your EC2 instance, you need to create what AWS calls an elastic IP. Elastic IPs are not free and are not included in the AWS free tier. Stopping and restarting your EC2 instance with a new IP address will not cause any loss of configuration or data related to the instance.

If you pursue AWS SageMaker for ML, on top of the overall free tier, AWS offers an additional monthly free tier of 250 hours for building models plus 50 hours for training on SageMaker.

3.4 Machine Learning APIs

There may be times when you don't need to build and deploy your own ML models. In these cases, you can leverage the cloud APIs provided by the big four cloud providers.

In the preceding section, I covered the AWS ML services. Figure 3-26 summarizes the high-level APIs provided by the big four cloud providers: Amazon, Google, IBM, and Microsoft. All of their APIs fall into five distinct categories: language, vision, data insights, speech, and search.

High-Level ML API Comparison

	AWS ML API	Google ML API	IBM Watson ML API	Microsoft Azure ML API
Language	Lex Comprehend	Language Cloud Translation	Alchemy Language Conversation Dialog Document Conversion Language Translator Nat. Lang. Classifier Nat. Lang. Understanding Personality Insights Retrieve and Rank Tone Analyzer	Bing Spell Check Language Understanding Linguistic Analysis Text Analytics Translator Text Web Language Model
Vision	Deep Lens Rekognition	Cloud Vision Video Intelligence Label Detection	Visual Recognition	Computer Vision Content Moderator Custom Vision Service Emotion Face Video Indexer
Knowledge /Data Insight	Machine Learning Sagemaker		Alchemy Data News Discovery Discovery News Tradeoff Analytics	Custom Decision Service QnA Maker Recommendations Knowledge Exploration Academic Knowledge Entity Linking Inteligence URL Preview Answer Search Anomaly Finder Conversation Learner
Speech	Polly Transcribe Translate	Cloud Speech	Speech to Text Text to Speech	Bing Speech Custom Speech Service Speaker Recognition Translator
Search/ Other		Cloud Jobs		Bing Search (7 APIs) Bing Autosuggest

Figure 3-26. *High-level ML API comparison*

While Google and AWS do a great job at providing the lower-level tools and building blocks we need to implement ML solutions, IBM and Microsoft do an equally fine job at providing higher-level models we can access by API. Figure 3-26 shows that they have many APIs to solve a wide variety of problems in each of the five categories.

Most of these APIs employ DL methods created from the massive amount of data the cloud providers own. The APIs are mostly free to try. If you decide to use these APIs commercially, you will typically just need to pay the cloud provider's inference fee per API call. Recall that the inference fee is the fee to make predictions. You can make real time predictions or batch predictions. See Table 1-5 for pricing approximations.

Using ML REST APIs

If you decide to use one of the services in Figure 3-26, they will most likely allow access to the service via a REST API call. Making predictions (inference) with ML model APIs using REST calls is easy. The APIs normally use the REST protocol with the JSON data format covered in Chapter 2.

When making a REST call to the API, both the request and response are in JSON format. For example, Listing 3-1 shows a GCP Cloud Vision API JSON request. The listing demonstrates only the most important fields: your API key, a reference to the image source, and the feature being requested. If you wish to implement this API call, refer to the following link for full details on the specific JSON requirements:

https://cloud.google.com/vision/docs/request

Listing 3-1. Example of GCP Cloud Vision API JSON Request

```
001   POST https://vision.googleapis.com/v1/images:annotate?key=YOUR_API_KEY
002   {
003      "requests": [
004         {
005            "images": {
006               "content": "your_image.jpg"
007            },
008            "features": [
009               {
010                  "type": "LABEL_DETECTION"
011               }
012            ]
013         }
014      ]
015   }
```

After you post the request, you will receive a JSON response. Listing 3-2 shows a successful JSON response; in this case, you are getting back the top two image label predictions for the image file submitted in the request.

Listing 3-2. Example of GCP Cloud Vision API JSON Response

```
001  {
002     "responses": [
003       {
004         "labelAnnotations": [
005           {
006             "mid": "/m/01yrx",
007             "description": "cat",
008             "score": 0.92562944
009           },
010           {
011             "mid": "/m/0307l",
012             "description": "cat like mammal",
013             "score": 0.65950978
014           }
015         ]
016       }
017     ]
018  }
```

To help you submit JSON requests and parse JSON responses, the Java SDK provides example code. Additionally, Java client libraries are available for each of the various APIs. For this example, refer the Cloud Vision API client library and select the Java tab, at **https://cloud.google.com/vision/docs/libraries**.

In the next section, you will use this approach to build a complete Android app using JSON to access the powerful GCP Cloud Speech API. The Google Cloud Speech API will allow you to transcribe audio files recorded by the device.

Alternative ML API Providers

There are times when you might want to consider alternative cloud API model providers. If you have a niche application not covered by the big cloud players, alternative providers who specialize in certain applications could provide a solution.

Sometimes you just wish to differentiate your product from competitors who all use the large cloud provider APIs. Using alternative smaller cloud API providers in these cases could be a viable strategy.

Table 3-6 shows some alternative cloud ML API providers.

Table 3-6. *Alternative Cloud ML API Providers*

Provider	Description
www.diffbot.com/products/automatic/	Data extraction
www.beyondverbal.com/api/	Emotion and vocal analytics from an Israeli company
www.kairos.com/face-recognition-api	Face recognition
https://wit.ai/getting-started	Chat bot
www.openalpr.com/cloud-api.html	Real-time license plate recognition

Whether you use alternative ML APIs or ML APIs from the big four cloud providers, there are a huge number of product offerings you can choose from. If you think back to the M-Gates, at MLG6, you must start with a well-defined problem. At that point, it is a best practice to scan the available APIs to see if any of them exactly match the problem. There is no need to reinvent the wheel. The large cloud providers have so much data, it would be hard to create a better solution than the models they make available to us. While the large four cloud providers have many APIs, it can be fruitful to explore if external alternatives are available.

3.5 Project: GCP Cloud Speech API for Android

In this project, you will implement the GCP Cloud Speech API Android app. You will use the Android Studio IDE. This project is copyrighted and released by Google (Apache license 2.0), and is available for download at the following link:

https://github.com/GoogleCloudPlatform/android-docs-samples/tree/master/speech/Speech

Cloud Speech API App Overview

Download the project from GitHub and import it into Android Studio. Table 3-7 shows the summary of the key project files.

Table 3-7. *GCP Cloud Speech API Project File Summary*

Project Name: GCP Cloud Speech API
Source: GitHub Google Cloud Speech Platform
Type: Android Application

File	Description
app->src->main->java *MainActivity.java*	The main activity that checks for device permissions, launches the voice recorder and speech service, and sets up the main view.
app->src->main->java *SpeechService.java*	Service for handling API access. This Android service implements the interface to the GCP Cloud Speech API, including authentication and real-time streaming of spoken words.
app->src->main->java *MessageDialogFragment.java*	A simple Android **Dialog** class that the app uses to display messages to the user.
app->src->main->java *VoiceRecorder.java*	This class implements the Android **AudioRecord** class for voice recording.
app->src->main-> *res->layout* *main.xml*	Main XML layout.
app->src->main->res->raw *credential.json*	JSON credential file created on the GCP Cloud API Center. Place the file into the **res/raw** folder.
app->src->main->res->raw *audio.raw*	A sample audio file stored into the **/res/raw** folder that can be sent to the API for classification. The audio file is a recording of the spoken words "How old is the Brooklyn Bridge?"
app->src->main *AndroidManifest.xml*	App manifest file. Defines the activity and the service.

Figure 3-27 shows a screenshot of the Android app. The app's concept is straightforward. The app accepts audio input from the user and uses the Google Cloud Speech API to translate the audio and display a text translation. The app supports two methods for audio input:

- The app can record audio from the device microphone. Audio is recorded in raw PCM format. In Chapter 2, you saw that digitized voice is a form of data. I will discuss more about audio file formats later. Recorded audio is sent up the Cloud Speech API in real time for translation.

- The user can also press the **LOAD FILE** button to load a prerecorded audio file which will then be sent to the API for translation.

The Cloud Speech API uses DL to translate the recorded audio to text. The app receives the translated text and displays the translation in real time as the user is speaking. Because the API uses deep learning, it does a really impressive job at translating voice input.

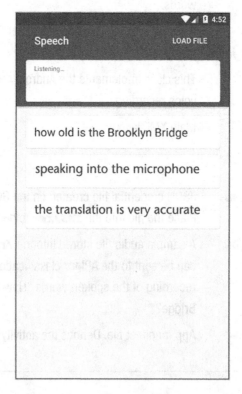

Figure 3-27. *The GCP ML Cloud Speech API Android app*

Running the app on the device allows you to record audio using the microphone. The app batches spoken words in real time and passes them up to the API. If you are using the emulator to run the app, you will be restricted to pressing the *LOAD FILE* button to provide audio for the API to translate.

GCP Machine Learning APIs

Before you can get the app running on your Android device, you need to perform the following two actions on the Google Cloud Platform dashboard:

- Enable the Cloud Speech API.

- Create the authentication key required by the Android app.

In order to enable the API, visit the following link:

https://console.cloud.google.com/apis/library?filter=category:machine-learning

Figure 3-28 shows the currently available GCP Cloud ML APIs, including the Cloud Speech API you wish to implement. Click the Cloud Speech API and enable it.

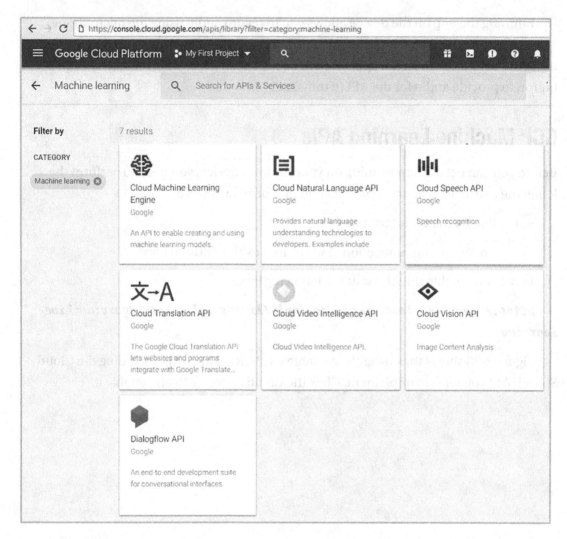

Figure 3-28. *GCP Cloud ML APIs*

Next you need to create the authentication key that is required for the Android app.

Cloud Speech API Authentication

The Cloud Speech API Android app requires you to provide a JSON file authentication key. The file will be named ***credential.json*** and will be placed in the app's ***raw*** folder. Follow these steps to create the file.

The first step is to create a service account key. The service account is required for authentication. Figure 3-29 shows the *Credentials* tab within the API dashboard. Choose *Create credentials*, and then select *Service account key* from the drop down list.

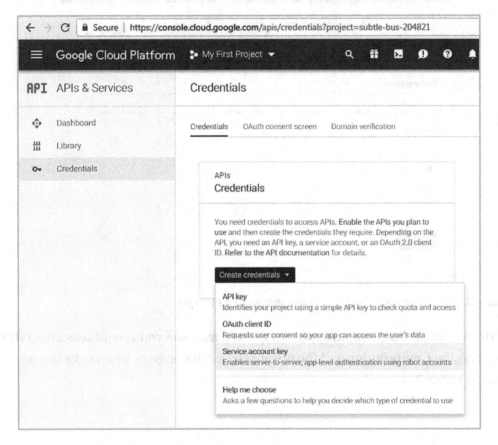

Figure 3-29.   *GCP creating a service account key*

The *Create service account key* dialog box will be displayed, as shown in Figure 3-30.

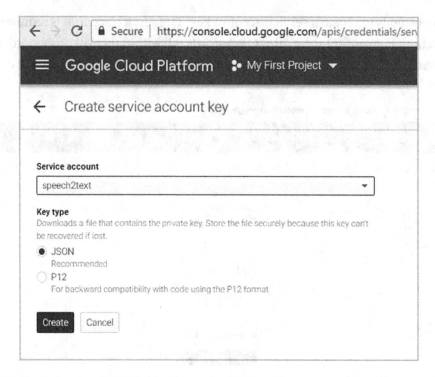

Figure 3-30. *Selecting JSON service account key type*

The service account should appear as ***speech2text,*** and you should select the ***JSON*** type. Press the ***Create*** button and the private key will be saved to your computer, as shown in Figure 3-31.

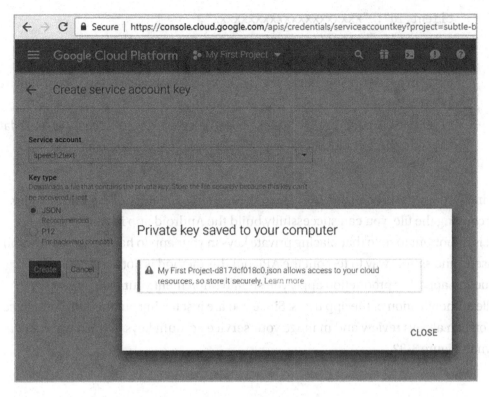

Figure 3-31. *Saving the JSON private key file*

The private key will be saved to your computer with a filename based on the name of the project. If you leave the project name as the default value, it will appear similar to the following:

My First Project-D817dcf314.json

Rename this file to

credential.json

The JSON configuration file contents will look similar to the following and is required to access the API from Android:

```
001    {
002       "type": "service_account",
003       "project_id": "subtle-bus-204821",
004       "private_key_id": "xxxxxxxxxxxxxxxxxxxxxx",
005       "private_key": "-----BEGIN PRIVATE KEY-----\nxxxxxxxx\n-----END
          PRIVATE KEY-----\n",
006       "client_email": "speech2text@subtle-bus-204821.iam.gservice
          account.com",
```

```
007       "client_id": "xxxxxxxxxxxxxxxxxxxxxx",
008       "auth_uri": "https://accounts.google.com/o/oauth2/auth",
009       "token_uri": "https://accounts.google.com/o/oauth2/token",
010       "auth_provider_x509_cert_url": "https://www.googleapis.com/oauth2/
          v1/certs",
011       "client_x509_cert_url": "https://www.googleapis.com/robot/v1/metadata/
          x509/speech2text%40subtle-bus-204821.iam.gserviceaccount.com"
012   }
```

Finally, copy the ***credential.json*** file to the ***res/raw*** directory of the Android app. After copying the file, you can successfully build the Android app in Android Studio.

It is important to note that placing private keys in your app to handle authentication is a useful and simple way to test out the API, but this method is not acceptable for production apps. For production apps, you should implement your own app server to handle authentication of the app users. Since you are just testing out the API, you can copy.

You can always review and manage your service account keys in the dashboard, as shown in Figure 3-32.

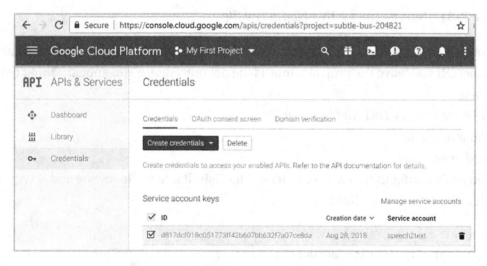

Figure 3-32. *Displaying active credentials*

Android Audio

With the backend setup complete, you can focus on the client Android app. In this section, you will cover the following key events:

- Recording raw audio
- Sending audio to the API
- Processing the API JSON response

Audio is a form of data. ML often uses audio data as input. Android devices are excellent for working with audio because the hardware supports many codecs for encoding and decoding.

> *Android devices are excellent tools for audio data processing. Android supports many codecs. The **AudioRecord** and **AudioTrack** classes support recording and processing of raw uncompressed audio. While latency is not great for Android audio, most ML Audio APIs support high throughput and do not require low latency.*

Table 3-8 shows a list of Android's supported audio formats. Note that Y indicates encoding or decoding is available in all SDK versions for a particular codec. N indicates encoding is not available for a codec.

Table 3-8. *Android Supported Audio Formats*

Codec	Encode	Decode	Details	File Type
AAC	4.1+	Y	Mono/stereo/5.0/5.1up to 48khz sample	3GPP,MP4,ADTS AAC
AMR	Y	Y	5-12 kbps12-24 kbps	3GPP
FLAC	Y	Y (3.1+)	Mono/stereo/up to 44.1/48khz	FLAC
MP3	N	Y	Mono/stereo/8-320kbps	MP3
MIDI	N	Y	Support for ringtones	MID
Vorbis	N	Y		OGG, Matroska
PCM	Y (4.1+)	Y	8-bit/16-bit Linear PCM rates to hardware limit	WAVE
Opus	N	Y (5.0+)		Matroska

161

The GCP Cloud Speech API can accept several types of audio data: FLAC (.flac), PCM (.wav) files, AMR, and Linear-16. The FLAC and PCM formats represent raw uncompressed audio data. While compressed audio data, such as MP3 files, would be smaller and faster to transmit to the cloud, the compression would introduce noise and possibly compromise accuracy.

The Android *AudioRecord* class is a very powerful low-level audio API. Any serious app that processes audio is most likely using *AudioRecord*. In the Cloud Speech API app, the *AudioRecord* class is used to record uncompressed raw audio, which is passed to the API for translation.

Listing 3-3 shows the key audio recording loop in the app. The *ProcessVoice* class shown resides inside the *VoiceRecorder.java* file. The code runs on a thread and is responsible for continuously reading uncompressed voice data from the *AudioRecord* object into the *mBuffer* byte array (line 013).

Listing 3-3. ProcessVoice Class within VoiceRecorder.java

```
001    private AudioRecord mAudioRecord;
002    private Thread mThread;
003    private byte[] mBuffer;
004
005    private class ProcessVoice implements Runnable {
006        @Override
007        public void run() {
008            while (true) {
009                synchronized (mLock) {
010                    if (Thread.currentThread().isInterrupted()) {
011                        break;
012                    }
013                    final int size = mAudioRecord.read(mBuffer, 0,
                           mBuffer.length);
014                    final long now = System.currentTimeMillis();
015                    if (isHearingVoice(mBuffer, size)) {
016                        if (mLastVoiceHeardMillis == Long.MAX_VALUE) {
017                            mVoiceStartedMillis = now;
018                            mCallback.onVoiceStart();
019                        }
```

```
020                     mCallback.onVoice(mBuffer, size);
021                     mLastVoiceHeardMillis = now;
022                     if (now - mVoiceStartedMillis > MAX_SPEECH_
                        LENGTH_MILLIS) {
023                         end();
024                     }
025                 } else if (mLastVoiceHeardMillis != Long.MAX_VALUE) {
026                     mCallback.onVoice(mBuffer, size);
027                     if (now - mLastVoiceHeardMillis > SPEECH_TIMEOUT_
                        MILLIS) {
028                         end();
029                     }
030                 }
031             }
032         }
033     }
034 }
```

The code in Listing 3-3 is a typical audio recording implementation. One of the features that makes the app so powerful is the use of the following callbacks:

- **onVoiceStart**: Called when the recorder starts hearing a voice.

- **onVoice**: Called when the recorder hears a voice.

- **onVoiceEnd**: Called when the recorder stops hearing a voice.

The use of these methods is how the app is able to provide real-time translations as the user speaks.

Raw audio from the microphone is sent to the Cloud Speech API by passing the data to the **recognizeInputStream** method in **SpeechService.java**.

SpeechService.java runs as an Android Service within the app. It is responsible for interfacing with the cloud API. The code in Listing 3-4 shows how the service builds the JSON request message for the API.

Listing 3-4. Building the API Request within SpeechService.java

```
001  public void recognizeInputStream(InputStream stream) {
002      try {
003          mApi.recognize(
```

```
004                     RecognizeRequest.newBuilder()
005                         .setConfig(RecognitionConfig.newBuilder()
006                             .setEncoding(RecognitionConfig.
                                AudioEncoding.LINEAR16)
007                             .setLanguageCode("en-US")
008                             .setSampleRateHertz(16000)
009                             .build())
010                         .setAudio(RecognitionAudio.newBuilder()
011                         .setContent(ByteString.readFrom(stream))
012                         .build())
013                         .build(),
014                 mFileResponseObserver);
015     } catch (IOException e) {
016         Log.e(TAG, "Error loading the input", e);
017     }
018 }
```

After processing each audio data stream through its DL model, the Cloud Speech API sends the text results back to the service. The service handles everything for you. The code in Listing 3-5 shows an excerpt from *MainActivity.java*. This code sets up a *SpeechService* listener and populates the UI with the text results as they are received.

Listing 3-5. Listening for Text Results in MainActivity.java

```
001     private final SpeechService.Listener mSpeechServiceListener =
002             new SpeechService.Listener() {
003                 @Override
004                 public void onSpeechRecognized(final String text, final
                    boolean isFinal) {
005                     if (isFinal) {
006                         mVoiceRecorder.dismiss();
007                     }
008                     if (mText != null && !TextUtils.isEmpty(text)) {
009                         runOnUiThread(new Runnable() {
010                             @Override
011                             public void run() {
```

```
012                         if (isFinal) {
013                             mText.setText(null);
014                             mAdapter.addResult(text);
015                             mRecyclerView.smoothScroll
                                ToPosition(0);
016                         } else {
017                             mText.setText(text);
018                         }
019                     }
020                 });
021             }
022         }
023     };
```

Cloud Speech API App Summary

The Google Cloud Speech API app is a powerful example of leveraging DL models in the cloud. It is an advanced implementation because it provides a service-based architecture to handle all of the API interfaces. The use of callbacks in conjunction with the service architecture provides real-time translation and creates a seamless user experience.

It is an architecture that can be replicated for the other GCP ML APIs. Keep in mind that is also can create significant network traffic and API access volume.

Once you successfully deploy a solution such as the Cloud Speech API, you should revisit the dashboard periodically to check on traffic and errors. Figure 3-33 shows the Cloud Speech API Dashboard with traffic recorded. Be careful to watch the API traffic volume, especially if working within the constraints of the free trial.

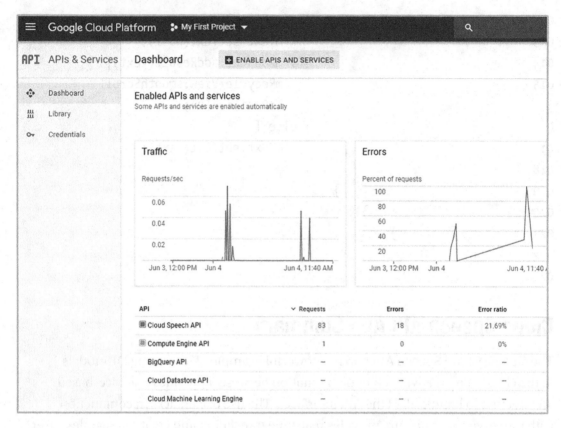

Figure 3-33. *GCP monitoring API access volumes*

3.6 Cloud Data for Machine Learning

The cloud service providers excel at storing data. While many of their ML services are relatively new, the data storage services they offer have been available from the beginning.

The data storage services they offer can take a variety of formats, including

- Container images

- Traditional databases

- NoSQL databases

- APIs and services

- Virtual machines

Earlier in the chapter, you saw two of these approaches. You used AWS S3 buckets object store when you demonstrated the AWS ML consoles with the PAMAP2_Dataset. You then used a virtual machine for storage when setting up Weka in the cloud. Next, you will examine how the explosion in unstructured data is leading to increased usage of NoSQL databases as a storage solution.

Unstructured Data

Chapter 2 discussed a megatrend: the explosion of data. We define unstructured data as data with little or no metadata and little or no classification. ML often uses unstructured data. Unstructured data includes many categories, such as videos, emails, images, IoT device data, file shares, security data, surveillance data, log files, web data, user and session data, chat, messaging, twitter streams sensor data, time series data, IoT device data, and retail customer data.

Unstructured data can be characterized by the three Vs: volume, velocity, and variety.

- Volume: Size of the data. See Table 2-2.

- Velocity: How fast the data is generated. Jet engine sensors, for example, can produce thousands of samples per second.

- Variety: There are many different kinds of data.

Figure 3-34 shows the exponential growth of unstructured data relative to structured data.

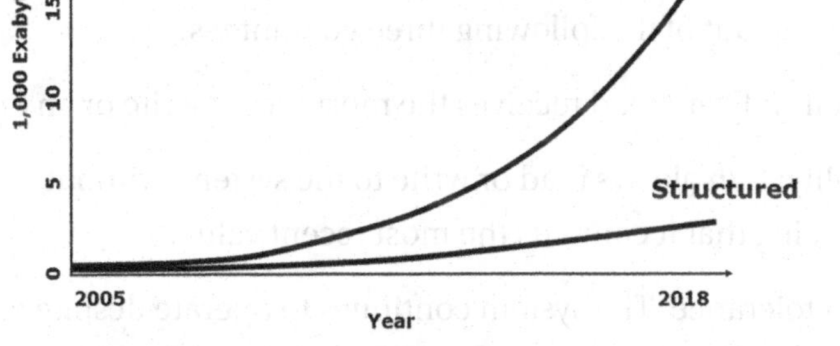

Figure 3-34. *Growth of unstructured data*

The problem with traditional databases is that they are hard to scale and not well suited for unstructured data. One of the best ways to store unstructured data in the cloud is with NoSQL databases because they do a much better job at handling this type of data.

NoSQL Databases

NoSQL stands for "not SQL." The approach is different from traditional relational database management systems (RDBMS). SQL is the query language used by relational databases. These databases rely on tables, columns, rows, or schemas to organize and retrieve the data. NoSQL databases do not rely on these structures and use more flexible data models. Many mainstream enterprises have adopted NoSQL.

The benefits of NoSQL databases include

- Scalability: Horizontal scaling architecture makes it easy to add commoditized nodes to increase capacity.

- Performance: You can easily increase performance by adding commoditized resources as required.

- High availability: NoSQL databases often use a master-less architecture, making them less prone to outages.

- Global availability: Distributed databases can be replicated across machines and geographic areas.

- Flexible modeling: Handling documents or unstructured data represented by JSON means there is no strict data typing, tables, or indexes.

To understand how NoSQL databases differ from traditional RDBMS databases, it is useful to review the CAP theorem, originally described by Eric Brewer. The CAP theorem states that for distributed database architectures, it is impossible to simultaneously provide more than two out of the following three guarantees:

- Consistency: Every read receives the most recent write or an error.

- Availability: Can always read or write to the system, without guaranteeing that it contains the most recent value.

- Partition tolerance: The system continues to operate despite an arbitrary number of messages being dropped or delayed by the network between nodes.

Figure 3-35 shows a graphical representation of the CAP theorem and includes a classification of many popular SQL (RDBMS) and NoSQL databases.

The traditional SQL databases are on the left side of the triangle. They support consistency and availability. However, they do not partition easily in a distributed fashion. Partitioning is the key ingredient behind the massive scalability of NoSQL architectures. The triangle shows popular NoSQL databases at the bottom and right side of the triangle.

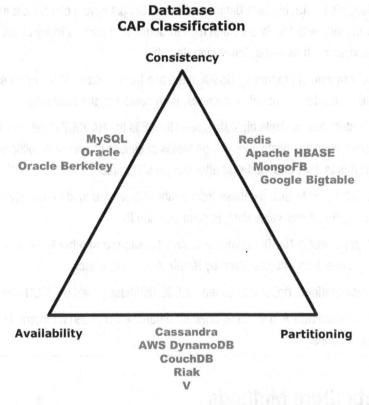

Figure 3-35. *Database classification per the CAP theorem*

Database theorists used two interesting terms to describe these database philosophies:

- ACID: Atomicity, Consistency, Isolation, Durability
- BASE: Basically Available, Soft state, Eventual consistency

RDBMS databases choose ACID for consistency and availability. Distributed NoSQL databases choose BASE for either partitioning/consistency or partitioning/availability. Many popular NoSQL databases use the BASE philosophy. Table 3-9 shows a summary of the most popular NoSQL databases.

Table 3-9. *Popular NoSQL Databases*

Database	Description
Google Bigtable	Google's NoSQL big data database service. Google says it can handle massive workloads with low latency and high throughput. It powers many of the Google services such as Maps, Gmail, and Search.
AWS DynamoDB	Fully managed proprietary NoSQL database from Amazon. DynamoDB supports key-value and document data structures. High durability and availability.
Apache HBASE	A distributed, scalable big data store. HBASE is the HADOOP database. The Apache project's goal is hosting very large tables of billions of rows and millions of columns. Written in Java and modelled after Google's Bigtable.
Riak KV	A distributed NoSQL database from Basho. Allows you to store massive amounts of unstructured key-value data. Popular solution for IoT.
Apache Cassandra	Highly scalable NoSQL database. Claims to outperform other NoSQL databases due to architectural choices. Used by Netflix, Apple, EBay, etc.
MongoDB	Cross-platform, document-based, NoSQL database based on JSON-like documents.
CouchDB	Distributed NoSQL document-oriented database optimized for interactive applications.

NoSQL Data Store Methods

The NoSQL databases shown in Table 3-8 have differences. When choosing a NoSQL database, the key consideration is how they store the data. There are four types of NoSQL data stores:

- Key-value data stores

- Document stores

- Wide column stores

- Graph stores

Table 3-10 shows how the poplar NoSQL products fall into these categories.

Table 3-10. *NoSQL Data Store Methods*

Data store type	Characteristics	Examples
Key/Value	A hash table indexed by key. Entirely in memory or combination of memory and disk. Does not support secondary indexes.	Memcache
Document	Principle storage object is a document, usually in JSON format. Supports secondary indexes. Offers small to medium scalability. Internally objects are stored in binary as BSON or BLOBs.	MongoDB CouchDB CouchBase DynamoDB Redis
Graph	Used for storing connected datasets.	Neo
Wide Column	Provides a wide or big table. Supports millions of columns. Offers large scalability. Supports big data.	HBase BigtableCassandra

Data size and performance are also important factors to consider when selecting a NoSQL database. MongoDB and CouchDB are excellent choices for small to medium dataset sizes, while Cassandra is excellent for large datasets.

Performance is a complex topic and beyond the scope of this chapter. For CML projects, you do not require top-tier performance. If you are interested in NoSQL performance benchmarking, Datastax has a great summary available at

www.datastax.com/nosql-databases/benchmarks-cassandra-vs-mongodb-vs-hbase.

The cloud providers include support for many NoSQL databases. Figure 3-36 show the AWS Database Quickstart page.

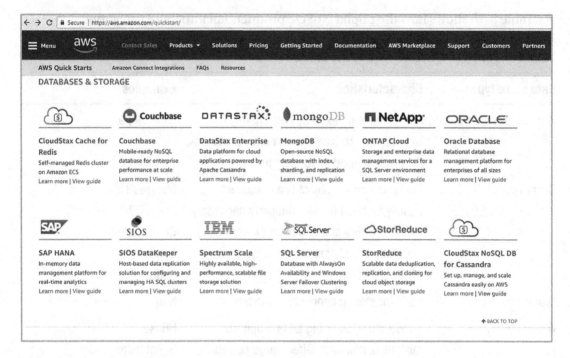

Figure 3-36. *AWS Database Quickstart options*

You can see AWS provides NoSQL Quickstart packages for Couchbase, MongoDB, two flavors of Cassandra, and its own DynamoDB NoSQL offering.

Apache Cassandra Java Interface

Using Quickstart packages makes it easy to deploy a NoSQL database on cloud providers such as AWS or GCP. In this final section, you will explore, at a very high level, how you can interface from your Java programs to the Apache Cassandra NoSQL database.

DataStax is one of the leading distributors of Apache Cassandra. It is available for AWS and Google Compute Engine at the following links:

> *https://aws.amazon.com/quickstart/architecture/datastax-enterprise/*
> *https://console.cloud.google.com/marketplace/details/datastax-public/*
> *datastax-enterprise*

Note that DataStax does not charge a fee for Datastax Enterprise, but the cloud providers will charge a fee for compute resources. The cloud providers and DataStax have teamed up to make it very easy to spin up a highly scalable Cassandra cluster in the cloud.

One of the great features of the DataStax distribution is the available of drivers for all the popular programming languages, including Java. The Datastax Java driver is available at

https://github.com/datastax/java-driver.

The DataStax Java driver GitHub site has an excellent **Readme.md** file with very helpful information for getting started with Java and Cassandra. Some highlights of the DataStax Cassandra distribution and Java driver:

- Open source drivers (Apache 2.0) available for all main languages, including Java.

- The DataStax Java driver contains the logic for connecting to Cassandra and executing a query.

- The DataStax Java driver supports synchronous and asynchronous queries.

- The driver is a feature-rich and highly tunable Java client library.

- The driver supports Apache Cassandra (2.1+).

- The driver supports Cassandra's binary protocol.

- The driver supports Cassandra Query Language v3.

The following code shows how to connect to a Cassandra database and execute a Cassandra query from Java using the DataStax driver:

```
001    Cluster cluster = null;
002    try {
003        // Connect to the cloud Cassandra cluster
004        cluster = Cluster.builder()
005                .addContactPoint("ip_address")
006                .build();
007        Session session = cluster.connect();
008
009        // Provide a Query String for the execute method
010        ResultSet rs = session.execute("select release_version from
           system.local");
011
```

```
012        // Get the first row
013        Row row = rs.one();
014        System.out.println(row.getString(0)); // The first column;
015    } finally {
016        if (cluster != null) cluster.close();
017    }
```

Cassandra uses the Cassandra Query Language (CQL). CQL is very similar to SQL. There are several ways to access CQL, including

- Starting *cqlsh*, the command-line client, on the command line of a Cassandra node.

- Using DataStax *DevCenter*, a graphical user interface.

- For developing applications, you can use one of the official DataStax Java drivers.

One of the most useful CQL commands is the *Copy* command. The CQL *Copy* command allows you to import and export CSV files. Recall from Chapter 2, these files are an integral part of the ML pipeline. With a single command, you are able to populate an entire Cassandra DB or back up the Cassandra NoSQL DB to a CSV file for offline processing. Complete details on the CQL *Copy* command are at

https://docs.datastax.com/en/cql/3.1/cql/cql_reference/copy_r.html.

For more details on other useful CQL commands including additional Java code examples, refer to the DataStax driver documentation at

https://docs.datastax.com/en/developer/java-driver/3.4/manual/.

One of the advantages of using a cloud-based NoSQL database like Cassandra is scalability. This can come in handy if you are collecting a lot of ML data and you need to store it. A few years ago, Google achieved 1 million writes per second using Cassandra on Google Compute Engine. You can learn about the deployment details in this blogpost:

https://cloudplatform.googleblog.com/2014/03/cassandra-hits-one-million-writes-per-second-on-google-compute-engine.html

According to the author, the cost to achieve this result in 2014 was only $0.07 per million writes. This illustrates the powerful value proposition of the cloud platforms.

3.7 Cloud Platform Summary

This chapter had the lofty goal of covering cloud platforms for ML. Cloud ML is a very fast moving space characterized by rapid developments. Keep in mind the following findings as you proceed to the next chapters to cover algorithms and ML environments:

- When building ML solutions, always scan the available cloud services first to see if one exists that can solve the problem with minimal model building or coding.

- Each of the cloud providers has been investing huge resources the past few years to deploy compute resources, storage solutions, model building platforms, and DL APIs that you can leverage for your applications.

- Leverage the free tier provided by the cloud platforms to see if a particular service works for your specific application.

- Google makes it easy for Android apps to leverage Google ML Engine services through published JSON APIs.

- NoSQL databases such as Cassandra allow you to achieve massive scale and are relatively easy to configure.

- Many services, especially those provided by open source packages offered by the cloud providers are free, but ultimately users will pay for any compute resources consumed. Fortunately, these costs have been driven down by fierce industry competition.

CHAPTER 4

Algorithms: The Brains of Machine Learning

Selecting the best algorithm for your ML problem is extremely important. This chapter will explore algorithms and meet the following objectives:

- Explain the terminology used by the scientists who create ML algorithms.

- Show you how to select the best algorithm by considering multiple factors.

- Summarize the three high-level styles of algorithms.

- Provide a complete index list of CML algorithms so you can easily identify which style of ML a particular algorithm utilizes.

- Present a decision flowchart and a functional flowchart that will help you to choose the best algorithm for your problem.

- Present an overview of the seven most important ML algorithms.

- Compare the performance of CML algorithms, including summary of CML and DL algorithms on the MNIST dataset.

- Review the Java source code of popular algorithms.

4.1 Introduction

When asked why they fail to deploy ML solutions, developers often express two main reasons:

- It takes too much manual work.

- Algorithms and model creation are too complicated.

177

© Mark Wickham 2018
M. Wickham, *Practical Java Machine Learning*, https://doi.org/10.1007/978-1-4842-3951-3_4

The manual work typically refers to data wrangling. In Chapter 2, I covered some tools that can help to make this simpler. Chapter 5 will present additional tools integrated as part of Java ML environments. With ML, it is hard to avoid manual work with data. I refer back to Mr. Silver's interesting quote about expecting more from ourselves before we expect more from our data.

In Figure 1-20, you saw that algorithms are rooted in the scientific domain. One of the main reasons developers shy away from deploying ML is that algorithm selection and model creation are too complicated. Fortunately, you can overcome the algorithm complexity issue by learning some basic principles and gaining an understanding of the scientific language associated with ML algorithms.

This book and chapter will mainly cover CML algorithms. In Chapter 3, you accessed a DL algorithm via the Google Cloud Speech API because the cloud providers tend to focus their ML APIs on DL solutions.

ML-Gate 3

MLG3 is the phase during which you generate the ML model. The most important action during this phase is the selection and validation of the ML algorithm. This chapter will help you to choose the best algorithm and determine how it is performing.

When you first embark on ML solutions, choosing the best algorithm seems somewhat arbitrary. In Chapter 5, you will see that it is actually quite easy to randomly select and apply any algorithm to a dataset. This is not a particularly good use of time. In Chapter 3, you saw disappointing results when the AWS Machine Learning wizard chose the wrong algorithm after misunderstanding the label data type. There is a conventional wisdom for algorithm selection. Answers to the following questions help to determine which algorithm is best suited for your model:

- How much data do you have?

- What are you trying to predict?

- Is the data labeled or unlabeled?

- Do you require incremental or batched training?

As you gain experience, you can quickly determine which algorithm is the best match for your problem and data.

4.2 Algorithm Styles

The world of ML algorithms is bifurcated into two equally important and useful categories. Before introducing the fancy terminology scientists use to describe each category, let's first look at the types of data that define each category.

Labeled vs. Unlabeled Data

You will recall in Chapter 2, I defined the term *label* as what you are attempting to predict or forecast. In Chapter 2, the PAMAP2_Dataset was labeled. Column 1 contained the label values. At the time of the data collection, the participants wearing sensors were asked to record their activity. This label value was then stored along with all of the other data from the sensors.

Many datasets used in ML consist of labeled data. The majority of the datasets in the UC Irvine repository have labels. Most of the ML competitions hosted by the ML site *Kaggle.com* use labelled data. In the real world, this is not always the case.

Some organizations consider labeled data as more valuable than unlabeled data. Organizations sometimes even consider unlabeled data as worthless. This is probably shortsighted. You shall see that ML can use both labeled and unlabeled data.

Whether or not the data contains labels is the key factor in determining the ML algorithm style. ML algorithms fall into three general ML styles:

- Supervised learning

- Unsupervised learning

- Semi-supervised learning

Figure 4-1 summarizes these three ML algorithm styles.

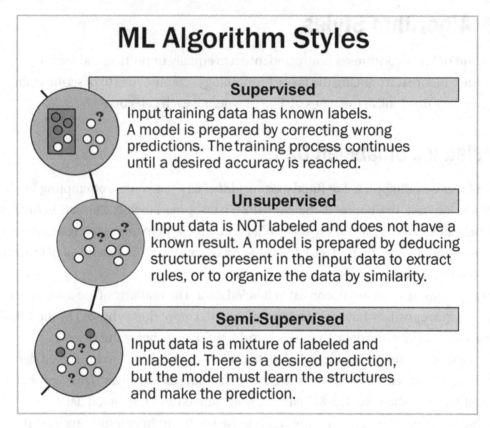

Figure 4-1. ML algorithm styles

All of the algorithms I will discuss fall into one of these categories. Supervised algorithms use data with labels. Unsupervised algorithms use data without labels. Semi-supervised algorithms use data with and without labels.

4.3 Supervised Learning

Supervised learning is the easiest ML learning style to understand. Supervised learning algorithms operate on data with labels. Because each sample includes a label, a function (which we will call a critic) is able to calculate an error value for each sample. Figure 4-2 shows a graphical representation of the supervised learning process.

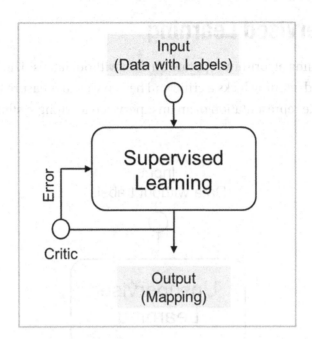

Figure 4-2. Supervised learning logic

The term "supervision" refers to the critic-error operation. This operation enables the algorithm to compare actual vs. desired and learn from this. There are many algorithms under the supervised learning umbrella. Later in this chapter, you will explore some of the most useful supervised algorithms:

- Support vector machines (SVM)

- Naive Bayesian (NB) networks

- Random forest (RF) decision trees

When you combine supervised learning with labeled data, you are able to classify samples. The terms "supervised learning" and "classification" are thus highly correlated.

Supervised learning classification usually happens in two phases. You divide the data into two parts: training data and testing data. Both sets of data contain fully labeled samples. In the first phase, you train the mapping function with the training data until it meets some level of performance (actual vs. desired output). In phase two, you use the testing data as input to the mapping function. Phase two provides a good measure of how well the model performs with unseen data.

4.4 Unsupervised Learning

Unsupervised learning algorithms operate on data without labels. The key difference is that unsupervised learning lacks a critic and has no way to measure its performance. Figure 4-3 shows the representation of an unsupervised learning system.

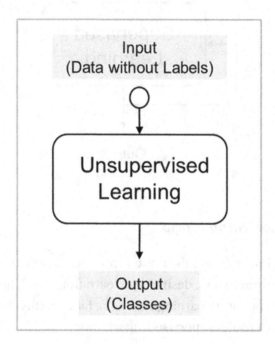

Figure 4-3. *Unsupervised learning logic*

In this system, you do not have the necessary label to perform classification of individual samples. Instead, you accept data without labels as input and perform the task of outputting classes. Unsupervised learning is all about finding the structure of the data, a task commonly described as clustering, or knowledge discovery.

A common example often cited to help explain clustering is the unknown Excel spreadsheet. Consider a spreadsheet that contains columns of data but no headers to identify the data. What can you determine? You need to analyze the data contained in each column and attempt to discover what it means. You are essentially trying to uncover the structure of the data in the spreadsheet. If a new sample arrives, you would like to make some decisions about how it might connect to the rest of the data in the spreadsheet. This is clustering.

Clustering algorithms involve determining a mapping function that categorizes the data into classes based on the features hidden within the data. With unsupervised learning, because no labels are present, you lack the knowledge to know what you wish to get out of the model. Instead, you look for relationships or correlations in the data.

Unsupervised learning algorithms work their magic by dividing the data into clusters. In Figure 2-10, you saw an interesting dataset that contained erroneous value. If you pass this dataset into a clustering algorithm, you might possibly obtain a result like that shown in Figure 4-4.

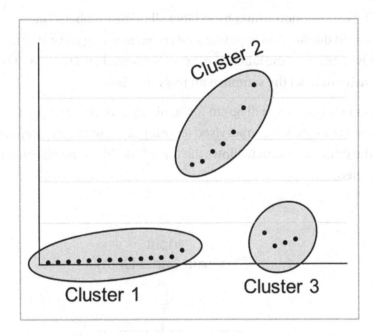

Figure 4-4. *Clustering of a dataset*

Visualization is very helpful in understanding clusters. Obviously, Cluster 2 represents the erroneous data in the dataset. Algorithms have many different techniques to determine what constitutes a cluster. Later in this chapter, you will explore the pros and cons of the following clustering algorithms:

- DBSCAN

- Expectation-maximization (EM)

- K-means clustering

In Chapter 5, you will implement clustering with Java and Weka.

4.5 Semi-Supervised Learning

Semi-supervised learning algorithms operate on mixed data where only some of the data contains labels. This is often the case for real-world data. Semi-supervised learning is becoming increasingly popular for two reasons:

- The data explosion megatrend has led to the increasing collection of unstructured data that does not have a consistent application of labels.

- One possible option would be to label all of the unlabeled data in a mixed dataset and then use supervised learning algorithms. However, because the labeling process is manual and tedious, it is too expensive to label the sample with missing labels.

Figure 4-5 shows the process diagram for semi-supervised learning. The input and outputs are the same as with the supervised learning style, with the exception of a switch placed before the critic. The switch allows the critic function to be disabled when a data sample is unlabeled.

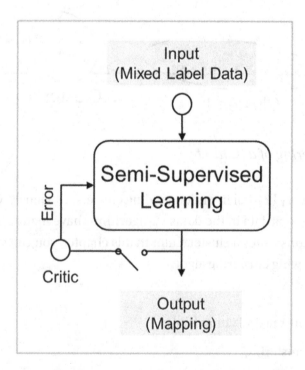

Figure 4-5. *Semi-supervised learning logic*

As with the supervised and unsupervised learning styles, semi-supervised learning has many algorithms. In Chapter 5, you will implement semi-supervised learning using a collective classification set of algorithms. There is a growing amount of academic research showing that semi-supervised algorithms can outperform supervised algorithms. However, the main advantage of using semi-supervised algorithms remains the time-savings gained by not needing to label unlabeled data.

4.6 Alternative Learning Styles

Regression, deep learning, and reinforcement learning are learning styles with unique algorithms that I will not cover in this chapter, with one exception: the support vector machine algorithm that performs wells for supervised learning classification.

Linear Regression Algorithm

Regression is useful for predicting outputs that are continuous, rather than outputs confined to a set of labels. Linear regression is the most popular regression algorithm. All of the cloud and desktop ML environments support the linear regression algorithm. It is one of the more simple algorithms. If you recall back to the statistics class you suffered through, linear regression is the process of finding the best fit line through a series of data points. Figure 4-6 shows a linear regression example.

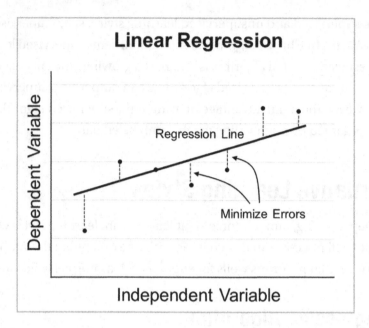

Figure 4-6. *Linear regression*

The regression line minimizes the error values associated with each data point. The resulting best-fit line can successfully generate or "predict" a value for any independent variable value along the line.

Recall in Chapter 2, you applied the AWS ML regression algorithm to the PAMAP2_ Dataset. The result was poor because this dataset was not a good match for the regression algorithm. In the example, the AWS ML wizard mistakenly considered your target label to be a continuous value rather than an integer label. Later you will see how to choose a better algorithm for this dataset.

In the rest of this text, you will mainly focus on CML algorithms for supervised and unsupervised learning, but keep in mind the linear regression algorithm if you have a simple problem that requires continuous value prediction rather than discrete labels.

Deep Learning Algorithms

DL styles rely on neural networks with hidden layers. There are several families of algorithms popular in DL, including convolutional neural networks (CNN) and recurrent neural networks (RNN). One of the best summary resources for DL algorithms is "The Mostly Complete Guide to Deep Learning Algorithms," available at ***https:// asimovinstitute.org***.

Figure 4-7 displays a simplified summary of the cells and hidden layers that comprise some of the most popular neural networks.

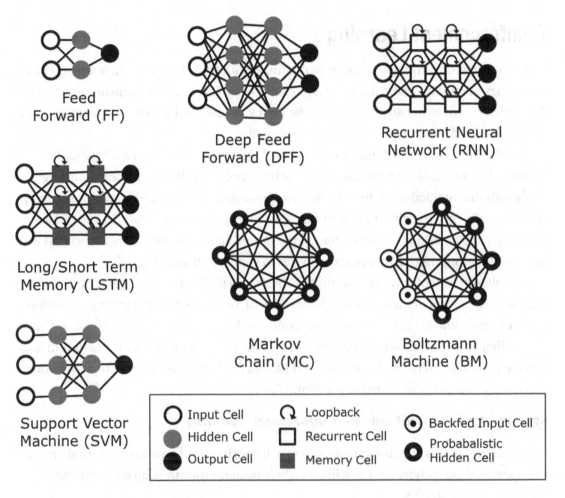

Figure 4-7. *DL algorithm summary*

Neural networks have many types of hidden layers. Refer to the link to distinguish the different hidden layer types because it is hard to visualize the layer types in the greyscale image.

In the bottom left corner of Figure 4-7 is the support vector machine DL algorithm. The SVM DL algorithm is a supervised ML algorithm you can also apply to CML. You will take a closer look at the performance of this algorithm later in this chapter and again in Chapter 5.

Reinforcement Learning

Semi-supervised learning is sometimes confused with the reinforcement learning (RL) style. They are not the same. RL is a type of supervised learning with a distinction. With RL, each input does not always generate feedback. While semi-supervised learning uses data with mixed labels, with RL, there are no labels.

In RL, the supervision comes from a reward signal that tells the critic how well it is doing, but does not say what the correct action should be. Reinforcement learning deals with the interaction of the critic with its environment (state). The actions taken by the critic influence the distribution of states it will observe in the future. In supervised learning, each decision is independent of the others. In RL, the labels are associated with sequences, as opposed to individual samples in supervised learning.

Recall from Chapter 1, the Pokerbot problem was difficult to solve because poker is a game of uncertain or incomplete information. RL works well for navigating uncertain environments, and is thus often used for games such as poker, chess, blackjack, or Go.

Earlier, I mentioned Skymind, the creator of the Java-based DL library. Skymind also has some great content on RL. It described RL as a goal-oriented approach to ML. You can learn more about RL from the following link:

https://skymind.ai/wiki/deep-reinforcement-learning

In the rest of this chapter and book, you will restrict your focus to supervised and unsupervised algorithms with or without labels because they overlap well with your focus on CML problems.

4.7 CML Algorithm Overview

With an understanding of the major algorithm styles, supervised, unsupervised, and semi-supervised, and their relation to labeled vs. unlabeled data, it is now time to look at the specific algorithms within these styles. Table 4-1 provides an index of most of the popular supervised CML algorithms. The shaded cells indicate the key algorithms you will explore.

Table 4-1. *Supervised ML Algorithms*

Supervised ML Algorithm	Family/Class
Averages one-dependency estimator (AODE)	Outperforms Bayes
Analysis of variance (ANOVA)	Statistical
Artificial neural network (ANN)	Neural networks
Apriori algorithm	Association learning (databases)
Naive Bayesian	Bayes (probabilistic)
Bayesian statistics	Bayes (probabilistic)
Boosting	Ensemble learning
Conditional random field	Statistical
C45	Decision tree
CART	Decision tree
Random forest	Decision tree
Sliq	Decision tree
Sprint	Decision tree
Eclat algorithm	Association learning
Ensemble of classifiers	Ensemble learning
Information fuzzy network (IFN)	Decision tree but with directed graphs
Hidden Markov models	Statistical, Markov process
K-nearest neighbors (KNN)	Instance-based (lazy learning)
Learning automata	Reinforcement

(continued)

Table 4-1. (*continued*)

Supervised ML Algorithm	Family/Class
Learning vector quant (LVQ)	Neural network
Logistic model tree (LMT)	Combines regression and decision tree
Minimum message length	Instance-based
Probably approximately correct (PAC) learning	Statistical
Quadratic classifiers	Linear classifier
Support vector machines	Non-probabilistic linear classifier

Table 4-2 provides an index of most of the popular unsupervised ML algorithms.

Table 4-2. *UnSupervised ML Algorithms*

Unsupervised ML Algorithm	Family/Class
COBWEB	Conceptual clustering
Conceptual clustering	Data clustering
DBSCAN	Density-based clustering
Expectation-maximization (EM)	Iterative method
FP-growth algorithm (frequent pattern)	Recursive tree
Fuzzy clustering (FCM)	Similar to k-means
Generative topographic map	Probabilistic
HDBSCAN	Density-based clustering
Information bottleneck	Deep learning
K-means algorithm	Vector quantization, similar to KNN
Local outlier factor	Anomaly detection
OPTICS algorithm	Density-based clustering
Self-organizing map (ANN)	Neural network
Single-linkage clustering	Hierarchical clustering
Support vector clustering	Vector quantization, similar to SVM
Vector quantization	Vector quantization

Lastly, Table 4-3 shows a list of the semi-supervised algorithms.

Table 4-3. *Semi-Supervised CML Algorithms*

Semi-Supervised ML Algorithms	Family/Class
Co-training	Large amount of unlabeled data
Collective classification	WEKA
Generative models	Graph-based
Graph-based methods	Graph-based
SARSA (State-Action-Reward-State-Action)	Reinforcement
Temporal	Reinforcement

These tables are a nearly complete list of CML algorithms. It is not necessary to understand all of these algorithms to write successful ML applications. If you see a particular algorithm referenced in an ML solution, you can use the tables to identify the class or family of algorithms and the learning style. Wikipedia has decent reference pages for all of the algorithms if you wish to learn more about one of them.

The CML algorithm is a commodity. Algorithm innovation and performance gains have been widely achieved. However, CML algorithms prefer specific types of problems, so consider algorithm preference bias when choosing your algorithm.

While knowing the details of all the CML algorithms is not necessary, it is necessary to understand the following:

- What type of data you have?

- Which learning style is the most appropriate for your data?

- What is the preference bias for each ML algorithm?

Next, you will explore a process for choosing the best algorithm.

4.8 Choose the Right Algorithm

There is a popular saying among data scientists...

Algorithms are easy; the hard part is the data.

The part about data being hard was a theme of Chapter 2. At first glance, CML algorithms do not appear to be easy. Unlike DL algorithms, which are still undergoing significant development, CML algorithms are widely deployed and relatively stable. This allows us to define a decision flowchart for choosing the right CML algorithm. Figure 4-8 shows the algorithm decision process.

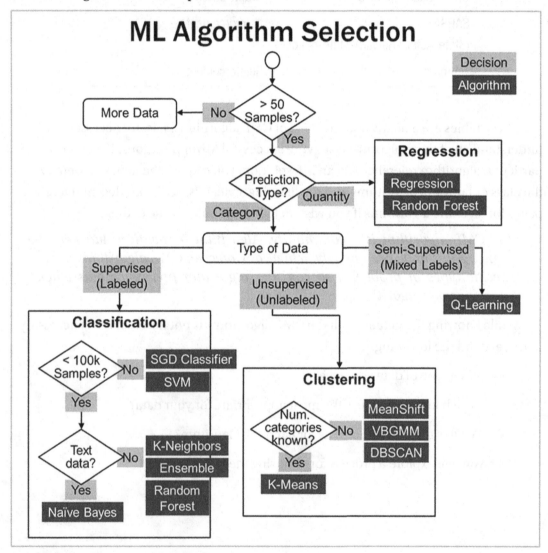

Figure 4-8. *ML algorithm decision flowchart*

This decision chart is a modified version of a more complex chart available on the Scikit-learn resources page. If you look closely at Figure 4-8, you will notice that simple decisions steer you into one of the three main learning style boxes: classification, clustering, and regression. Each of these boxes highlights the key algorithms you need to know.

As you navigate the flowchart, the decision nodes depend on the amount of data and the type of data. In some cases, you will find there is more than one algorithm that you could use. The general rule of thumb is to start simple by running the basic algorithms first.

Even though Table 4-1, Table 4-2, and Table 4-3 contain many algorithms, you really only need to consider the algorithms shown in Figure 4-8. You will take a closer look at these specific algorithms later in the chapter.

Functional Algorithm Decision Process

Sometimes ML practitioners take a more functional approach to algorithm selection. Cloud platforms use this approach when they wish to remove users from the complications associated with the data type decisions required to choose an algorithm. Microsoft Azure ML does a particularly good job of using this approach to help users choose the correct algorithm.

The idea is to ask yourself the simple question, "What do I want to find out?" The answer to the question will lead you to the correct learning style and then to specific algorithms. Figure 4-9 show a summary of this approach for each of five distinct answers to the question, including

- Predict values

- Discover structure

- Predict between several categories

- Find unusual occurrences

- Predict between two categories

Figure 4-9 shows examples and algorithms for each of the five categories. Some users appreciate this approach to algorithm selection, because it is simpler. "Discover structure" is an easier concept to understand than "clustering."

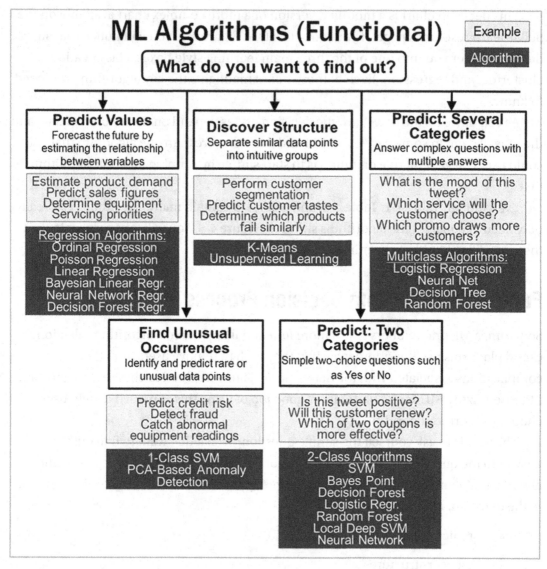

Figure 4-9. *Functional algorithm decision flowchart*

Organizing ML algorithms in this manner shows that the same algorithm can answer several of the different questions. The distinction lies in the number of output classes. Notice, for example, the case of the decision tree or random forest algorithms. You can apply these algorithms as multiclass algorithms to predict between several categories, as 2-class algorithms to predict between two categories, or as a regression algorithm to predict values.

The data-driven decision flowchart in Figure 4-8 and the functional approach in Figure 4-9 will both lead you to the same correct learning style and algorithm choice for your problem.

Next, you will take a closer look at the key algorithms you need to know for your CML problems.

4.9 The Seven Most Useful CML Algorithms

The algorithm decision charts in Figure 4-8 and Figure 4-9 guide you in the selection of the best ML algorithm. With experience, you will find that a handful of algorithms can solve most of your problems. This section will cover the seven most useful CML algorithms you need in your toolbox.

The following seven algorithms are the "go-to" algorithms for CML problems. The list includes four classifiers and three clustering algorithms.

- Naive Bayes (classify)

- Random forest (classify)

- K-nearest neighbors (classify)

- Support vector machine (classify)

- DBSCAN (cluster)

- Expectation-maximization (cluster)

- K-means (cluster)

Of course, the special case will arise when you need to reach for an obscure algorithm, but 95% of time, these seven algorithms will deliver excellent results. The best part of all, there is open source Java production code available for all of the algorithms.

Naive Bayes Algorithm (NB)

NB is a probability-based modeling algorithm based on Bayes' theorem. One of the goals of this book is to avoid mathematical equations. Because of its roots in probability, the NB algorithm represents one circumstance warranting the use of math equations, but we will avoid the temptation.

Bayes' theorem simply states the following:

- The probability of an event is based on prior knowledge of conditions that might be related to the event. Bayes' theorem discusses conditional probability. Conditional probability is the likelihood that event A occurs given that condition B is true.

For example, consider human eyesight and its relationship to a person's age. According to Bayes' theorem, age can help assess more accurately the probability that a person wears glasses, compared to an assessment made without knowledge of the person's age. In this example, the age of the person is the condition.

The reason for the "naive" part of the name is that the algorithm makes a very "naive" assumption about the independence of the attributes. NB algorithms assume that all the attributes are conditionally independent given the class. Even with this assumption, NB algorithms often outperform classifiers using techniques that are more elaborate.

Some advantages of NB algorithms include

- NB is good for spam detection where classification returns a category such as spam or not spam.

- NB can accept categorical and continuous data types.

- NB can work with missing values in the dataset by omitting them when estimating probabilities.

- NB is also effective with noisy data because the noise averages out with the use of probabilities.

- NB is highly scalable and it is especially suited for large databases.

- NB can adapt to most kinds of classification. NB is an excellent algorithm choice for document classification, spam filtering, and fraud detection.

- NB is good for updating incrementally.

- NB offers an efficient use of memory and fast training speeds. The algorithm is suitable for parallel processing.

Disadvantages of NB include

- The NB algorithm does not work well when data attributes have some degree of correlation. This violates the "naive" assumption of the algorithm.

You will implement document classification using naive Bayes in Chapter 5.

Random Forest Algorithm (RF)

If I could only choose one algorithm for my ML toolbox, I would choose the random forest algorithm.

To understand RF, it is first necessary to understand decision trees. Decision trees are a supervised learning method for classification. Decision tree algorithms grow trees using the training data set. The decision tree can classify instances in the test data set. Decision trees are a divide-and-conquer approach to learning.

A decision tree is a structure where "internal nodes" represent each attribute in the dataset. Each "branch" of the tree represents the result of a test, and the "leaf nodes" at the bottom of the tree represent the classification made.

The test can take on a variety of forms, including

- Comparing the attribute value with a constant.

- If the attribute is a nominal one, the number of children usually represents the categories that match.

- If the attribute is numeric, the children can represent ">" or "<" or "=" matches.

The CART (classification and regression trees) algorithm is one of the most basic decision tree algorithms. CART uses binary trees with exactly two outputs. C45 is an improved algorithm that handles missing values and has pruning to help with overfitting issues. With a decision tree, you can use classification trees for discrete value targets and regression trees for continuous value targets.

The RF algorithm is an improvement over the basic decision tree algorithms such as CART and C45. RF is an ensemble model because it uses multiple decision trees and bases each decision tree on a random subset of attributes (columns) and observations (rows) from the original data. Figure 4-10 shows a graphical representation of how the RF algorithm classifies an instance.

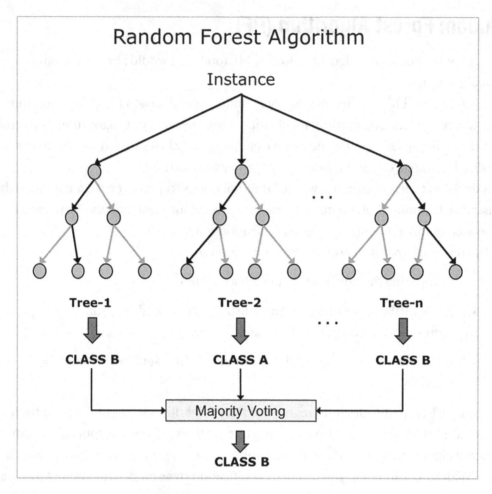

Figure 4-10. *Random forest algorithm*

Many trees make up the random forest, and a majority voting determines the final classification.

The RF algorithm has several advantages:

- RF is easy to visualize so you can understand the factors that lead to a classification result. This can be very useful if you have to explain how your algorithm works to business domain experts or users.

- Each tree in a random forest grows the structure on random features, minimizing the bias.

- Unlike the naive Bayes algorithm, the decision tree-based algorithms work well when attributes have some correlation.

- RF is one of the most simple, robust, and easily understood algorithms.

- The RF bagging feature is very useful. It provides strong fit and typically does not over-fit.

- RF is highly scalable and gives reasonable performance.

RF has some disadvantages:

- Decision trees can be slow with large training times when they are complex.

- Missing values can pose a problem for decision tree-based algorithms.

- Attribute ordering is important, such that those with the most "information gain" appear first.

The RF algorithm is a good compliment to the naive Bayes algorithm. One of the main reasons RF has become popular is because it is very easy to get good results. You will see later in this chapter that RF algorithm can generally outperform all of the other CML classifier algorithms.

K-Nearest Neighbors Algorithm (KNN)

The k-nearest neighbors algorithm is a simple algorithm that yields good results. KNN is useful for classification and regression. Recall from Table 4-1, the KNN algorithm is an instanced-based algorithm, a class of learning also known as lazy learning. The reason is that the work is done at the time you are ready to classify a new instance, rather than when a training set is processed. Instance-based learning is thus "lazy". KNN algorithms do not make any assumptions on the underlying data and do not build models from training data.

Because they rely on distance calculations, KNN algorithms work well with numeric attributes, but KNN can also support categorical attributes with transformation to numeric or binary values.

KNN algorithms classify each new instance based on the classification of its nearby neighbor(s). Figure 4-11 shows a graphical representation of a KNN algorithm with K=5.

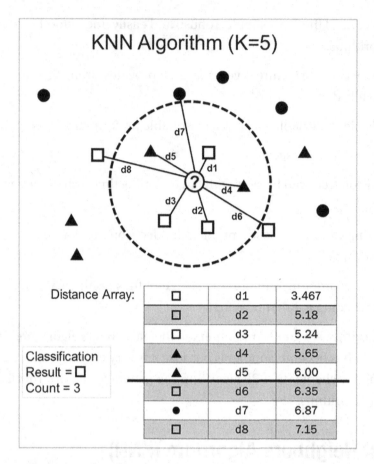

Figure 4-11. *KNN algorithm (k=5)*

Figure 4-11 shows two-dimensional data with three different classes. The algorithm scans outward from the instance it is trying to classify. The algorithm maintains a distance array that contains the distances from the unclassified instance to each classified neighbor. Because K=5, only the five nearest neighbors are considered for a majority vote that determines the class. In this example, a count of three classified the unknown instance, as shown.

The trick with KNN is determining the best value for K. If you pick a K that is too large, perhaps even equal to the total number of observations, then your classification result will simply be the most populous class. If K is too small, the result will simply be the class of the closest neighbor. There are many approaches to choosing K:

- Make a guess and refine with trial by error.

- Choose a K value related to the number of classes, for example, the number of classes + 1.

- Use another algorithm to choose K.

KNN advantages:

- KNN makes no assumptions on the underlying data.

- KNN is a simple classifier that works well on basic recognition problems.

- KNN is easy to visualize and understand how classification is determined.

- Unlike naive Bayes, KNN has no problem with correlated attributes and works well with noisy data if the dataset is not large.

KNN disadvantages:

- Choosing K can be problematic and you may need to spend time tuning K values.

- KNN is subject to the curse of dimensionality due to reliance on distance-based measures. To help combat this, you can try to reduce dimensions or perform feature selection prior to modeling.

- KNN is instance-based and processes the entire dataset for classification, which is resource intensive. KNN is not a great algorithm choice for large datasets.

- Transforming categorical values to numeric values does not always yield good results.

- As a lazy classifier, KNN is not a good algorithm choice for real-time classification.

KNN is a simple, useful classifier. Consider it for the initial classification attempt, particularly if the disadvantages listed above are not an issue for your problem.

Support Vector Machine Algorithm (SVM)

The support vector machine algorithm fills a useful place in your toolbox of seven algorithms. The SVM is technically a linear classifier, but there's a method that will also allow it to handle complex non-linear data.

For its input, the SVM is effective with numeric features only, but most implementations of the algorithm allow you to transform categorical features to numerical values. The SVM output is a class prediction.

The SVM works its magic similar to the linear regression algorithm discussed earlier. Figure 4-12 shows the SVM concept.

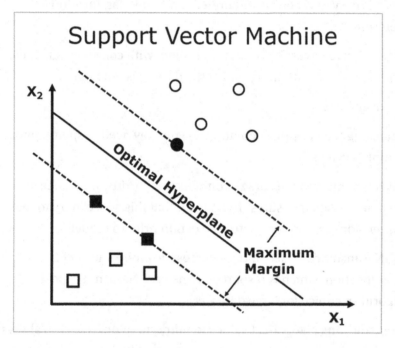

Figure 4-12. *Support vector machine*

The points on the dashed lines in Figure 4-12 are the support vectors. The algorithm tries to create the optimal hyperplane decision boundary between the classes by maximizing the margin between the support vectors.

The SVM algorithm has several advantages:

- SVMs have fewer parameters to set up when building the model.

- SVM algorithms have a good theoretical foundation.

- SVMs are extremely flexible in the type of data they can support.

- SVMs require less computational resources to get an accurate model than decision trees.

- SVMs are not sensitive to noisy data.

- SVM is a good algorithm for binary two-class outputs.

- You can accomplish non-linear classification with SVMs by using kernel transformation.

- SVMs can work well with a large number of features and less training data.

Disadvantages of SVM algorithms:

- SVMs are black boxes. Unlike decision trees, it is hard to interpret or explain what is happening under the hood.

- SVMs can consume a large amount of memory. They are considered $O(n^2)$ and $O(n^3)$, which means they scale exponentially with the number of instances, and thus scalability issues can result.

- SVMs are generally good for binary classification (two-class) but do not perform as well for multiclass classification.

You don't always have linear data as show in Figure 4-12. Fortunately, you can classify non-linear data with SVMs by using kernel transformation, also known as the "kernel trick." Using the kernel trick, SVMs can efficiently classify non-linear data by mapping the inputs into high-dimensional feature spaces.

To understand two-dimensional-to-three-dimensional transformation, consider the following example. A set of coins consisting of pennies and dimes are scattered randomly on a table. They will certainly land in a non-linear pattern, such that no line could separate them into two distinct classes. Imagine if you then raised (transform) all of the dimes a few inches above the table. You can do this because this is supervised learning and you have labeled data. After this transformation, you can now easily separate the classes with a plane. That is essentially the kernel trick and it is why SVMs have become so popular.

Spoiler alert: In the next section, you will discover that SVMs can perform almost as well as neural networks on the MNIST image classification problem. Because of such excellent performance, SVMs are becoming increasingly popular and many people are starting to ask if they are an alternative to neural networks. SVMs cannot match the performance of deep networks, but they do have some advantages worth mentioning:

- SVMs are less prone to overfitting than neural networks.

- SVMs require less memory than neural networks to store the predictive model.

- SVMs yield a more readable result because they have a geometrical interpretation.

You will explore the SVM further in Chapter 5.

K-Means Algorithm

Clustering is the main task of explorative ML, and when seeking a clustering algorithm, k-means is the usual starting point. It works well for many datasets. Figure 4-13 shows a simplified view of how the algorithm works.

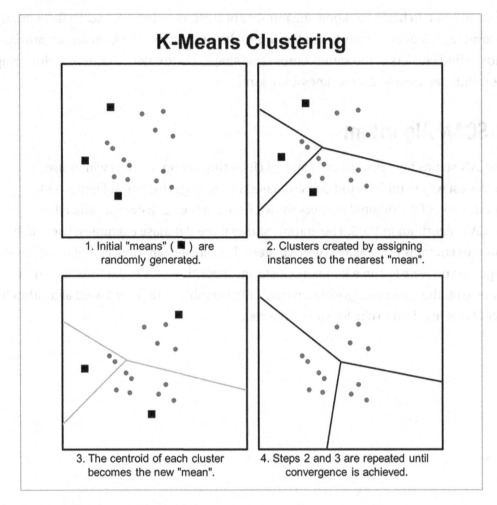

Figure 4-13. *K-means clustering algorithm*

As shown in the graphic, the k-means algorithm is iterative. The algorithm tries to partition the N observations into K clusters. You must start with the number of clusters. The main drawback of the k-means algorithm is that you are required to know upfront how many clusters there are. In the example shown, K=3. The algorithm then chooses three initial "means" randomly and creates the initial clusters by assigning each observation to the nearest mean. The centroid of each cluster becomes the new mean and the process repeats until convergence is achieved.

K-means has been around since 1967 and it is one of the simplest unsupervised algorithms for clustering problems. K-means performance is also relatively good.

In addition to having to know the number of clusters upfront, k-means faces another disadvantage: it does not work well for non-globular clusters. The k-means algorithm tends to find clusters of the same comparable shape. Fortunately, additional clustering algorithms can handle the weaknesses of k-means.

DBSCAN Algorithm

DBSCAN stands for density-based spatial clustering of applications with noise. The easiest way to understand density-based clustering is to look at Figure 4-14, a reproduction of the original clusters shown from Ester et al. Ester introduced the DBSCAN algorithm in 1996. The graphic shows three database examples. Each of the examples contains four easily visible clusters. The clusters are non-globular, inconsistent shapes. If you were to run a k-means clustering algorithm on the datasets shown in Figure 4-14, the k-means algorithm would fail miserably. A density-based algorithm like DBSCAN is required to cluster such datasets.

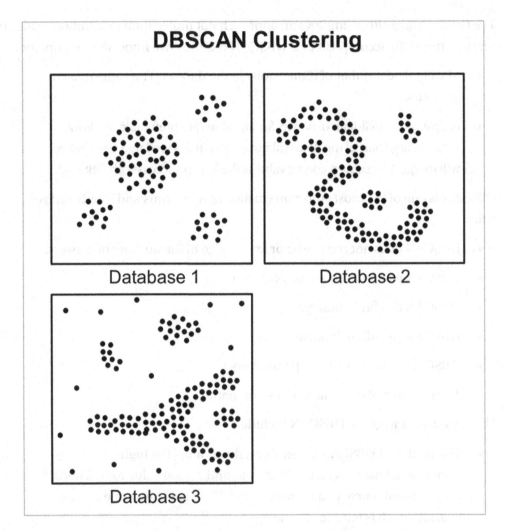

Figure 4-14. *DBSCAN clustering examples*

The three images shown highlight the strengths of density-based algorithms. In Database 1, the relative cluster size of the larger center cluster compared to the three surrounding clusters would be problematic for k-means. In Database 2, the S-shaped cluster surrounding the two smaller clusters would pose trouble for k-means. In Database 3, the random noise points dispersed throughout the area would be problematic for the k-means algorithm.

The DBSCAN algorithm employs an approach not unlike human intuition to identify clusters and noise. To accomplish this, DBSCAN requires two important parameters:

- MinPts: The number of dimensions in the dataset. The value must be at least 3.

- e: Epsilon is Euclidean distance. Small values are preferable. If e is too small, a large part of the data will not cluster. If e is too large, the clusters will merge. Choosing a good e value is the key to success with DBSCAN.

DBSCAN is one of the most common clustering algorithms and its advantages include

- DBSCAN does not require prior knowledge of the number of clusters.

- DBSCAN can find any shape of cluster.

- DBSCAN can find outliers.

- DBSCAN can identify noise.

- DBSCAN requires just two parameters.

- The ordering of the dataset does not matter.

The key disadvantages of DBSCAN include

- The quality of DBSCAN depends on the e value. For high-dimensional data, it can be difficult to find a good value for e. This is the so-called "curse of dimensionality." If the data and scale are not well known, it is hard to choose e.

- DBSCAN cannot cluster datasets well with large differences in density.

Note that the optics algorithm is a hierarchical version of DBSCAN. The HDBSCAN algorithm is a faster version of the optics algorithm.

Expectation-Maximization (EM) Algorithm

When k-means fails to achieve desirable results, consider the EM algorithm. EM often gives excellent results for real-world datasets, especially if you have a small region of interest.

EM is an iterative algorithm that works well when the model depends on unobserved latent variables. The algorithm iterates between two steps: expectation (E) and maximization (M). In the expectation step (E), a function is created for the expectation of likelihood. In the maximization step (M), parameters are created to maximize the expected likelihood in the E step.

The theory behind the EM algorithm is difficult to understand. With EM clustering, you are probabilistically assigning candidates to clusters. The EM algorithm tends to run comparatively slow since it needs to calculate a lot of covariances and means.

You will explore how to implement the EM algorithm on real-world data in the next chapter.

4.10 Algorithm Performance

Whether you are classifying or clustering, algorithm prediction accuracy is the key measure of the chosen algorithm's performance. The degree of accuracy you require is relative to the problem you are trying to solve. If you are building an ML model to determine the best day to play golf, a 90% confidence rate is acceptable. If you are trying to determine if a photograph of a skin spot is cancerous, or if a plot of land contains a landmine, 90% would not be acceptable.

The rise of deep learning has, to some extent, been the result of an ever-increasing search for algorithm accuracy. The users of CML algorithms were in search of higher degrees of accuracy, which led them to DL algorithms.

The MNIST database is one of the most popular "Hello World" applications in ML. MNIST is a large database of handwritten digits used to train neural networks and CML algorithms in image recognition. Because image recognition is well suited for DL algorithms, you will not implement MNIST. However, as MNIST has been around for a long time, you can gain insight about the algorithm's performance.

MNIST Algorithm Evaluation

MNIST is the abbreviation for Mixed National Institute of Standards and Technology. The MNIST database consists of 60,000 handwritten digits. Figure 4-15 shows what these images look like.

MNIST Sample Images

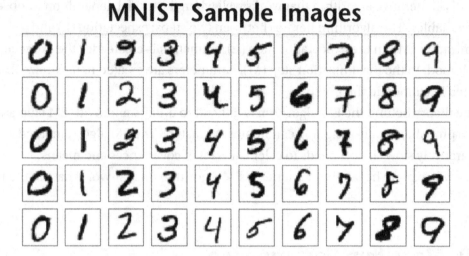

Figure 4-15. *MNIST sample images*

Characteristics of the MNIST image database:

- 60,000 training instances

- 10,000 test instances

- Each image dimension is 28x28 pixels

- All images are greyscale

In addition to the image files, the MNIST database includes labels for each image. Because the MNIST dataset contains labels, MNIST is a classification ML problem.

Figure 4-16 shows a visualization of the MNIST dataset. You can distinguish the 10 unique digits. Digits that have similar appearance appear in close proximity. For example, x and y appear together at the top left. Digits 1 and 2 are also similar and appear in close proximity to each other at the center of the visualization.

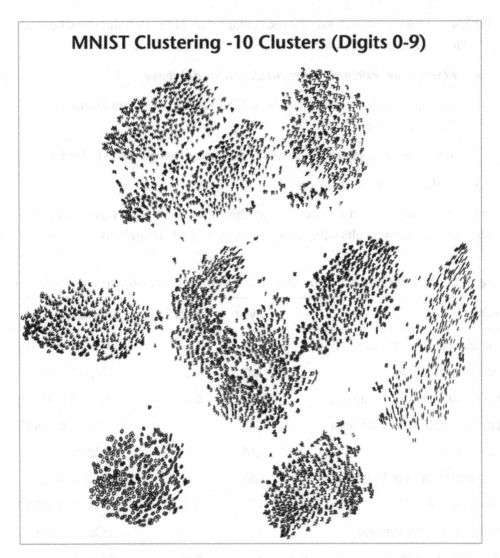

Figure 4-16. *MNIST visualization*

There is a rich amount of academic research on the MNIST database. You can utilize the results to help you understand the algorithm. Because you have labeled data, you can understand how the supervised learning classifiers stack up against one another.

In order to evaluate a ML model on the MNIST database, it is necessary to train the model with the 60,000 training instances. Evaluation uses the additional 10,000 test instances. Because MNIST is such a popular dataset, many models and algorithms have solved MNIST. You can use the results of this work to gain some insights about relative algorithm performance.

Table 4-4 shows a summary of the results for many of the popular classifiers on MNIST. The table summarizes MNIST results from the following references:

- *https://en.wikipedia.org/wiki/MNIST_database*

- *Summary of Performance on the MNIST Evaluation, Data Mining,* Witten et al., pp 421

- MNIST website, *www.nist.gov/itl/iad/image-group/emnist-dataset*

- Author MNIST evaluation

The second column in the table displays the algorithm category as either CML or DL. Most of the recent results with error rates < 1% use DL algorithms.

Table 4-4. *MNIST Classification Algorithm Performance Summary*

Classifier	Type	Error (%)	References
Linear classifier (1-layer neural net)	CML	12.0	LeCun et al. (1998)
Linear classifier (pairwise)	CML	7.6	Wikipedia
K-nearest-neighbors, Euclidean (L2)	CML	5.0	LeCun et al. (1998)
2-layer neural net, 300 hidden units	CML	4.7	LeCun et al. (1998)
Random forest	CML	2.8	Wickham
Support vector machine, Gaussian	CML	1.4	MNIST website
Convolutional net, LeNet-5	DL	0.95	LeCun et al. (1998)
Virtual support vector machine	DL	0.56	DeCoste (2002)
KNN (shiftable edge preprocessing)	CML	0.56	Wikipedia
Convolutional neural net	DL	0.4	Simard (2003)
6-layer feed forward neural net GPU	DL	0.35	Ciresan (2010)
Large deep convolutional neural net	DL	0.35	Ciresan (2011)
Committee of 35 convolutional neural nets	DL	0.23	Ciresan (2012)

Recall from Figure 4-8, k-nearest neighbor and support vector machine were two of the recommended algorithms for classification problems. The MNIST performance of KNN is 95% classification accuracy while SVM achieves a 98.6% accuracy. These are very impressive results, especially for the SVM. The SVM result rivals the results seen with several of the DL algorithms. Scanning down the bottom half of the table, you can see the top results are obtained with DL algorithms, >99.5% accuracy.

MNIST is an image recognition problem. While the accuracy results presented are useful, you also need to consider different problem types before reaching any conclusions.

Earlier in the book, I discussed leveraging academic research papers as a means to gain a competitive advantage. One of the common metrics published by researchers is algorithm classification accuracy. Figure 4-17 shows the my summary of CML algorithm performance across a wide variety of ML classification problems published in academic research.

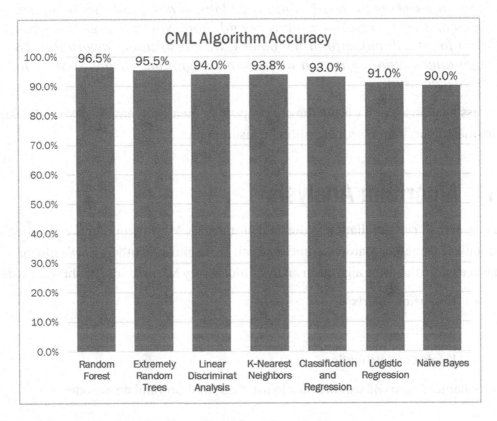

Figure 4-17. *CML classification algorithm comparison*

You saw earlier in the chapter that different algorithms are useful for different types of problems. The data in Figure 4-17 represents a very wide snapshot, and it is not very scientific to aggregate the results, but you can use it to make some general insights:

- With the zero-based Y-axis used in the chart, it is apparent the differences between algorithms are not great. All of these CML algorithms achieve accuracy in the 90% - 95% range.

- Random forest often does an excellent job, typically outperforming the other classifiers. This makes random forest the go-to algorithm for most CML classification purposes.

You saw with MNIST results that the SVM algorithm outperformed all of the non-DL algorithms, including random forest. This is likely because decision trees do not work as well for high-dimensional problems like MNIST. Depending on the problem, random forest and SVM are two very important, yet different, algorithms for your toolbox.

If you are seeking to classify multi-class labeled data, just choose random forest and save yourself precious time and effort. Nine out of ten times, random forest will outperform the other CML classification algorithms. For high-dimensional data such as pattern recognition, choose SVM as the go-to algorithm.

Classification accuracy is not the only important measurement. Next, you will look at additional important tools for algorithm measurement.

4.11 Algorithm Analysis

Because of their close affiliation to the field of statistics, ML environments are loaded with statistical analysis features, some of which are useful, and others not so much. Next, you will explore the three algorithm analysis tools every ML practitioner should master:

- Confusion matrix

- ROC curves

- K-fold cross validation

In Chapter 5, you will explore how to use these tools to validate a model.

Confusion Matrix

One of the most important outputs of the ML model is the confusion matrix. You saw the following confusion matrix in Chapter 3 when you ran a Weka classifier in the cloud:

```
001    === Confusion Matrix ===
002
003     a  b  c   <-- classified as
004    50  0  0 |  a = Iris-setosa
005     0 49  1 |  b = Iris-versicolor
006     0  2 48 |  c = Iris-virginica
```

The confusion matrix is a two-dimensional plot with a row and column for each class. The example above had three classes. You can generate a confusion matrix for any number of dataset classes. Figure 4-18 shows a generic 2-class confusion matrix.

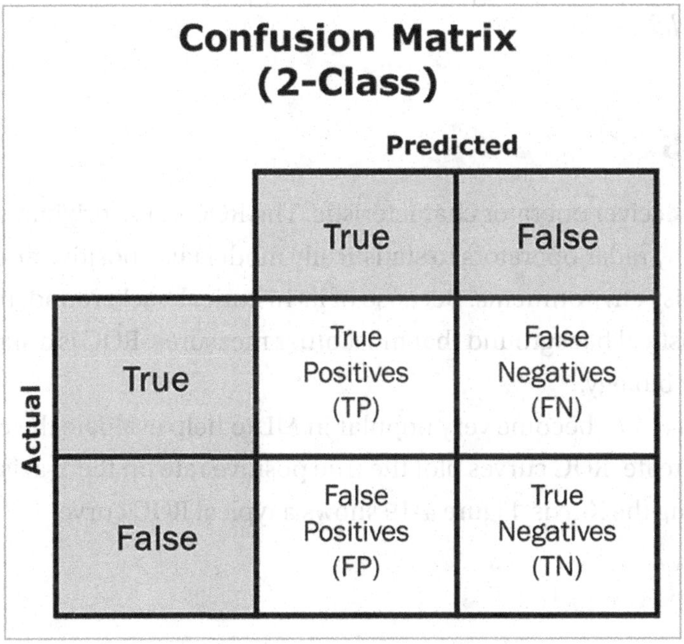

Figure 4-18. *A 2-class generic confusion matrix*

Each element in the confusion matrix shows the number of test examples for which the actual class is the row and the predicted class is the column. Good results correspond to large numbers running down the diagonal of the matrix. In the 2-class confusion matrix, the diagonal values represent true positives and true negatives.

Glancing at the values not on the main diagonal can give you excellent feedback on how the model is performing, or more specifically, when the model is getting "confused". You can gain the following insights from the 3-class confusion matrix shown earlier:

- Two instances of iris-virginica (type c) were misclassified as iris-versicolor (type b).

- One instance of iris-versicolor (type b) was misclassified as iris-virginica (type c).

- All fifty instances of iris-sentosa were correctly classified.

Each time you run a classifier, an ML-Gate 2 best practice is to check the confusion matrix results against values you predetermine to be acceptable for the model.

ROC Curves

ROC stands for receiver operator characteristic. The ROC curve originated in World War II and was used by radar operators to statistically model false positive and false negative detections in noisy environments. Because of its historical background, the ROC curve has a better statistical background that most other measures. ROC is a standard measure in medicine and biology.

The ROC curve has become very popular in ML to help evaluate the effectiveness of the models we create. ROC curves plot the true positive rate on the Y-axis and the false positive rate along the X-axis. Figure 4-19 shows a typical ROC curve.

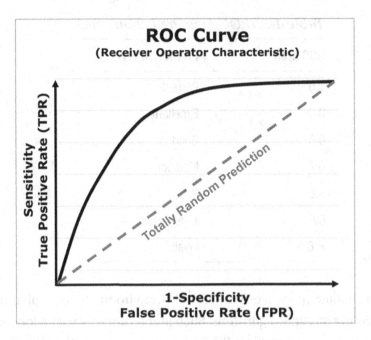

Figure 4-19. *ROC curve*

ROC curves have some interesting properties:

- The slope of the ROC curve is non-increasing. The slope typically decreases. Steeper ROC curves represent better classification. A perfect classifier would produce a vertical line ROC curve.

- Each point on the ROC curve represents a different tradeoff, or cost ratio, between false positives and false negatives.

- The slope of the line tangent to the ROC curve defines the cost ratio.

- The ROC area is the area under the ROC curve. The ROC area represents the performance averaged over all possible cost ratios.

The ROC area represents the area under the ROC curve. Table 4-5 shows the prediction level that is associated with the ML model given its corresponding ROC area.

Table 4-5. *ROC Area Prediction Levels*

ROC area	Prediction level
1.0	Perfect
0.9	Excellent
0.8	Good
0.7	Mediocre
0.6	Poor
0.5	Totally random
< 0.5	Invalid

In the next chapter, you will use the Weka ML environment to graph multiple ROC curves representing multiple algorithms. Such graphs are very useful for comparing algorithms. When graphing multiple ROC curves, you can gain the following additional insights:

- If two ROC curves do not intersect, one method dominates the other and you should choose its corresponding algorithm.

- If two ROC curves intersect, one method (algorithm) is better for some cost ratios, and the other method (algorithm) is better for the other cost ratios.

As you will see, ML environments make it easy to visualize multiple ROC curves.

K-Fold Cross-Validation

In the real world, it seems we never have enough data. The amount of data available for training and testing our models is often times limited. You saw with MNIST that the standard training method is 60,000 defined instances for training and an additional 10,000 instances for testing. This approach is called the ***holdout method*** because you are holding out part of the data for testing purposes. It is common to hold out one-third of the data for testing. The holdout method worked fine for MNIST because the dataset was large. With smaller datasets, it can be problematic. How do you know which part of the data to hold out?

Choosing a particular set of data for testing can lead to a bias. For example, if you are unlucky, and a particular class is completely missing in the training data, how could you expect the classifier to predict such a value when it appears in the testing data? The solution to bias caused by particular samples chosen for holdout is to repeat the process several (K) times, where K can be any number such as three, five, or ten. If you desire to train on two-thirds of the data and test on one-third, then K equals three. If you wish to train on nine-tenths and test on one-tenth, then K equals ten.

This approach is called k-fold cross-validation. Figure 4-20 shows the example of a 5-fold cross-validation process.

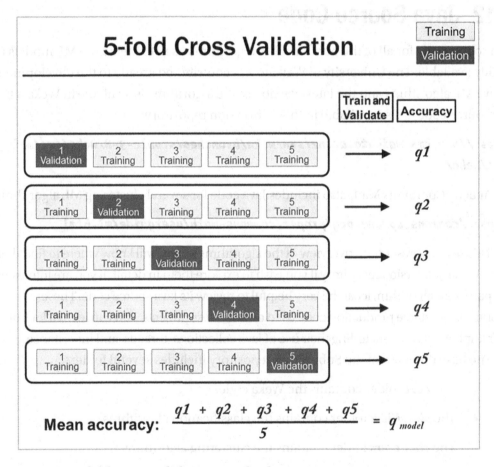

Figure 4-20. *5-fold cross-validation method*

When you perform an n-fold cross-validation, you are actually performing multiple (K) passes of the training and validation cycle. The resulting accuracies of each pass are averaged to obtain the mean accuracy for the model.

> *K-fold cross-validation is a simple but powerful concept. The standard way of predicting the error rate on a learning technique is to use a 10-fold cross-validation where the dataset is divided randomly into 10 parts. 10-fold cross-validation should be part of every ML-Gate 2 model evaluation.*

Extensive tests have shown that K=10 gives the best results independent of dataset size.

4.12 Java Source Code

Java source code for all of the popular CML algorithms used to create the ML models is readily available. The University of Waikato has contributed greatly to the development of Java ML algorithms and the latest version of the algorithms is available in Weka 3.8. The source code is also available in this Subversion repository:

https://svn.cms.waikato.ac.nz/svn/weka/branches/stable-3-8/weka/src/main/java/weka/

Apache Commons Math also includes Java code for several clustering ML algorithms:

https://commons.apache.org/proper/commons-math/userguide/ml.html

This section presents an overview of the algorithms so you will know where to find them in the Weka Subversion repository if you wish to explore them in detail. If you are interested in a particular algorithm, it can be very helpful to review its Java source code. These algorithms are stable production code used on countless projects. You can learn a lot from their implementation, including their use of Java collections, threads, and inheritance.

The base directory of the Subversion repository includes several folders:

- The *core* folder contains the Weka code.

- The *classifiers* folder contains the classification algorithms.

- The *clusterers* folder contains the clustering algorithms.

The Java files structure is hierarchical. The algorithms inherit from other underlying algorithms. For example, if you wish to implement a random forest algorithm, each of the following files will be included when you construct the random forest:

RandomForest.java will set the base classifier as **RandomTree**:

```
001    /**
002     * Constructor that sets base classifier to RandomTree
003     */
004    public RandomForest() {
005        RandomTree rTree = new RandomTree();
006        rTree.setDoNotCheckCapabilities(true);
007        super.setClassifier(rTree);
008        super.setRepresentCopiesUsingWeights(true);
009        setNumIterations(defaultNumberOfIterations());
010    }
```

The **RandomTree.java** class will extend the **AbstractClassifier** class:

```
001    /**
002     * Constructor for Random Tree that extends AbstractClassifier
003     */
004    public class RandomTree extends AbstractClassifier implements
       OptionHandler,
005        WeightedInstancesHandler, Randomizable, Drawable, PartitionGenerator {
006    }
```

The **AbstractClassifier.java** class will implement the **Classfier** class:

```
001    /**
002     * Abstract classifier. All schemes for numeric or nominal prediction
           in Weka
003     * extend this class. Note that a classifier MUST either implement
004     * distributionForInstance() or classifyInstance().
005     */
006    public abstract class AbstractClassifier implements Classifier,
       BatchPredictor,
007        Cloneable, Serializable, OptionHandler, CapabilitiesHandler,
           RevisionHandler,
008        CapabilitiesIgnorer, CommandlineRunnable {
009    }
```

221

Classifier.java

```
001   /**
002    * Classifier interface. All schemes for numeric or nominal prediction in
003    * Weka implement this interface. Note that a classifier MUST either implement
           implement
004    * distributionForInstance() or classifyInstance().
005    */
006   public interface Classifier {
007   }
```

To view the Java code for any of the CML algorithms, simply navigate through the repository into the *classifiers* or *clusterers* folders.

Classification Algorithms

Within the *classifiers* folder, the algorithms fall into three categories:

- *bayes*: Contains several variants of the naive Bayes algorithms.

- *pmml*: Predictive Model Markup Language is an XML-based interchange format. This folder contains PMML based-models such as SVM and regression algorithms.

- *trees*: Contains all the decision tree-based algorithms, such as random forest.

Figure 4-21 shows an expanded view of the key classifier algorithms.

Figure 4-21. *Java classifier algorithms (Weka Subversion repository)*

The most useful classifiers, listed earlier in Figure 4-8, are included in the repository. Figure 4-21 shows that naive Bayes, random forest, and SVM source code are all included in the ***classifiers*** directory.

Clustering Algorithms

Figure 4-22 shows the Java clustering algorithms available in Weka.

Figure 4-22. *Java clusterers (Weka Subversion repository)*

In Figure 4-8, you saw that k-means and DBSCAN were the go-to algorithms for clustering problems with unlabeled data. Source code for these algorithms is within *SimpleKMeans.java* and *DensityBasedCluster.java*.

Just as you saw with the classification algorithms, the clustering algorithms also build upon other higher-level clustering classes in the directory, such as *Cluster.java* and *HeirarchicalClusterer.java*.

Java Algorithm Modification

I stated earlier that CML algorithms are commodities. The source code of the Java algorithms in the Weka Subversion repository shows the algorithm code has been stable for several years. All of the Java code in the Weka repository is licensed under the GNU General Public License. The code is free and you can distribute or modify it under the terms of the license.

www.gnu.org/licenses/

Due to advances in the Java platform, there are several areas where these algorithms could be improved:

- **Lambda expressions**: The addition of *lambda expressions* is starting to reshape Java. Lambda expressions allow for new capabilities in the Java API library. For example, lambda expressions simplify the handling of *for-each* style operations, allowing us to take greater advantage of parallel processing capabilities of multi-core environments. There exists an opportunity to improves the performance of most of the Java algorithms by introducing lambda expressions.

- **Stream API**: The new stream API introduced in Java 8 allows us to manipulate data in much more powerful ways. The new Stream API works in conjunction with the Java collections class and lambda expressions. The new Stream API can handle advanced data queries and provides a higher level of efficiency especially for large datasets.

- **Concurrency**: If you look into the Java code, you will see that many of the algorithms use the Java *ThreadPoolExecutor* to handle their multi-threaded operations. *ThreadPoolExecutor* is one of the services that make up the Java *ExecutorService*. JDK 7 saw the introduction of a new service, the *ForkJoinPool*. The *ForkJoinPool* class enables the implementation of parallel programming such that threads can run on multiple CPUs/GPUs. The main idea behind a *ForkJoin* task is the divide-and-conquer strategy, which is very suitable for the decision tree family of algorithms, including random forest. Updating the Java algorithms to utilize *ForkJoin* could significantly improve performance.

These potential enhancements are performance-related improvements. As discussed in Chapter 2, cloud-based providers make it easy to scale CPU resources on demand. For this reason, when building models in the cloud, it is typically easier to add CPU resources, rather than optimize the algorithms to take advantage of the latest JAVA API features. The enhancements would be useful in an environment where you have limited CPU constraints at model build time, such as building models on a mobile or embedded device.

CHAPTER 5

Machine Learning Environments

You have learned about data and algorithms. Next, you will put the pieces together and build the CML model. ML environments perform a critical function. They act as an important piece of middleware, enabling you to create ML models from the data for later use by your application. This chapter will cover the following:

- Introduce the steps required during the model creation phase.

- Review the Java-based ML environments, including a high-level overview of the RapidMiner and KNIME Java ML environments.

- Offer a detailed review, including complete setup instructions for the Weka ML environment.

- Implement the seven most important CML models using Weka.

- Cluster the Old Faithful geyser dataset using three clustering algorithms.

- Classify the large PAMAP2_Dataset using four classification algorithms.

- Review the accuracy performance of the four classification algorithms.

- Create a combined graph representing four multiple ROC curves using Weka KnowledgeFlow.

- Demonstrate how to import and export Weka ML models.

© Mark Wickham 2018
M. Wickham, *Practical Java Machine Learning*, https://doi.org/10.1007/978-1-4842-3951-3_5

5.1 Overview

In Chapter 3, you saw how easy it is to create ML and DL solutions using cloud-based APIs. In this chapter, you will bring the solution to the desktop. Java-based ML environments allow you to create your own models using your own computing resources. This provides two huge advantages:

- You do not incur incremental costs for compute resources required to create the models.

- You retain control of the models you create. This can lead to a competitive advantage.

In this chapter, I will present several Java-based ML environments, but the focus will be primarily on the Weka environment. If you decide to use one of the other ML environments, the detailed implementation steps with respect to data import, algorithms supported, and model creation/import/export should be similar.

ML Gates

In the ML-Gates methodology, the most important task of the ML environment is to create the ML model you will use in your application.

Creating the best possible model is an iterative process. You saw in Chapter 4 how to choose the best algorithm. In this chapter, you will explore how to create the best possible model by tuning the available parameters of the algorithm.

Figure 5-1 shows the key steps involved with the model at ML-Gates 3 and ML-Gates 2.

Machine Learning
ML-Gate 3/ML-Gate 2

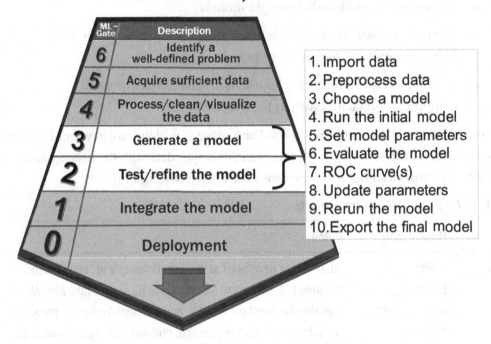

Figure 5-1. *ML-Gates 3/2 model activity*

Many ML environments can accomplish these tasks. The number of Java packages is smaller, and I will cover them next.

5.2 Java ML Environments

In Chapter 1, you saw how widespread Java has become. I also discussed the build vs. buy decision process for data science platforms.

One of your main goals is to apply ML solutions at the edge. This requires you to produce lightweight models that you can deploy into portable devices, such as mobile phones. Java ML environments meet these requirements.

Java ML environments check all the boxes:

- They are free and open source.

- You can easily produce lightweight models.

- You can run Java ML environments on the desktop or in the cloud if higher compute resources are required.

- It is easy to export the model for use in mobile devices or small computer form factors such as the Raspberry Pi.

In effect, the Java ML environment acts like a piece of middleware in your ML pipeline. Models created by the ML environment connect the input data with the user application.

Table 5-1 shows a summary of the Java-based ML environments.

Table 5-1. *Java ML Environments*

Name	Description	Notes
Weka	Waikato Environment for Knowledge Analysis	ML platform developed at Waikato University in New Zealand. Includes GUI, command line interface (CLI), and Java API. Weka is arguably the most popular ML environment. Weka is a great ML environment to start or practice, and you can export models for Android. Weka is free and open source.
KNIME	Konstanz Information Miner	Konstanz University (Germany) developed KNIME. It has a focus on pharmacy research and business intelligence. KNIME bases its GUI on Eclipse. KNIME also contains an API interface.
RapidMiner	RapidMiner	The Technical University of Dortmund (Germany) developed RapidMiner. RapidMiner contains a GUI and a Java API. RapidMiner supports data handling, visualization, modeling, and algorithms. RapidMiner has free and commercial distributions.
ELKI	Environment for developing KDD applications	Data mining workbench developed at Ludwig Maximillion University in Munich. ELKI focuses on data and knowledge discovery from data (KDD) applications. ELKI provides a mini-GUI, CLI, and Java API. ELKI is research software.
Java-ML	The Java Machine Learning Library	Java-ML is a collection of ML algorithms. Java-ML does not contain a GUI.
DL4J	Deep Learning4 Java	DL4J is the deep learning library for Java from Skymind. DL4J does not support CML algorithms. See Chapter 1 for additional detail.

The first five entries in Table 5-1 are mainly Java-based CML environments, and I will discuss them briefly next, before taking a deep dive into Weka. The last entry, DL4J, is a dedicated Java DL environment. Table 5-2 provides links for each of the Java ML environments.

Table 5-2. *Java ML Environment Links*

Name	Link
Weka	www.cs.waikato.ac.nz/ml/weka/
KNIME	www.knime.com/knime-analytics-platform
RapidMiner	https://rapidminer.com/
ELKI	https://elki-project.github.io/
Java-ML	http://java-ml.sourceforge.net/
DL4J	https://deeplearning4j.org/index.html

There are several factors to consider in choosing the best Java ML environment. The factors include

- **License and commercial terms**: You should favor free open sources packages that allow you to create models you can use for commercial applications.

- **Availability of algorithms**: You should look for packages that support the seven most important algorithms discussed in Chapter 4.

- **Ongoing support**: You should look for a community of users or a long-term commitment by the creators.

- **Portability of models**: You should look for the ability to export models so Java clients in any device can use the models you create. This helps you to achieve ML at the edge.

- **Flexibility**: Java continues to grow with each major release. You need a Java-based ML environment that can grow with the language. Perhaps in the future, we will see ML features directly included with Java, much the same way that JSON and other features are now candidates for inclusion.

Weka

Weka is an abbreviation for Waikato Environment for Knowledge Analysis. The University of Waikato, in New Zealand, created Weka. Interestingly, Weka is also the name of a flightless bird in New Zealand (Gallirallus Australis), hence the logo. New Zealand seems to have many cute flightless birds.

Weka, the ML environment, has been around a while. Ported to Java in 1997, it has been a mainstay in the data mining industry. In 2005, Weka received the Data Mining and Knowledge Discovery Service Award from ACM at the SIGKDD Conference. The decision to migrate Weka to Java has allowed it to stay relevant.

Recently, Weka added a package manager. Many third-party packages and algorithms are available through the package manager. All of the important CML algorithms are available for Weka. You will explore the Weka algorithms later in this chapter.

The University of Waikato, which maintains a stable release (currently 3.8.2) and a development release (3.9.2), supports Weka. Unlike Android Studio, the Weka releases are infrequent. It is safe to run the development channel release, which includes some useful GUI improvements and support for DL4J. As Weka gains support with the ML community, it is becoming increasingly easy to find help for problems on the popular forums, such as Stack Overflow and YouTube videos.

Weka has a friendly license, the GNU General Public License (GPL). Therefore, it is possible to study how the algorithms work and to modify them.

The Weka GUI looks dated. The Weka GUIs and visualization tools are not nearly as slick as RapidMiner. However, under the hood, it lacks nothing. Weka is a very capable ML environment that can deliver the models your ML apps require. Despite its inferior GUI relative to RapidMiner, Weka checks all of the boxes.

To address one of the Weka weaknesses, later in the chapter I will discuss a Weka add-on to improve the Weka charting capabilities.

RapidMiner

RapidMiner is an incredible ML environment. Recall according to Figure 1-4, RapidMiner is a leader in data science platforms. Java-based RapidMiner excels at the following:

- RapidMiner is lightning fast.

- RapidMiner has many tools.

- RapidMiner is excellent at preparing data.

- RapidMiner allow you to build predictive ML models.

Figure 5-2 shows a screenshot of the RapidMiner main interface.

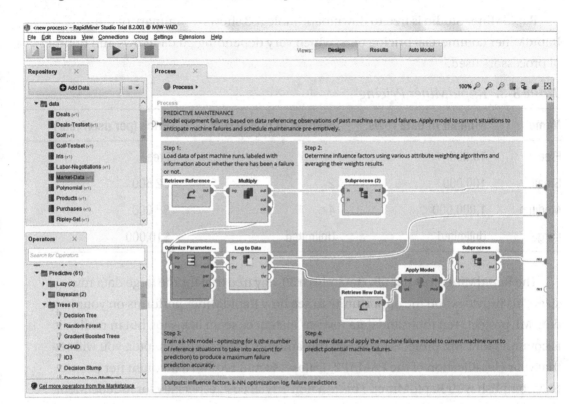

Figure 5-2. *RapidMiner main interface*

As shown in Figure 5-2, RapidMiner has a nice modern GUI. The RapidMiner's ease of use has led to its increase in popularity. RapidMiner has a large community of users and all of the usual support resources associated with widespread popularity.

The core of RapidMiner is open source Java code and is available on GitHub at ***https://github.com/rapidminer/rapidminer-studio***.

As you saw with Weka in Chapter 4, all of the ML algorithm Java code is part of core RapidMiner and is available at the GitHub repository. Close inspection will show the Java code base of the algorithms is not the same, although you can expect the algorithms to achieve nearly similar results. In many algorithm cases, the RapidMiner algorithm implementations rely on less inheritance and are easier to follow.

Aside from the RapidMiner GUI advantages, other key differences between RapidMiner and Weka are the licensing and commercial pricing terms. RapidMiner is licensed under the GNU AGPL 3.0 license. It has free and commercial offerings.

https://opensource.org/licenses/AGPL-3.0

RapidMiner Studio is free to download. Table 5-3 shows a summary of the RapidMiner commercial pricing tiers, which vary depending on data rows and number of processors used.

Table 5-3. *RapidMiner Pricing*

Name	Number of data rows	Number of processors	Price (per user/year)
Free	10,000	1	Free
Small	100,000	2	$2,500
Medium	1,000,000	4	$5,000
Large	Unlimited	Unlimited	$10,000

The RapidMiner free tier also includes a 30-day free trial for the large data row size. This provides you the opportunity to see how RapidMiner performs on your large data ML project. Ten thousand data rows or instances seem like a lot, but in reality, it is common for CML projects to exceed this amount. Later in this chapter, you will see that your classification of the PAMAP2_Dataset would require a medium tier license to accomplish with RapidMiner. This is a non-trivial cost, especially for independent developers without large resources. The RapidMiner licensing costs are the primary reason you will proceed with Weka.

In terms of flexibility, both Weka and RapidMiner provide jar file libraries that you can integrate into your Java projects. This allows you to leverage prebuilt models in your Java applications.

Weka and RapidMiner each have their own approach to implementing model generation. With any software platform, there is an initial time investment in learning how to navigate them. Fortunately, the high-level steps involved at this phase in the ML-Gates are identical.

KNIME

Like RapidMiner, KNIME was included a leader among the data science platforms shown in Figure 1-4. Some key selling points for KNIME:

- KNIME is a toolbox for data scientists.
- KNIME contains over 2,000 modules.

- KNIME is an open platform.

- KNIME can run locally, on the server, or in the cloud, which is the kind of flexibility you seek.

The latest free-download version of KNIME is 3.6.0. KNIME is licensed under GNU GPL Version 3. KNIME has a very intuitive workbench that is similar to Weka. The GUI is very comprehensive, which make KNIME useful for people who wish to explore ML but do not want to code. Figure 5-3 shows the KNIME workbench.

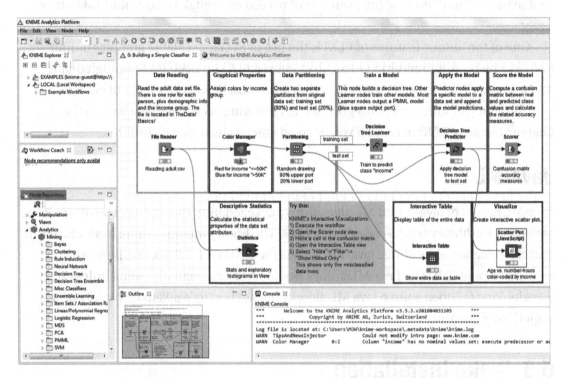

Figure 5-3. *KNIME workbench*

The KNIME interface looks very similar to RapidMiner, especially in the knowledge flow area where users can graphically connect modules to form processes.

KNIME uses PMML (Predictive Model Markup Language) to export models. PMML is a popular standard. You saw it referenced as a category title for some of the Weka classification algorithms. PMML is not quite as flexible for exporting prebuilt models for use on Android mobile devices. For this reason, Weka remains your preferred ML environment.

ELKI

ELKI is a Java platform that excels at clustering and outlier detection. While Weka and RapidMiner are general frameworks, ELKI does one thing and one thing well: clustering. It contains a huge number of clustering algorithms. If the basic clustering algorithms contained in the general frameworks are not sufficient for your ML clustering problem, ELKI probably is the solution.

ELKI has a research and education focus. It has helped to solve real-world clustering problems such as clustering the positions of whales and rebalancing public bike share programs.

One of the unique features of ELKI is the use of SVG for scalable graphics output and Apache Batik for rendering of the user interface. If you need lossless, high quality, scalable graphics output for your clustering problems, ELKI is an excellent choice.

The general frameworks do a great job at clustering, as you will see later in the chapter, but keep ELKI in mind if you need advanced clustering algorithms.

Java-ML

Java-ML is a set of Java-based ML algorithms packaged into a jar library. The most recent version of the library is 0.1.7, released in 2012. The library includes some basic clustering and classification algorithms. Java-ML carries the GNU GPL 2.0 license. Java-ML does not include any GUI. The Java-ML library would not be particularly useful unless you were looking for open source Java ML algorithms not tied to Waikato University or the RapidMiner license.

5.3 Weka Installation

To install Weka, visit the Weka download page and choose a package for your platform:

www.cs.waikato.ac.nz/ml/weka/downloading.html

You can download Weka with or without Java. Managing Weka independently of your Java install, as shown in Chapter 1, gives you the advantage of knowing which version of Java you are running.

There are two current versions of Weka:

- 3.8.2 is the latest stable release of Weka.

- 3.9.2 is the latest development release of Weka.

Weka follows the Linux model of release numbering. Even digits after the decimal point (such as 3.8.2) indicate a stable release, while odd digits (such as 3.9.2) indicate a development release.

The Weka team maintains links that summarize the bug fixes and new features in each new release. To see the new features in 3.9.2, look under the Documentation section shown here:

https://wiki.pentaho.com/display/DATAMINING/Pentaho+Data+Mining+Community+Documentation

The Weka development releases are generally very safe.

After you decide on a version, the download page contains packages for the three major platforms: Windows, Mac O/S, and Linux. Choose your package and install Weka.

1. Install Java on your system.

2. Download your desired Weka package.

3. Unzip the zip file into the new directory called ***weka-3-9-2***.

4. Set the Java CLASSPATH environment variable. The CLASSPATH environment variable tells Java where to look for classes to include.

5. Change into the directory and run Weka with ***java -jar weka.jar***.

The Weka logo, Figure 5-4, appears during the initialization.

Figure 5-4. *Weka logo*

After the Weka initialization completes, the main Weka GUI chooser appears, as shown in Figure 5-5.

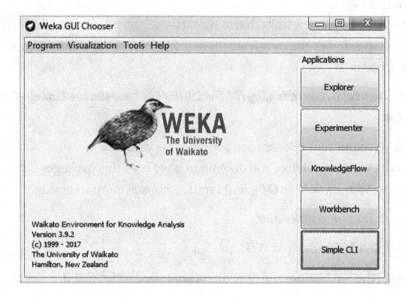

Figure 5-5. *Weka GUI Chooser*

Before starting with the main Weka applications, you need configure Weka.

Weka Configuration

Weka is mostly ready to go after the initial install. I will address a few configuration updates next. Figure 5-6 shows the contents of the main Weka directory after you unzip the install file.

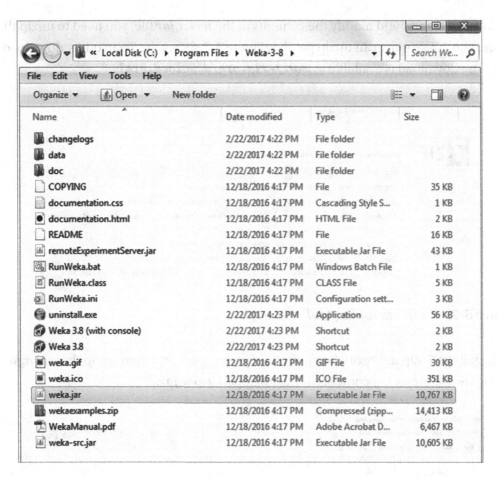

Figure 5-6. *Weka.jar*

The ***weka.jar*** file is of interest for two reasons:

- The ***weka.jar*** file contains all of the Java source code for the algorithms in Weka. You saw in Chapter 4 how to explore them in the online Subversion repository. By unzipping the ***weka.jar*** file, you can explore them locally.

- Weka uses a file named ***Visualize.props*** for many GUI configuration properties. In order to modify the configuration, you must make a local copy of this file.

In order to view and modify the contents of the *weka.jar* file, you need to unzip the jar file. The 7-Zip utility can unzip jar files. Figure 5-7 shows the 7-Zip utility download page. The download is available at *www.7-zip.org/download.html*.

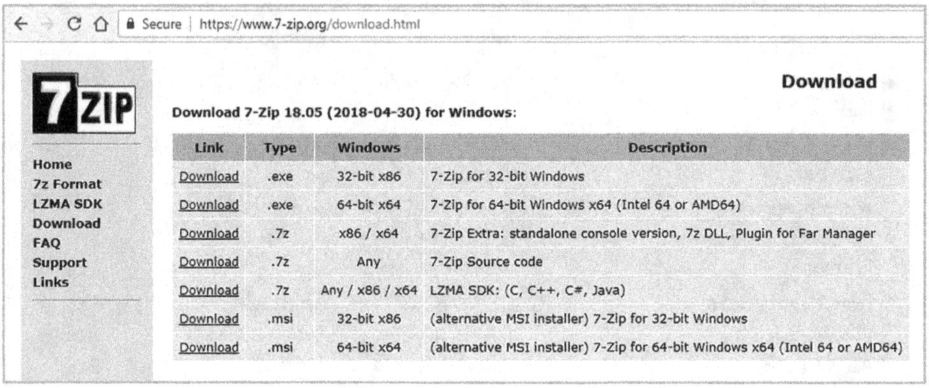

Figure 5-7. *7-Zip unzipping tool*

Install the 7-Zip utility on the platform of your choice and then unzip the *weka.jar* file. Figure 5-8 shows the contents of the unzipped *weka.jar*.

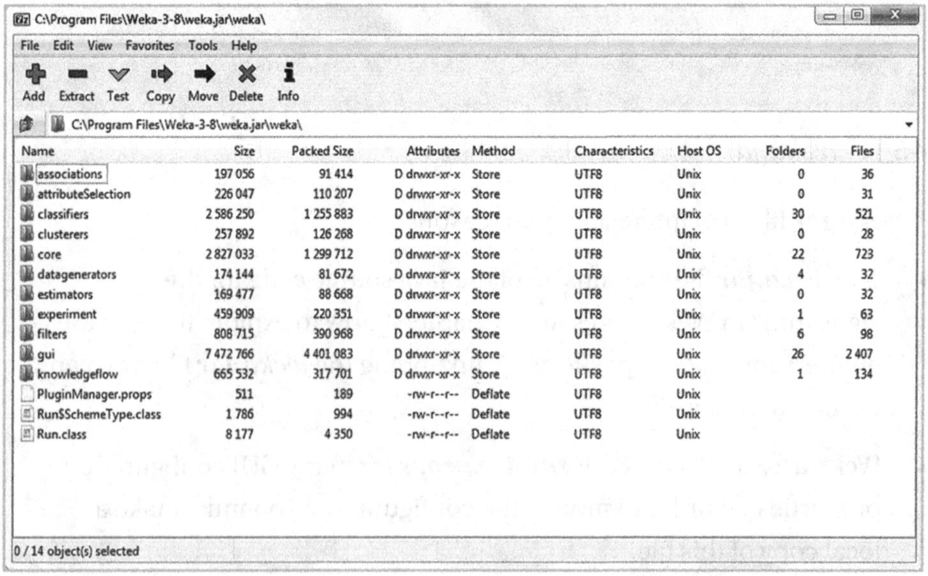

Figure 5-8. *Weka.jar contents*

Weka.jar includes directories for cluster algorithms, classifier algorithms, and the *gui* directory which contains the *Visualize.props* file you want to modify.

Java Parameters Setup

One of the issues with Java is high memory usage. Weka always displays a status box at the bottom of the Weka Explorer window. The status box displays messages about what is happening within Weka. Right-clicking inside the status box brings up a menu with two helpful options:

- *Memory information*: Shows the amount of memory available to Weka

- *Run garbage collector*: Forces the Java garbage collector to perform a garbage collection task in the background

You can use these options to monitor the Weka memory usage. If you should get *Out Of Memory* errors, you should increase the heap size for your Java engine. The default setting of 64MB is usually too small. You can set the memory for Java using the *–Xmx* option in the Java command line. For example, increase the Java memory to 1024MB with the following:

```
001    java -Xmx1024m -jar weka.jar
```

If you are running Windows and wish to make the change globally, you can set the *javaOpts* parameter in the *RunWeka.ini* file like so:

```
001    javaOpts= -Xmx1040m
```

If you get *Class Not Found* errors, you will need to verify your CLASSPATH variable settings. The best way to confirm your CLASSPATH setting is to use the Weka *Sysinfo* display, shown in Figure 5-9.

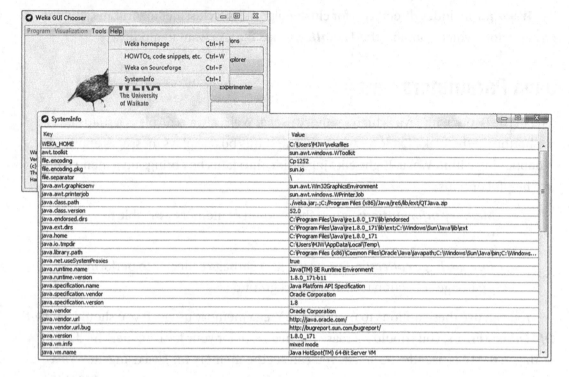

Figure 5-9. *Weka Help ➤ SystemInfo Display*

In addition to the ***java.class.path*** setting, the Weka Sysinfo page also displays the ***WEKA_HOME*** and ***memory.max*** settings.

Modifying Weka .prop Files

If the default setup of Weka is not to your liking, you can tweak the ***.prop*** files to modify Weka behavior. There are many ***.prop*** files to configure Weka.

The following steps show how to modify the ***Visualize.props*** file to change the default colors of the X-axis and Y-axis from green to black. The responsible ***.props*** file for charts and graphs in Weka is ***weka/gui/visualize/Visualize.props***.

1. Close Weka.

2. Extract the ***.props*** file from the ***weka.jar***, using an archive manager that can handle ZIP files, such as 7-Zip under Windows.

3. Place this ***.props*** file in the ***$WEKA_HOME/props***.

4. Open the local ***.props*** file with a text editor, making sure that CRLF and BOM characters are correct for your platform.

5. Modify the parameters you wish to change. The property name is on the left side of the "=" and the property value is on the right side.

6. Save the file and restart Weka.

Figure 5-10 shows the local copy of the ***Visualize.props*** file you are updating.

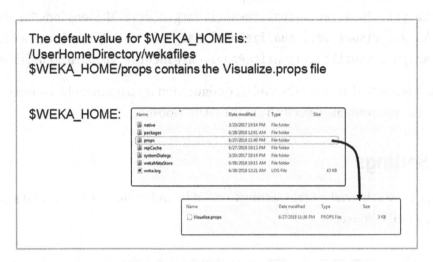

Figure 5-10. *Weka Visualize.props local file copy*

There are many customizable values inside the Weka *.props* files. The following listing shows line 009 with the updated axis color setting:

```
001    # Properties for visualization
002    #
003    # Version: $Revision: 5015 $
004
005    # Maximum precision for numeric values
006    weka.gui.visualize.precision=10
007
008    # Colour for the axis in the 2D plot (can use R,G,B format)
009    weka.gui.visualize.Plot2D.axisColour=black
010
011    # Colour for the background of the 2D plot (can use R,G,B format)
012    weka.gui.visualize.Plot2D.backgroundColour=white
013
014    # The JFrame (needs to implement the interface weka.gui.visualize.
       InstanceInfo)
```

```
015    # for displaying Instance information.
016    weka.gui.visualize.Plot2D.instanceInfoFrame=weka.gui.visualize.
       InstanceInfoFrame
017
018    # Defaults for margin curve plots
019    weka.gui.visualize.VisualizePanel.MarginCurve.XDimension=Margin
020    weka.gui.visualize.VisualizePanel.MarginCurve.YDimension=Cumulative
021    weka.gui.visualize.VisualizePanel.MarginCurve.ColourDimension=Margin
```

Using this method, most of the Weka configuration is customizable. However, there are some settings available directly from the GUI Chooser.

Weka Settings

Figure 5-11 shows the Weka main settings available under the Program menu selection in the Weka GUI Chooser.

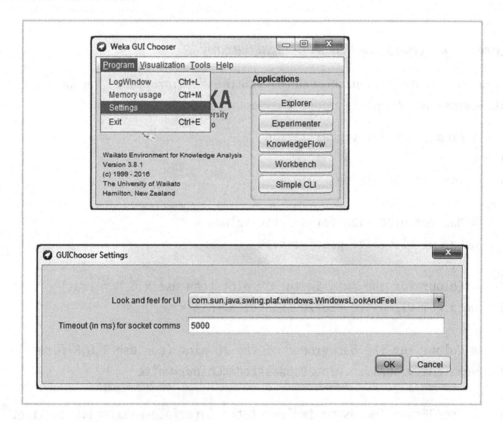

Figure 5-11. *Weka main settings*

There are only two settings available: *LookAndFeel* of the GUI and *SocketTimeout* for communications. For Windows platforms, the preferred *LookAndFeel* setting is *WindowsLookAndFeel*. It is not necessary to change this default *SocketTimeout* value.

Weka Package Manager

Weka recently introduced a package manager. When you initially run Weka, there are many preinstalled algorithms for clustering and classification. There are also many uninstalled packages that are available for installation with the package manager. Figure 5-12 shows the Weka package manager available from the Weka GUI Chooser.

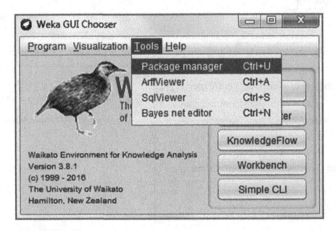

Figure 5-12. *Weka Package Manager Chooser*

When you launch the package manager, Weka gives you the option to show both the installed and available packages.

For these projects, you must install the following two packages using the package manager:

- jFreeChart: A graphical extension for Weka

- DBSCAN: A density-based clustering algorithm

Figure 5-13 shows the installation of jFreeChart, which provides improved chart rendering over the basic Weka renderer. You will use jFreeChart to render the multiple ROC curve comparison chart later in the chapter. This add-on is not required; the built-in Weka renderer will work fine, but jFreeChart provides a much more attractive charting option.

Figure 5-14 shows that package manager and highlights the recently installed DBSCAN algorithm. You will use the DBSCAN algorithm in a clustering example later in the chapter.

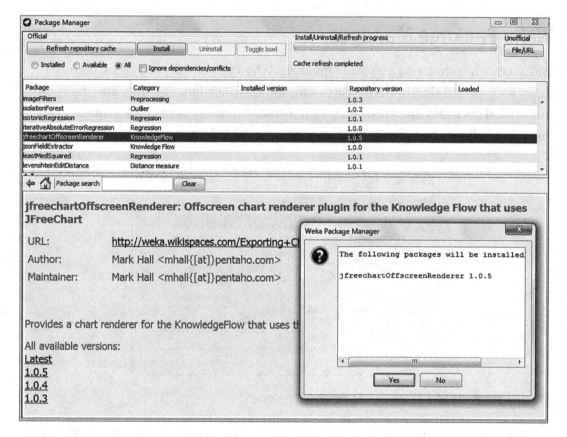

Figure 5-13. *Weka package manager and FreeChart extension*

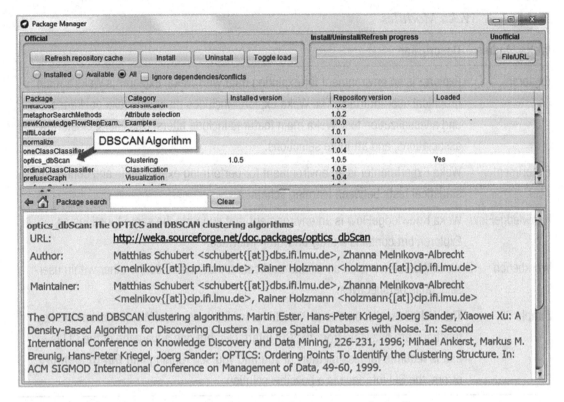

Figure 5-14. *Weka package manager and DBSCAN algorithm*

5.4 Weka Overview

Weka is a comprehensive suite of Java class libraries. The Weka package implements many state-of-the-art machine learning and data mining algorithms. Table 5-4 shows a summary of the Weka modules available from the GUI Chooser, shown earlier in Figure 5-5.

Table 5-4. *Weka Modules*

Weka Module	Description
Explorer	Explorer is an environment for exploring data with Weka. Explorer is Weka's main graphical user interface. The Weka Explorer includes the main Weka packages and a Visualization tool. Weka main features include filters, classifiers, clusterers, associations, and attribute selections.
Experimenter	Weka Experimenter is an environment for performing experiments and conducting statistical tests between learning schemes.
KnowledgeFlow	Weka KnowledgeFlow is an environment that supports the same functions as Explorer, but contains a drag-and-drop interface.
Workbench	Weka Workbench is an all-in-one application that combines the other within user-selectable perspectives.
Simple CLI	The Weka team recommends the CLI for in-depth usage of Weka. Most of the key functions are available from the GUI interfaces, but one advantage of the CLI is that is requires far less memory. If you find yourself running into **Out Of Memory** errors, the CLI interface is a possible solution.

As shown in Table 5-4, there is some redundancy in the Weka modules. You are going to focus on the following three Weka modules because they are more than sufficient to create the models you need for your Java applications.

- Weka Explorer

- Weka KnowledgeFlow

- Weka Simple CLI

I have excluded the Experimenter and the Workbench. Later in the chapter, you will use the KnowledgeFlow module to compare multiple ROC curves of different algorithms. The Experimenter could do this as well, but even though Weka does not have the best graphical interface, I prefer the graphical approach of the KnowledgeFlow module to the Experimenter. You can use the Workbench module if you are seeking a customized perspective for the Weka modules.

Weka Documentation

The Weka team does provide official documentation in the form of PDF file distributed with each release, and the University of Waikato has many videos and support resources for developers who want to learn Weka. The Weka manuals are 340+ pages and are essential reading if you wish to get serious about Weka.

The following represent the official Weka documentation from the Weka creators:

- Weka manual: The Weka manual for the current release (such as *WekaManual-3-8-2.pdf* and *WekaManual-3-9-2.pdf*) is always included within the distribution. For any particular Weka release, the manual filename is *WekaManual.pdf*.

- Weka book: The Weka team has published a book, *Data Mining - Practical Machine Learning Tools and Techniques*, written by Witten, Frank, and Hall. The book is a very good ML reference book. While it does not cover Weka in detail, it does cover many aspects of data, algorithms, and general ML theory.

- YouTube: The Weka YouTube channel, *WekaMOOC*, contains many useful Weka how-to videos.

Weka Explorer

The Explorer is the main Weka interface. Figure 5-15 shows the Weka Explorer upon initialization.

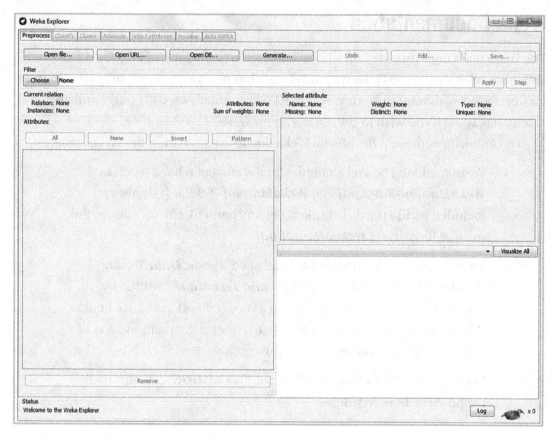

Figure 5-15. *Weka Explorer*

Across the top of the Explorer, you will see tabs for each of the key steps you need to accomplish during the model creation phase:

- **Preprocess**: "Filter" is the word used by Weka for its set of data preprocessing routines. You apply filters to your data to prepare it for classification or clustering.

- **Classify**: The **Classify** tab allows you to select a classification algorithm, adjust the parameters, and train a classifier that can be used later for predictions.

- **Cluster**: The **Cluster** tab allows you to select a clustering algorithm, adjust its parameters, and cluster an unlabeled dataset.

- **Attributes**: The **Attributes** tab allows you to select the best attributes for prediction.

- **Visualize**: The **Visualize** tab provides a visualization of the dataset. A matrix of visualizations in the form of 2D plots represents each pair of attributes.

Weka Filters

You load and prepare your data during ML-Gate 4, the preprocessing phase. Weka uses the term *filters* to describe the process of transforming your data. In Chapter 2, you explored data preprocessing in general. Within Weka, you have an additional set of internal filters you can use to prepare your data for model building. Table 5-5 shows a summary of the Weka filters grouped by filter type.

Table 5-5. *Weka Filters*

Filter type	Filter name
General	AllFilter
General	MultiFilter
General	RenameRelation
Supervised Attribute	AddClassification, AttributeSelection, ClassConditionProbabilties, ClassOrder, Discretize, MergeNominalValues, NominalToBinary, PartitionMembership
Supervised Instance	ClassBalancer, Resample, SpreadSubsaple, StratifiedRemoveFolds
Unsupervised Attribute	Add, AddCluster, AddExpression, AddID, AddNoise, AddUserFields, AddValues, CartesianProduct, Center, ChangeDateFormat, ClassAssigner, ClusterMembership, Copy, DateToNumeric, Discretize, FirstOrder, FixedDictionaryStringToWordVector, InterquartileRange, KernelFilter, MakeIndicator, MathExpression, MergeInfrequentNominalValues, MergeManyValues, MergeTwoValues, NominalToBinary, NominalToString, Normalize, NumericCleaner, NumericToBinary, NumericToDate, NumericToNominal, NumericTransform, Obfuscate, OrdinalToNumeric, PartitionedMultiFilter, PKIDiscretize, PrincipalComponents, RandomProjection, RandomSubset, Remove, RemoveByName, RemoveType, RemoveUseless, RenameAttribute, RenameNominalValues, Reorder, ReplaceMissingValues, ReplaceMissingWithUserConstant, ReplaceWithMissingValue, SortLabels, Standardize, StringToNominal, StringToWordVector, SwapValues, TimeSeriesDelta, TimeSeriesTranslate, Transpose,
Unsupervised Instance	NonSparseToSparse, Randomize, RemoveDuplicates, RemoveFolds, RemoveFrequentValues, RemoveMisclassified, RemovePercentage, RemoveRange, RemoveWithValues, Resample, ReservoirSample, SparseToNonSparse, SubsetByExpression

As you can see, there are a large number of filters available for data preprocessing with Weka, especially for unlabeled data used for unsupervised learning.

You can apply filter to data in Weka by pressing the ***Choose*** button under the filter section at the top of the ***Preprocess*** tab, shown in Figure 5-15.

> *Weka, like all good ML environments, contains a wealth of Java classes for data preprocessing. If you do not find the filter you need, you can modify an existing Weka filter Java code to create your own custom filter. Unzip the **weka-src.jar** file to access the Weka filter Java code.*

In the classification example later in this chapter, you will use the Weka ***NumericToNominal*** filter to convert the data type of an attribute from numerical to nominal.

If you need a Java class to modify your data before building your model, Weka probably has a Java class filter for you. If not, you can easily create your own by modifying the existing Weka filters.

Weka Explorer Key Options

The Weka Explorer is where the magic happens. You use the Explorer to classify or cluster. Note that the ***Classify*** and ***Cluster*** tabs are disabled in the Weka Explorer until you have opened a dataset using the ***Preprocess*** tab.

Within the ***Classify*** and ***Cluster*** tabs at the top of the Weka Explorer are three important configuration sections you will frequently use in Weka:

- Algorithm options
- Test options
- Attribute predictor selection (label) for classification

Figure 5-16 shows these areas highlighted within the Weka ***Classify*** tab.

Weka Explorer
Classify/Cluster Options

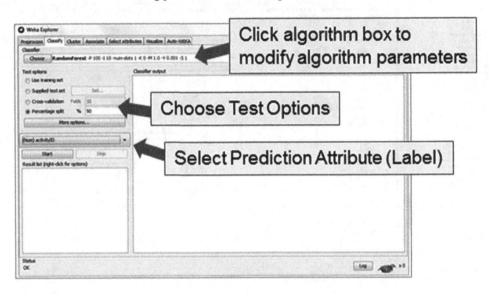

Figure 5-16. *Weka Explorer classify options*

After you confirm these three settings, press the ***Start*** button and Weka will classify or cluster using the selected algorithm.

Weka KnowledgeFlow

The Weka KnowledgeFlow is an alternative graphical front-end to core Weka. KnowledgeFlow implements a dataflow-inspired graphical interface for Weka. Figure 5-17 shows a predefined KnowledgeFlow template opened in Weka KnowledgeFlow. All of the Weka filters, classifiers, clusterers, and data tools are available in the KnowledgeFlow. KnowledgeFlow also includes some extra tools.

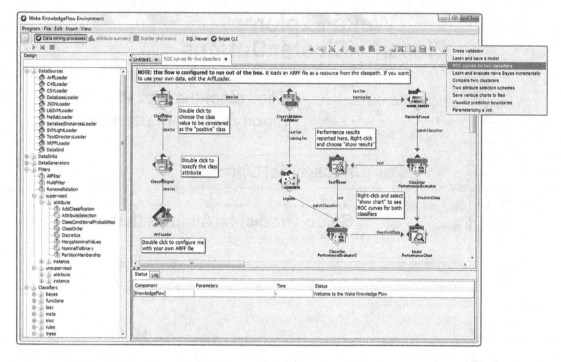

Figure 5-17. *Weka KnowledgeFlow template*

Using KnowledgeFlow, you can select Weka steps from a palette and place them onto the layout canvas. The Weka building blocks can then be connected together to form a knowledge flow, which can process and analyze the data.

The left side of the GUI contains all of the available Weka modules. You can place these modules onto the canvas as nodes. You can configure each node individually by right-clicking to access its configuration parameters. You create the flow by connecting the nodes. Executing a flow produces the results, typically a model generation or often times a visualization.

Later in the chapter, you will see how to compare multiple models with different algorithms. You will use Weka KnowledgeFlow to compare multiple clustering algorithms, and then use KnowledgeFlow to evaluate multiple classifiers by producing multiple ROC curves.

Weka Simple CLI

It is very easy to use graphical tools like KnowledgeFlow to build ML models. However, Java GUI applications often require a large amount of memory and system resources, resources you might prefer to reserve for your data, algorithms, and models. Figure 5-18 shows an alternative to KnowledgeFlow, the Weka Simple CLI Shell.

Figure 5-18. *Weka Simple CLI Shell*

The Weka Simple CLI Shell provides access to all Weka classes, including algorithms (classifiers and clusterers) and filters. It is a simple Weka shell with separated output and command line.

In Chapter 3, you saw an example of the Weka command line interface when you ran Weka in the AWS cloud. The Simple CLI Shell provides the same capabilities within your local desktop Weka environment.

The following commands are available in the Simple CLI:

- ***java <classname> [<args>]***: Invokes a Java class with the given arguments

- ***break***: Stops the current thread, such as running a classifier, in a friendly manner

- ***kill***: Stops the current thread in an unfriendly manner

- ***cls***: Clears the screen

- ***capabilities <classname> [<args>]***: Lists the capabilities of the specified class

- ***exit***: Exits the Simple CLI Shell

- ***help***: Provides an overview of the available commands

The Weka Simple CLI Shell is powerful because all of the filters and implementations of the algorithms have a uniform command-line interface. The following example shows how to train and test a random forest classifier with multiple filters from the command line. The ***MultiFilter*** operation handles the concatenation of filters.

```
001   java -classpath weka.jar weka.classifiers.meta.FilteredClassifier
      -t data/ReutersCorn-train.arff -T data/ReutersCorn-test.arff -F
      "weka.filters.MultiFilter -F weka.filters.unsupervised.attribute.
      StringToWordVector -F weka.filters.unsupervised.attribute.
      Standardize" -W weka.classifiers.trees.RandomForest -- -I 100
```

It is also possible to train and save a model using the *–t* and *–d* options:

```
001   java -classpath weka.jar weka.classifiers.meta.MultiClassClassifier
      -t data/iris.arff -d rf.model -W weka.classifiers.trees.RandomForest
      -- -I 100
```

A serialized model can also be loaded and used for predictions using the *–serialized* option to load the model and the *–i* option to load the input data:

```
001   java -classpath weka.jar weka.filters.supervised.attribute.
      AddClassification -serialized rf.model -classification -i data/iris.
      arff -o predict-iris.arff
```

It can become complicated if you try to string too many functions together on the command line. If you wish to load models, train models, apply filters, and save models, it is easier to use the Weka KnowledgeFlow interface to connect the various nodes. You will see how to do this next.

5.5 Weka Clustering Algorithms

In Chapter 4, I discussed clustering, the process of discovering structure in unlabeled data sets. Weka, like most of the good ML environments, has a broad array of clustering algorithms.

In this section, you will see how to implement clustering for the three most useful clustering ML algorithms as presented in Chapter 4:

- K-means clustering

- Expectation-maximization (EM) clustering

- Density-based clustering (DBSCAN)

If you are interested in exploring other clustering algorithms, just substitute the algorithm of your choice.

Clustering with DBSCAN

The DBSCAN algorithm is included as an "available" package in the Weka package manager. After you install the DBSCAN clustering algorithm it will be available as a clustering option in the Weka packages.

For this clustering example, you will use the Old Faithful geyser dataset. The original dataset is available at ***www.stat.cmu.edu/~larry/all-of-statistics/=data/ faithful.dat***.

Old Faithful is the famous geyser in Yellowstone National Park that erupts regularly approximately once per hour. The dataset, collected in 1990, includes 272 observations on two variables. The two variables are

- Eruption time: A numeric value representing the eruption time in minutes

- Waiting time: A numeric value representing the waiting time until the next eruption in minutes

Table 5-6 shows the first ten instances of the dataset. The original data file name is ***old-faithful-data.dat***. It does not contain a header row and contains fields separated by spaces. The modified file used in this example is ***old-faithful-data.csv***. The file is contained in the book resources in the Chapter 5 folder. It does contain a header row and comma-separated values. The OpenCalc spreadsheet program created the CSV file.

Table 5-6. *Old Faithful Geyser Dataset (first 10 instances), (Azalini and Bowman, 1990)*

Instance ID	Eruption time	Waiting time
1	3.600	79
2	1.800	54
3	3.333	74
4	2.283	62
5	4.533	85
6	2.883	55
7	4.700	88
8	3.600	85
9	1.950	51
10	4.350	85

Using the Weka Explorer, it is straightforward to perform a DBSCAN cluster on the data, as shown in the steps below.

1. Launch the Weka Explorer application from the Weka GUI Chooser.

2. In the ***PreProcess*** tab, click ***Open File*** and Open the ***old-faithful-data.csv*** file. You may have to tell the Weka CSV loader that the values are " , " separated and ***NoHeaderRowPresent*** is false. When the data loads, you will see a summary of the instances, including the two attributes, eruptions and waiting.

3. Click the ***Cluster*** tab.

4. Under ***Clusterer***, click the ***Choose*** button to select the algorithm.

5. Select the DBSCAN algorithm from the list of available clustering algorithms. If DBSCAN is not available, you will need to install it using the Weka package manager.

6. Click the text in the DBSCAN algorithm box. You will be able to enter the DBSCAN algorithm parameters. Enter .11 for Epsilon and 6 for NumPts. Click **OK**.

7. Click **Start** to execute the DBSCAN clustering algorithm on the dataset. After the processing is complete, the results will display.

Figure 5-19 shows the completed DBSCAN clustering results.

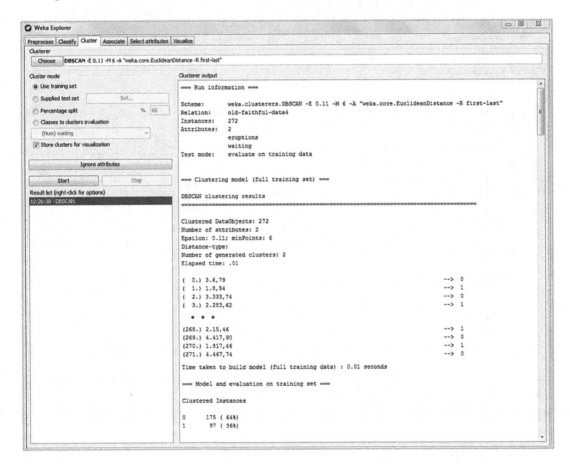

Figure 5-19.   *DBSCAN clustering of the Old Faithful dataset*

The results show that the algorithm identified two clusters for all of the 272 instances. In total, cluster0 received 175 instances, while cluster1 received 97 instances.

Each time you run a cluster or classification in Weka, the ***Results list*** on the left panel updates with a new entry. Right-clicking a results entry provides the option to visualize the results. You can also click the ***Visualize*** tab at the top of the Weka Explorer. Figure 5-20 shows the visualization of the two DBSCAN clusters. When you first click the ***Visualize*** tab, you will see a matrix of visualizations. Weka prepares charts for all combinations of the attributes. In this case, the one you are interested in maps the waiting time and eruption time on the X and Y axes. You can select this specific chart from the matrix, or you can use the X and Y drop-down boxes to populate the desired attributes for the X and Y axes.

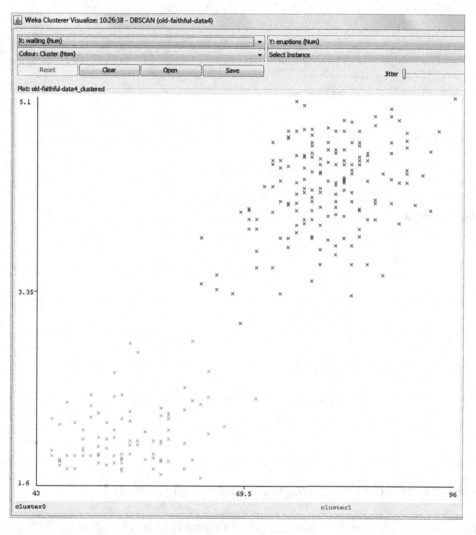

Figure 5-20. *Visualization of DBSCAN clustering*

You can visualize any two of the attributes, one on the X-axis and another on the Y-axis. In this case, there are actually four attributes:

- The eruption time interval

- The waiting time interval

- The instance ID

- A newly created attribute that holds the generated cluster ID. In effect, you now have a labeled dataset and you will take advantage of this later.

When visualizing the data, select the plot that places the eruption and waiting times on the axis. Plotting the other attributes is not particularly interesting. With the correct attributes selected, as shown in Figure 5-20, the visualization provides a key insight. The two clusters identified by the algorithm are color-coded.

The key insight you can gain from the visualization is that the two distinct clusters represent two "modes" in which the Old Faithful geyser operates.

You can adjust the algorithm parameters if you wish to fine-tune the clusters. Notice that some of the data points in the middle area are borderline in determining to which cluster they belong. Figure 5-21 shows adjustments to the DBSCAN algorithm parameters. Some algorithms have many parameters; the DBSCAN algorithm only has two parameters.

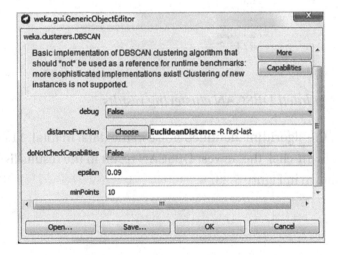

Figure 5-21. *DBSCAN algorithm parameter adjustment*

By changing the ***epsilon*** parameter and the ***numPoints*** parameter, you can tighten up the tolerance of the clusters. After changing the parameters, click ***OK*** and then press ***Start*** to commence another clustering. Figure 5-22 shows the new results.

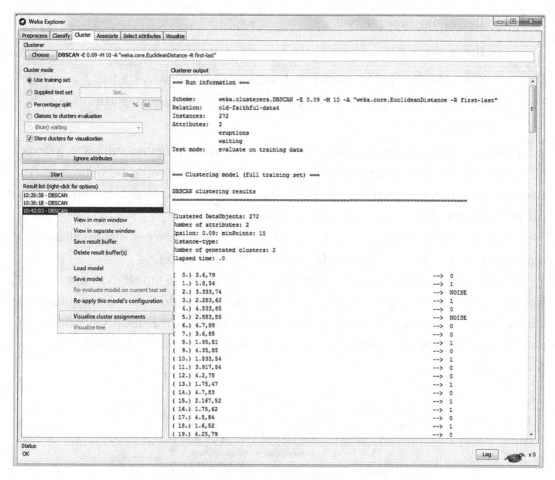

Figure 5-22. *Updated DBSCAN clustering results*

In this case, the algorithm identified noise in the data. In total, 11 instances fell in the boundary area. Right-click the newest DBSCAN result in the results list to show the new visualization, shown in Figure 5-23.

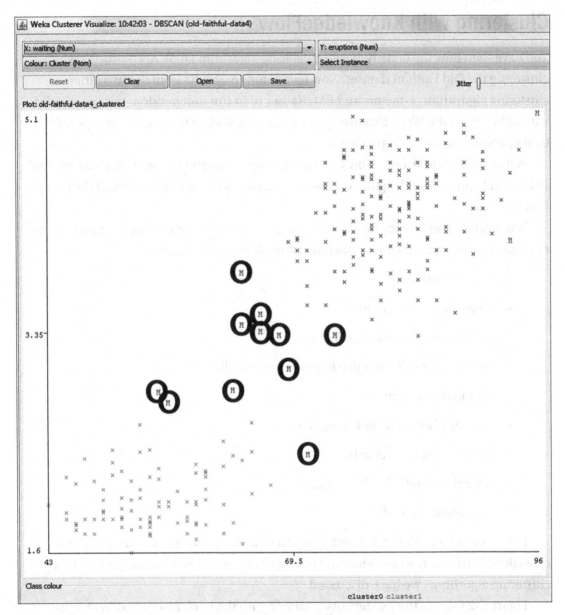

Figure 5-23. *Noise in the data identified by DBSCAN*

The circled data points did not cluster into either of the two clusters. In this example, you have much tighter clusters. By adjusting the algorithm parameters, you have essentially used the DBSCAN algorithm to identify outliers, one of the algorithm's strengths, if you recall from Chapter 4.

Clustering with KnowledgeFlow

You have seen how the density-based clustering algorithm DBSCAN performs when clustering the Old Faithful dataset. Now let's compare results from the two other clustering algorithms, k-means and EM. Rather than run independent tests as you did with DBSCAN in the Weka Explorer, you can use the Weka KnowledgeFlow application to simplify the comparison process.

Although the KnowledgeFlow GUI is not as stylish as you saw with RapidMiner and KNIME in Figure 5-2 and Figure 5-3, the KnowledgeFlow application has all the same functionality.

The KnowledgeFlow application contains several very useful templates you can use to build layouts. KnowledgeFlow includes the following templates:

- Cross-validation

- Learn and save a model

- ROC curves for two classifiers

- Learn and evaluate naive Bayes incrementally

- Compare two clusters

- Two attribute selection schemes

- Save various charts to files

- Visualize prediction boundaries

- Parameterize a job

Layouts can be loaded, modified, and saved. KnowledgeFlow layouts use the .kf extension. The book resources include two layouts you can load to compare all three clustering algorithms we have discussed.

Figure 5-24 shows the two layouts available with the book resource download: ***cluster-3-csv-cross-fold.kf*** uses k-fold cross-validation while ***cluster-3-csv-split.kf*** uses a simple split of the data for training and testing. Both of the KnowledgeFlow examples load the CSV dataset ***old-faithful-data.csv***.

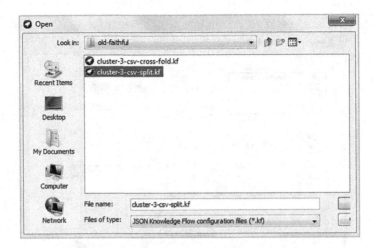

Figure 5-24. *KnowledgeFlow layouts: Comparing three clustering algorithms*

The process of constructing a KnowledgeFlow is straightforward. You simply choose nodes from the left-hand panel and add them to the canvas. The KnowledgeFlow application organizes nodes into expandable categories including DataSources, Filters, Classifiers, Clusterers, Visualization, and others.

When nodes placed onto the canvas, there are two configuration operations:

- Double-clicking a node will provide access to the node configuration parameters, including algorithm parameters.

- Right-clicking a node will provide access to the node options, including the important task of connecting the node to other nodes.

Figure 5-23 shows the ***cluster-3-csv-splt.kf*** loaded into the Weka KnowledgeFlow application.

Descriptive notes can also be included on the canvas, as shown in Figure 5-25.

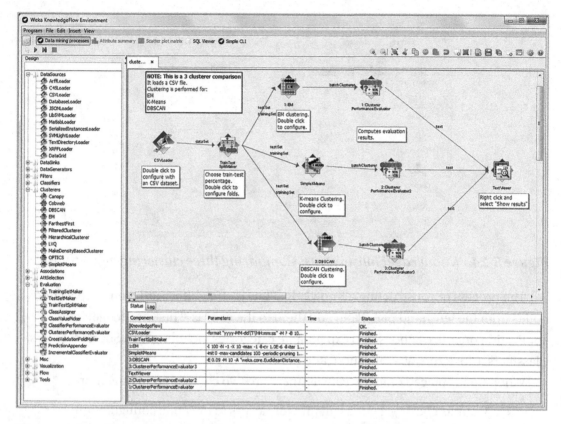

Figure 5-25. *KnowledgeFlow layout: three-clusterer comparison*

The following steps illustrate how to create the three-cluster comparison starting with a blank canvas:

1. Add the following nodes to the KnowledgeFlow canvas, arranging them as shown in Figure 5-25:

    CSVLoader,

    TrainTestSplitMaker,

    EM Clusterer,

    K-Means Clusterer,

    DBSCAN Clusterer,

    3 x ***ClustererPerformanceEvaluator,***

    TextViewer

2. Double-click the ***CSVLoader*** and set the filename to the ***old-faithful-data.csv*** file.

3. Right-click the ***CSVLoader*** and choose ***dataset***. Drag the ***dataSet*** connector to the ***TrainTestSplitMaker***.

4. Double-click the ***TrainTestSplitMaker*** and set the training percentage to 66% or a number of your choosing.

5. Right-click the ***TrainTestSplitMaker***, choose ***trainingSet***, and drag the ***trainingSet*** connector to the ***EM*** Clusterer node. Repeat for the other two clusterers.

6. Right-click the ***TrainTestSplitMaker***, choose ***testSet***, drag the ***testSet*** connector to the ***EM*** Clusterer node, and repeat for the other two clusterers.

7. Right-click the ***EM*** Clusterer node, choose ***batchClusterer***, and drag the ***batchClusterer*** connector to the first ***ClustererPerformanceEvaluator***. Repeat for the other two Clusterer nodes.

8. Right-click each ***ClustererPerformanceEvaluator***, choose text, and drag the text connector to the ***TextViewer***.

With the KnowledgeFlow fully configured, you can execute the flow by clicking the right Play arrow at the top of the layout. KnowledgeFlow records the progress status in the bottom panel as the flow executes.

When all of the tasks successfully complete, KnowledgeFlow will mark status as ***OK***, as shown in Figure 5-25. At this point, you can right-click the ***TextViewer*** to show the results. Figure 5-26 shows the ***Result List***.

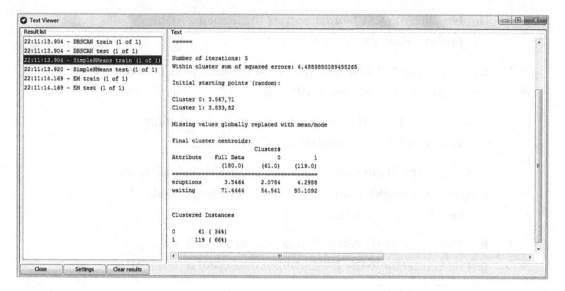

Figure 5-26. *KnowledgeFlow TextViewer results*

The **Result List** includes reports for each of the three clustering algorithms: DBSCAN, EM, and k-means.

The Weka KnowledgeFlow interface provides a very useful way for you to experiment with clustering algorithms. You can easily double-click a clustering algorithm, update its parameters, and rerun the flow. It is a very useful tool when deciding which algorithms works best for your CML clustering problem.

5.6 Weka Classification Algorithms

Implementing clustering algorithms to discover hidden patterns in unlabeled data, as you saw with Old Faithful, is very interesting. However, classification problems present an even more practical use of CML algorithms. Next, you will review the four go-to classification algorithms and see how well they can classify the PAMAP2_Dataset from Chapter 2.

Before you get started, you must make sure you have a well-defined problem.

Your goal in this section is build a model that can predict the current activity of a person based on the sensor data of the device they are carrying. In Chapter 6, you will create an Android app that can accurately determine the current active state of the device user by making a prediction with the prebuilt model. Android mobile devices have similar sensor functionality as the specialized hardware used by the participants in the PAMAP2_Dataset collection. If you build a reasonably accurate model, you should be able to predict the current activity of the mobile device user. Such an activity-monitoring app could have potential uses for healthcare, fitness, or security applications.

Preprocessing (Data Cleaning)

Recall that PAMAP2_Dataset was a large, labeled dataset generated by subjects wearing sensors while performing 19 different activities.

The dataset contains data from multiple subjects. Not all subjects recorded all of the activities. To train your model, you will use the data from *Subject101*. The dataset provides a document, *PerformedActivitiesSummary.pdf*, to summarize the activities of each subject.

You will clean the dataset to produce a subset that is appropriate for your well-defined problem. There are two reasons why you want to clean the dataset:

- To reduce the size of the dataset. The files are huge and there is a lot of redundant information contained within them.

- Your target Android devices do not have all the sensors used by the subjects in the original data collection. There is no sense retaining sensor data that the Android device cannot replicate.

Table 2-4 shows the structure of the original dataset. The *readme.pdf* file accompanying the dataset documents this structure. The original dataset files are large. They each contain over 300,000 instances (rows) and 54 attributes (columns). Before you proceed with creating the model, you need to clean the data.

Follow the steps below to produce the cleaned dataset, *subject101-cleaned.csv*. Note that the column numbers shown are 1-relative values.

1. Open the original *subject101.dat* file in Open Office Calc and save the CSV file as *subject101.csv*. Figure 2-5 shows the dataset loaded into the Open Office Calc spreadsheet. Calc converted the original *subject101.dat* file to the comma-separated version, *subject101.csv*. You will clean this CSV file.

2. Delete the time stamp attribute (column 1). This dataset is not intended as time series data. Each instance can stand on its own as a predictor for the current activity.

3. Delete any instance where the heart rate attribute (column 2) is a missing value (NaN). Sensors in the collection provided rapid data streams and only 1 in 10 samples included the heart rate. Filtering the data when this attribute is missing will reduce the size, but not the significance of the data.

4. Delete the heart rate attribute (column 2). You do not have a way of using this attribute on Android.

5. Delete columns 21-37, the chest sensor data. The Android device only has one sensor so let's assume it is hand-based. The hand-based sensor data is included in columns 4-20.

6. Delete columns 38-54, the foot sensor data. The Android device only has one sensor so let's assume it is hand-based. The hand-based sensor data is included in columns 4-20.

7. In the hand-based sensor data, you only need to keep the accelerometer, gyroscope, and magnetometer data. Delete columns 1, 5-7, and 14-17.

8. Add a header row to describe the remaining 10 columns.

The resulting cleaned file has only 10 attributes (columns) and 22,846 instances. It is much smaller at 1.8MB compared to the original file of 138MB. The first few records of the new structure of ***subject101-cleaned.csv*** are shown below, including the header row:

```
001   activityID,accelX,accelY,accelZ,gyroX,gyroY,gyroZ,magnetX,magnetY,
      magnetZ
002   1,2.301,7.25857,6.09259,-0.0699614,-0.01875,0.004568,9.15626,
      -67.1825,-20.0857
003   1,2.24615,7.4818,5.55219,-0.431227,0.002686,-0.06237,9.14612,
      -67.3936,-20.5508
004   1,2.3,7.10681,6.09309,0.07569,-0.0307922,0.005245,9.69163,-67.0898,
      -21.2481
005   1,2.49455,7.52335,6.17157,-0.259058,-0.267895,-0.03858,9.58694,
      -67.0882,-20.8997
006   1,2.71654,8.30596,4.78671,0.377115,-0.0236877,-0.02095,8.59622,
      -67.1486,-20.1947
```

```
007    1,2.54954,7.63122,5.55623,-0.487667,-0.0199,-0.0894,9.00159,
       -66.0543,-22.5021
008    1,2.82407,6.1449,5.06502,-0.781563,0.198873,-0.213285,10.5845,
       -63.7955,-27.5879
009    1,2.73626,7.94195,6.52017,-0.472414,0.279868,0.03655,12.2658,
       -64.6618,-27.0379
010    1,2.38894,7.4883,6.40103,0.3579,1.04661,0.346204,12.1033,-62.2186,
       -30.1344
011    1,1.8132,6.85639,7.35672,0.360442,1.2873,0.1226,14.9204,-62.7273,
       -28.6676
012    1,0.0125249,5.2733,6.95022,0.440524,1.19843,0.1064,16.6466,-63.2981,
       -25.9161
013    1,-0.530751,7.62191,6.04895,0.179548,1.05112,0.23129,18.111,
       -64.9924,-19.2388
014    1,-1.65419,7.6992,5.22362,1.51583,0.83644,0.283502,18.1058,-65.8251,
       -13.6928
015    1,-1.09215,7.20128,5.19524,1.22541,0.65619,0.19038,17.0806,-68.1161,
       -8.61366
```

The file contains the important *ActivityID* in the first column. This attribute is the label. Columns 2-10 contain accelerometer(X,Y,Z), gyroscope(X,Y,Z), and magnetometer(X,Y,Z) data.

Table 5-7 shows a list of the *ActivityIDs* and their occurrences in the cleaned dataset. There are 22,846 total instances in the cleaned dataset, which should be a sufficient dataset size to produce a good model. The Android app will use the model to predict these *ActivityIDs* based on the device sensor input.

Table 5-7. *ActivityID Occurrence - Subject101*

ActivityID	Activity name	Number of instances
1	Lying	2.486
2	Sitting	2,146
3	Standing	1,984
4	Walking	2,035
5	Running	1,941
6	Cycling	2,156
7	Nordic walking	1,852
12	Ascending stairs	1,452
13	Descending stairs	1,362
16	Vacuum Cleaning	2,097
17	Ironing	2,155
24	Rope jumping	1,180

With a much smaller and more relevant data file, you are now ready to load the ***subject101-cleaned.csv*** file into Weka.

Start Weka, select the Weka Explorer from the GUI Chooser, and click ***Open File*** under the ***Preprocess*** tab. Browse to the location of ***subject101-cleaned.csv*** and select it.

Because you imported a CSV file, you did not have full control over how the data types of the attributes were treated. For this dataset, all of the attributes are numbers, except for the ***ActivityID,*** which is a nominal value. Recall from Table 5-7, each of the values represents an activity. To correct this issue, you need to use a Weka ***filter*** to convert the numeric ***ActivityID*** attribute to a nominal data type.

Figure 5-27 shows the Weka Explorer after the data import and after the ***ActivityID*** attribute was converted to a nominal data type.

Figure 5-27. *Cleaned PAMAP2_Dataset with filter*

Figure 5-26 shows the Weka ***NumericToNominal*** filter applied to ***Attribute1***. Note that in the filter option box, the filter only applies to the ***first*** attribute.

If you import CSV data into Weka and then apply preprocessing filters, it is helpful to resave the data as ARFF format. The ARFF file format can store data types along with the data so data conversion filters are not required at later stages in the process.

The data is now ready for classification. Next, you start the classification analysis with the random forest algorithm.

Classification: Random Forest Algorithm

Classifying data is easy once the data is prepared. In Chapter 4, anecdotal evidence suggested the RF algorithm often performs the best. You will see if this holds true for the cleaned PAMAP dataset.

To classify data in the Weka Explorer, follow these steps:

1. Select the *Classify* tab in the Weka Explorer.

2. Press the *Choose* button to choose the classification algorithm.

3. Choose the test option. You will try both 2/3 split and 10-fold cross-validation to evaluate the chosen algorithms.

4. Select the *ActivityID* as the attribute to classify.

5. Click in the options box to change any of the algorithm-specific options if needed.

6. Press the *Start* button and wait for the classification to finish. It might be quick, or it could take a long time depending on factors such as data size, number of attributes, algorithm complexity, or algorithm options such as iterations.

7. Click the *Results List* to view the results, including the classification accuracy and confusion matrix.

Each algorithm has its own parameters with which you can experiment. For RF, one of the most important parameters is *iterations*, which determines how many decision trees the algorithm will use. Figure 5-28 shows the RF algorithm option box.

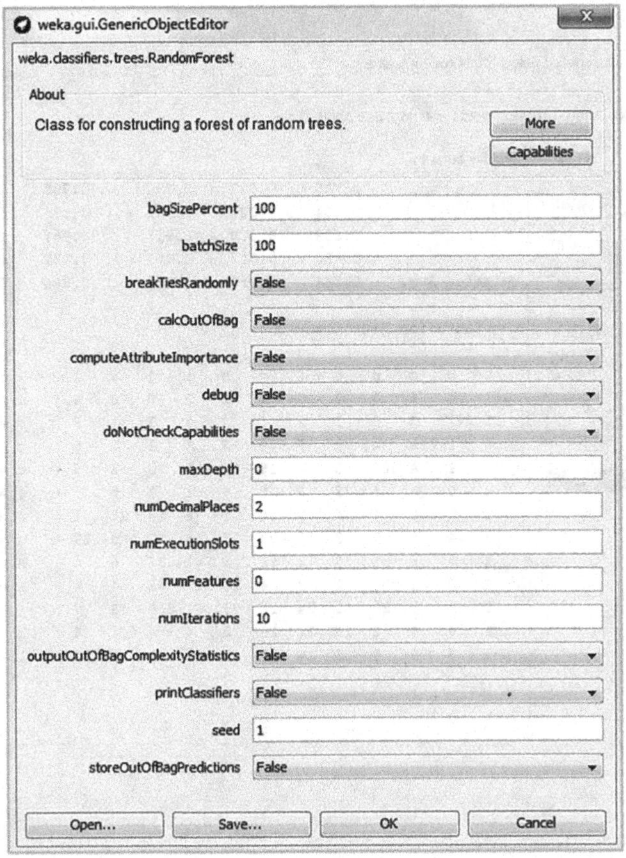

Figure 5-28. *Random forest algorithm options*

The default value for *iterations* is 100. For your testing, you will run four tests, using the values of 10 and 100 for iterations, and using two test options, 2/3 split and 10-fold cross-validation.

Figure 5-29 shows the results of one RF classification with iterations=100 and using the 10-fold cross-validation test option.

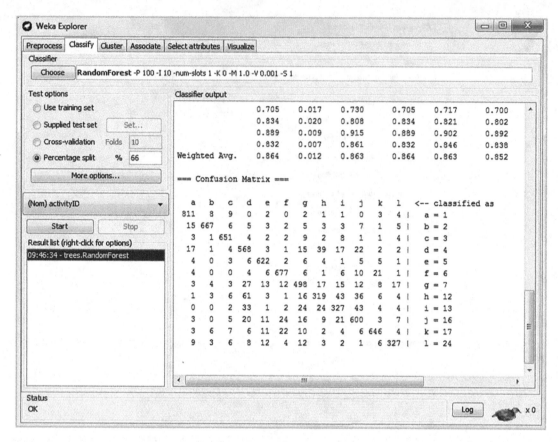

Figure 5-29. *Random forest algorithm classification*

Because your predictive attribute is a nominal data type, Weka provided a confusion matrix. The confusion matrix is included last. You can scroll back through the results window to see the classification accuracy. Right-click the Results List entry if you wish to save the results to a file. The following results show that the RF classification was very successful.

```
001    === Run information ===
002
003    Scheme: weka.classifiers.trees.RandomForest -P 100 -I 100 -K 0 -M 1.0
       -V 0.001 -S 1
004    Relation:      subject101-cleaned-weka.filters.unsupervised.attribute.
                       NumericToNominal-Rfirst
005    Instances:     22846
006    Attributes:    10: activityID, accelX, accelY, accelZ, gyroX,
```

```
007                    gyroY, gyroZ, magnetX, magnetY, magnetZ
008    Test mode:    10-fold cross-validation
009
010    === Classifier model (full training set) ===
011
012    RandomForest
013    Bagging with 100 iterations and base learner
014    weka.classifiers.trees.RandomTree -K 0 -M 1.0 -V 0.001 -S 1 -do-not-
       check-capabilities
015    Time taken to build model: 16.45 seconds
016
017    === Stratified cross-validation ===
018    === Summary ===
019
020    Correctly Classified Instances        20678              90.5104 %
021    Incorrectly Classified Instances       2168               9.4896 %
022    Kappa statistic                        0.8961
023    Mean absolute error                    0.0405
024    Root mean squared error                0.12
025    Relative absolute error               26.6251 %
026    Root relative squared error           43.4728 %
027    Total Number of Instances             22846
028
029    === Confusion Matrix ===
030
031        a      b      c      d      e      f      g      h      i      j      k      l    <--
       classified as
032    2433    17     15      1      2      2      4      2      2      3      0      5 |    a = 1
033      27  2041     14      3      1      6      9     10      4     18      7      6 |    b = 2
034      14     6   1910      5      2      7     11      4      7      2     12      4 |    c = 3
035      56     2      2   1737      1      0     34     99     38     58      8      0 |    d = 4
036      20     2      0      2   1856      5      5      9      2      9     23      8 |    e = 5
037      10     0      2      2     10   2026     21      2     13     18     51      1 |    f = 6
038      14     8      1     55     11     24   1615     28     19     25     22     30 |    g = 7
039       0     3      2    137      6      5     31   1064     86    105      7      6 |    h = 12
```

040	1	2	3	53	1	7	42	61	1063	120	7	2		i = 13
041	0	3	9	33	14	42	37	22	23	1886	10	18		j = 16
042	3	6	10	6	8	22	24	4	3	12	2051	6		k = 17
043	29	3	11	11	36	7	41	2	8	5	31	996		l = 24

The classification accuracy was 90.5%. If you look down the diagonal of the confusion matrix, it is obvious from the relatively large values that the RF algorithm did a very good job.

You can see a few relatively large numbers off the main diagonal, such as the 137 instance on line 039. These instances represent ActivityID 12 (Ascending stairs) being wrongly classified as ActivityID 4 (Walking). The next highest number was 120 instances (line 040) representing Activity 13 (Descending stairs) wrongly classified as ActivityID 16 (Vacuum Cleaning).

The 90% accuracy achieved by the RF algorithm is a good indication that your Android app will be successful in classifying the user's activity. Next, you will see if the other classification algorithms can match the performance of RF.

Classification: K-Nearest Neighbor

Recall that the KNN algorithm is a lazy learning algorithm. Weka contains an excellent modified version of KNN called KStar, or K*. You can learn the details of K* and how it improved KNN from this University of Waikato research paper:

www.cs.waikato.ac.nz/~ml/publications/1995/Cleary95-KStar.pdf

KStar is available under the *lazy* folder when you select *Choose* under the classifier section of the Weka Explorer. Figure 5-30 shows the default KStar options.

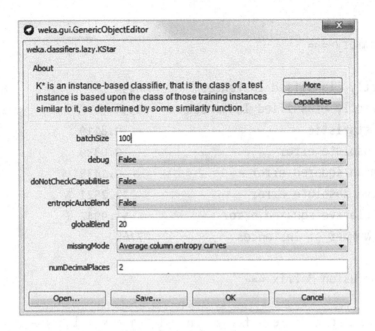

Figure 5-30. *Weka KNN algorithm (KStar) options*

Classifying the ***subject101-cleaned.arff*** data with the KStar algorithm achieves the following results:

```
001   === Run information ===
002
003   Scheme:       weka.classifiers.lazy.KStar -B 20 -M a
004   Relation:     subject101-cleaned-weka.filters.unsupervised.attribute.
                    NumericToNominal-Rfirst
005   Instances:    22846
006   Attributes:   10
007   Test mode:    split 66.0% train, remainder test
008
009   === Classifier model (full training set) ===
010
011   KStar options : -B 20 -M a
012   Time taken to build model: O seconds
013
014   === Evaluation on test split ===
015
016   Time taken to test model on test split: 2512.94 seconds
```

```
017
018    === Summary ===
019
020    Correctly Classified Instances          6434                    82.827 %
021    Incorrectly Classified Instances        1334                    17.173 %
022    Kappa statistic                            0.8119
023    Mean absolute error                        0.0339
024    Root mean squared error                    0.1435
025    Relative absolute error                   22.2521 %
026    Root relative squared error               51.9942 %
027    Total Number of Instances               7768
028
029    === Confusion Matrix ===
030
031      a    b    c    d    e    f    g    h    i    j    k    l   <-- classified as
032    806   20    9    2    0    0    1    0    2    0    1    0 |   a = 1
033     11  689    8    4    0    3    4    0    1    1    0    1 |   b = 2
034      4    4  669    3    1    1    3    0    0    1    1    1 |   c = 3
035     17    7   25  566    2    2   10   35   11   11    3    2 |   d = 4
036      4    2    7    4  612    3    5    5    2    7    2    6 |   e = 5
037      7    4    2    2    6  677    4    1    7    6   20    0 |   f = 6
038      5   15    9   37    5   27  447   13   19   20   16   16 |   g = 7
039      0   11   22   74    0    6   11  305   35   28    3    4 |   h = 12
040      0    8   46   40    0    8    9   31  289   28    4    1 |   i = 13
041      0   10   24   53    3   30   13   22   46  512    3    3 |   j = 16
042      3   11   23    7   13   54   11    7    4   20  563   11 |   k = 17
043     12    5   19   10   13    4   14    4    6    7    0  299 |   l = 24
```

The KStar algorithm achieved an impressive 82.8% accuracy. The confusion matrix main diagonal looks clean, containing much larger numbers than the erroneous classifications off the main diagonal.

The main issue with KNN-style algorithms is the testing time with large datasets. You have a large dataset, and if you look closely, you can see this model required over 2,500 seconds (41 minutes) to classify the data (Intel i7 CPU in a Windows desktop). As a result, it was not viable to use the 10-fold cross-validation test option. Instead, you specified the split (2/3 train, 1/3 test) test option. Using 10-fold cross validation would have taken approximately 10x longer.

Overall, the KNN accuracy was comparable to RF, but the time taken to predict is problematic for this dataset.

Classification: Naive Bayes

The NB algorithm is the probability-based approach to classification. To classify in Weka using NB, select the algorithm from the classifier **Choose** section. If naive Bayes is not available, make sure you select the **ActivityID** as the attribute to classify. Naive Bayes requires the attribute to be a nominal data type, and only the **ActivityID** meets this criterion.

Recall from Chapter 4, NB is well suited for 2-class classification. In order to use NB for multi-class data, you need to use the kernel trick. Figure 5-31 shows the kernel setting in the NB options screen. You need to set **useKernelEstimator** to true. Failure to do this will result in random output from the classifier.

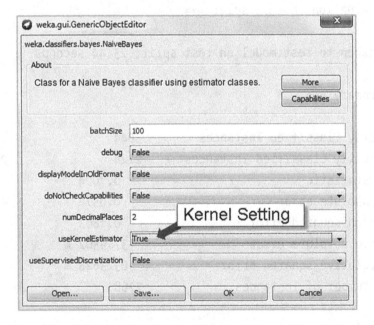

Figure 5-31. *Naive Bayes kernel setting option*

Start the classification and you will see the following naive Bayes classification results:

```
001    === Run information ===
002
003    Scheme:        weka.classifiers.bayes.NaiveBayes -K
004    Relation:      subject101-cleaned-weka.filters.unsupervised.attribute.
                      NumericToNominal-Rfirst
005    Instances:     22846
006    Attributes:    10
007    Test mode:     split 66.0% train, remainder test
008
009    === Classifier model (full training set) ===
010
011    Naive Bayes Classifier
012    Time taken to build model: 0.09 seconds
013
014    === Evaluation on test split ===
015
016    Time taken to test model on test split: 25.44 seconds
017
018    === Summary ===
019
020    Correctly Classified Instances          5644              72.6571 %
021    Incorrectly Classified Instances        2124              27.3429 %
022    Kappa statistic                            0.7004
023    Mean absolute error                        0.0578
024    Root mean squared error                    0.1803
025    Relative absolute error                 37.9502 %
026    Root relative squared error             65.3628 %
027    Total Number of Instances               7768
028
029    === Confusion Matrix ===
030
031        a    b    c    d    e    f    g    h    i    j    k    l   <-- classified as
032      762   21   15    0    7    3    5    1    2    6   16    3 |    a = 1
```

033	0	635	25	6	0	4	5	1	6	9	22	9		b = 2
034	1	15	603	7	7	12	16	0	16	5	6	0		c = 3
035	17	31	16	406	16	8	21	67	42	53	10	4		d = 4
036	6	8	5	3	540	4	12	5	6	22	22	26		e = 5
037	6	13	6	1	6	660	4	1	8	4	27	0		f = 6
038	6	23	5	67	38	34	292	29	30	29	42	34		g = 7
039	0	24	15	96	5	12	31	201	62	39	10	4		h = 12
040	0	27	15	60	6	19	8	38	234	38	18	1		i = 13
041	0	11	9	54	14	33	32	11	22	508	12	13		j = 16
042	2	23	13	3	24	84	13	0	5	4	542	14		k = 17
043	8	9	22	5	25	6	21	0	14	11	11	261		l = 243

The algorithm achieved 72.7% accuracy. Not bad, but not quite as good as RF and KNN. However, NB did run much faster than KNN, taking only 25 seconds to complete the classification using the 2/3 split test mode.

Classification: Support Vector Machine

SVM algorithms are gaining popularity against neural network DL algorithms. Weka provides the SMO (sequential minimal optimization) algorithm to implement a support vector classifier.

If you run the SMO algorithm using default options, the results will be poor. Weka makes it easy to tune the algorithm options. Figure 5-32 shows the option panel for the SMO algorithm. In order to achieve better results, change the following options:

- Set the Complexity parameter c = 2.0.

- Set the Calibrator to SMO.

- Change the Tolerance parameter to 0.1.

- Set the kernel to PUK with default parameters.

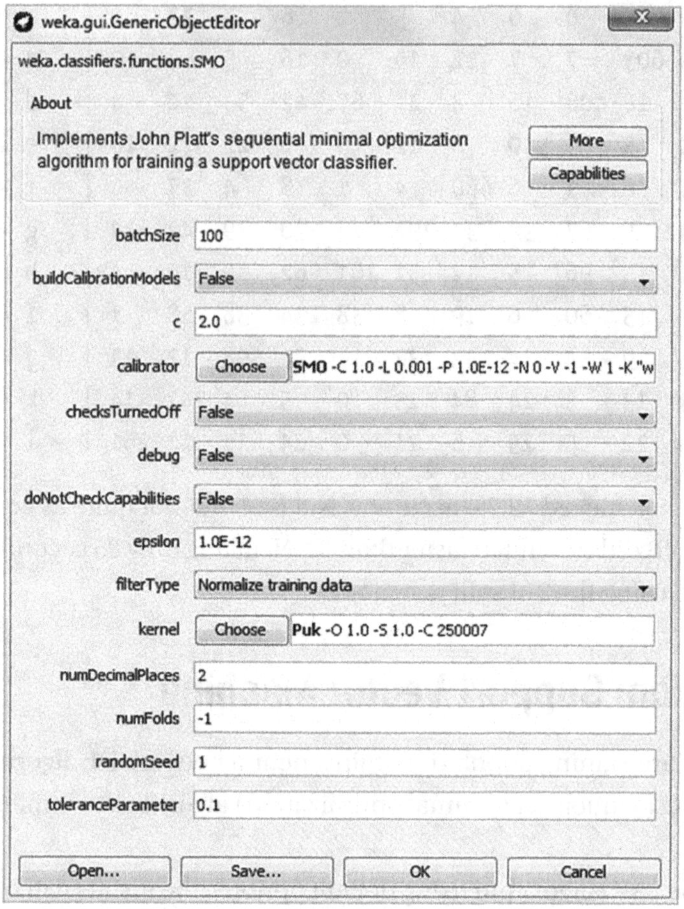

Figure 5-32. *Weka SMO algorithm options*

The SMO classifier output:

```
001   === Run information ===
002
003   Scheme:        weka.classifiers.functions.SMO -C 2.0 -L 0.1 -P 1.0E-
                      12 -N 0 -V -1 -W 1 -K "weka.classifiers.functions.
                      supportVector.Puk -O 1.0 -S 1.0 -C 250007" -calibrator
                      "weka.classifiers.functions.SMO -C 1.0 -L 0.001
                      -P 1.0E-12 -N 0 -V -1 -W 1 -K \"weka.classifiers.
                      functions.supportVector.PolyKernel -E 1.0 -C 250007\"
                      -calibrator \"weka.classifiers.functions.Logistic -R
                      1.0E-8 -M -1 -num-decimal-places 4\""
```

```
004    Relation:       subject101-cleaned-weka.filters.unsupervised.attribute.
                       NumericToNominal-Rfirst
005    Instances:      22846
006    Attributes:     10
007    Test mode:      split 66.0% train, remainder test
008
009    === Classifier model (full training set) ===
010
011    SMO
012    Kernel used:
013       Puk kernel
014    Classifier for classes: 1, 2
015    BinarySMO
016    Time taken to build model: 108.91 seconds
017
018    === Evaluation on test split ===
019
020    Time taken to test model on test split: 28.28 seconds
021
022    === Summary ===
023
024    Correctly Classified Instances         6426                  82.724  %
025    Incorrectly Classified Instances       1342                  17.276  %
026    Kappa statistic                           0.8107
027    Mean absolute error                       0.1399
028    Root mean squared error                   0.2571
029    Relative absolute error                  91.8675 %
030    Root relative squared error              93.177  %
031    Total Number of Instances              7768
032
033    === Confusion Matrix ===
034
035      a    b    c    d    e    f    g    h    i    j    k    l   <-- classified as
036    801    5   21    0    0    4    1    1    8    0    0    0 |   a = 1
037     19  665   14    3    0    6    3    5    1    3    1    2 |   b = 2
```

038	2	15	640	8	1	5	7	2	5	1	2	0	c = 3
039	2	4	14	493	8	1	22	45	20	70	12	0	d = 4
040	0	0	9	2	605	13	1	5	1	4	18	1	e = 5
041	3	12	6	2	2	658	4	0	4	14	30	1	f = 6
042	7	28	2	35	8	25	456	33	11	5	8	11	g = 7
043	1	11	20	68	0	2	7	297	29	60	3	1	h = 12
044	0	6	12	28	0	2	21	66	260	64	5	0	i = 13
045	0	5	14	15	6	23	16	10	10	618	1	1	j = 16
046	1	15	23	3	1	29	9	5	2	4	633	2	k = 17
047	2	6	28	7	10	5	12	2	6	9	6	300	l = 24

The Weka SMO algorithm achieved 82.7% accuracy on the cleaned dataset. The result was about the same as the KNN algorithm, but the elapsed time for training and testing was only 2 minutes for the 22,000+ instances.Next, you will take a more detailed look at these classification algorithm results.

5.7 Weka Model Evaluation

There are many factors to consider when evaluating a ML model.

You are trying to place ML models at the edge, so you need to think carefully about how your model affects the limited resources of the target device. While accuracy is the most visible performance measure, build time and test time also are important. Table 5-8 shows a summary of the classifier's performance for the *subject101-cleaned.arff* dataset.

Table 5-8. *Classification - Algorithm Performance Summary*

Algorithm	Training method	Build time (sec.)	Test time (sec.)	Accuracy (%)
RF (i=10)	10-fold cross-val.	1.7	NR	87.7%
RF (i=10)	2/3 split	1.8	0.2	86.4%
RF (i=100)	10-fold cross-val.	16.5	NR	90.5%
RF (i=100)	2/3 split	16.5	1.3	90.0%
KNN	10-fold cross-val.	DNF	DNF	DNF
KNN	2/3 split	0.1	2,513	82.8%
Naive Bayes	10-fold cross-val.	0.1	NR	72.9%
Naive Bayes	2/3 split	0.1	25.4	72.7%
SVM/SMO (c=2)	10-fold cross-val.	111	NR	83.4%
SVM/SMO (c=2)	2/3 split	109	28	82.7%

Note the DNF (Did Not Finish) entry for KNN with 10-fold test option. This means it aborted the operation because it was taking too long.

Note the NR (Not Reported) entries for the test times with 10-fold cross validation. Weka does not report the total training time when using the k-fold cross-validation test option. However, if you recall from Figure 4-10, you could multiply the test training time by k to determine an estimate for the test time, assuming you used a 90/10 split for a 10-fold cross-validation.

A summary of observations from the table of results:

- RF achieves the best accuracy result.

- RF sits in a sweet spot considering the accuracy vs. time to train/test tradeoff.

- Using the 10-fold cross-validation test option over the split improves the accuracy of the classifier by up to 1%.

- The KNN test time is large. The algorithm performs a lot of computation for every prediction due to the lazy nature of the algorithm.

- The SVM/SMO training time is large. This is because the algorithm creates so many support vectors.

The findings confirm the relative performance of the algorithms shown in Figure 4-17. Although only RF achieved 90% accuracy, it is likely the results for all the algorithms can improve by further adjusting the algorithm options.

One additional factor is extremely important in choosing the best model that I have not discussed yet is model size. You need a model that can be stored in a device at the edge. Such devices often have constrained memory and CPU resources due to their size. I will discuss this important factor further in Chapter 6.

Multiple ROC Curves

In addition to algorithm accuracy, let's look at the ROC curve(s) of your classification results. The ROC curve plots the true positive rate (TPR) against the false positive rate (FPR). ROC curves work best in a 2-class case, but you can make a multi-class problem like **subject101-cleaned.arff** into a 2-class case by singling out one class and evaluating it against the others.

You will use to Weka KnowledgeFlow application to generate the ROC comparison chart. Open a KnowledgeFlow window from the Weka GUI Chooser and open the **Classify-4.kf** file from the book resources.

Classify-4.kf is a knowledge flow example that performs the following actions when executed:

- It loads the data from **subject101-cleaned.arff**.

- It prepares a 10-fold cross-validation of the data to send to the RF and NB classifiers.

- It prepares a 2/3 split of the data to send to the KNN and SVM/SMO classifiers. These classifiers take a longer time to test instances, so avoid the 10-fold cross-validation test option.

- The four classifiers perform their classification.

- The results are sent to the charting module that can display the image of the multiple ROC curves.

- The results also saved in a text file.

Figure 5-33 shows the **Classify-4.kf** layout including the status window after the flow executes.

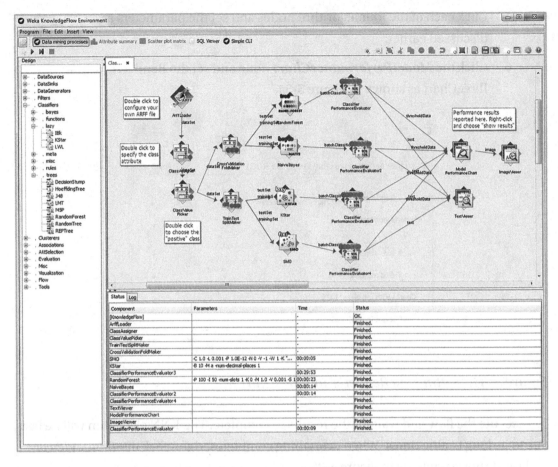

Figure 5-33. *KnowledgeFlow clustering multiple ROC output*

Before executing the flow, click the following nodes to set or confirm their parameters:

1. Click the ***ARFFLoader*** and verify the data file is ***subject101-cleaned.arff***.

2. Click the ***ClassAssigner*** and verify that ***ActivityID*** is the class attribute.

3. Click the ***ClassValuePicker*** and select the class to use for the ROC curve. In the example, you chose class 3 (Standing). This is how you map multi-class data for 2-class ROC curves.

4. Select the ***FoldMaker*** and the ***SplitMaker*** nodes to set the test divisions for 10 fold and 2/3 split.

289

5. Click each of the four algorithm nodes and set the parameters as discussed earlier.

6. Click the *ModelPerformanceChart* node and set the Renderer to JFreeChart as shown in Figure 5-34.

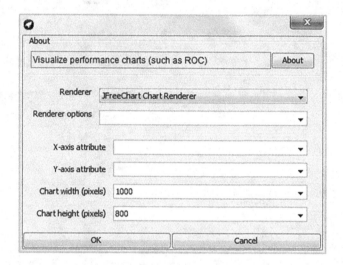

Figure 5-34. *Setting the Renderer to JFreeChart*

Execute the flow and wait for the results to complete. The KNN algorithm will be last due to its long testing times. When everything completes, right-click the *ImageViewer* node and show results, as in Figure 5-35.

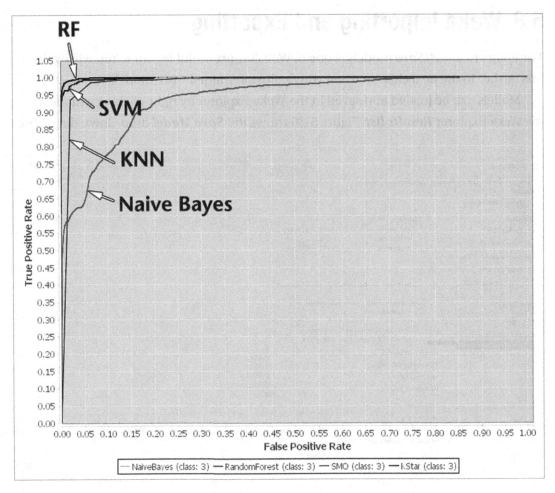

Figure 5-35. *Weka ROC curve comparison (Class: 3)*

Recall from Chapter 4, to interpret the multiple ROC curves, straight vertical line are the best. For this particular Class=3, the RF and SVM/SMO algorithms look great. The NB algorithm is lagging, which is reasonable because it had the lowest percentage accuracy.

The accuracy and ROC curve results give you confidence these models can work when integrated into your final application.

5.8 Weka Importing and Exporting

The ability to **Load/Save** models is one of Weka's most useful features. You will explore this further in the next chapter when you deploy pretrained CML models to devices.

Models can be loaded and saved in the Weka Explorer by right-clicking a model in the Weka Explorer **Results list**. Figure 5-36 shows the **Save Model** drop-down dialog box.

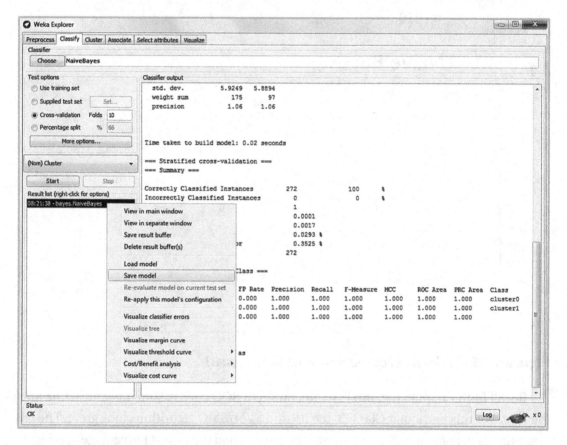

Figure 5-36. *Weka Explorer: saving a model*

Weka saves models as serialized Java objects with the **.model** extension. You can import saved Weka models into your Java applications by using the Weka Java API. Once imported, the model enables you to make predictions. In Chapter 6, you will explore the size and structure of **.model** files further.

One of the key issues with using prebuilt CML models on devices is the size of the model. Model size and model accuracy are trade-offs you must carefully consider whenever you build and export models. I will discuss this in detail in the next chapter.

In addition to saving models, Weka allows you to save data files with a variety of formats. When you click the **Save** button in the Weka Explorer **Preprocess** tab, the following file formats are available:

- ARFF file export

- ARFF data files (*.arff)

- ARFF data files (*.arff.gz)

- C4.5 file format (*.names)

- CSV files (*.csv)

- Plain text or binary serialized dictionary files (*.dict)

- JSON data files (*.json)

- JSON data files (*.json.gz)

- libsvm data files (*.libsvm)

This is a particularly useful feature because it allows you to convert files between formats. For example, in the Old Faithful clustering example, you started by importing the dataset in *.csv* format. After completing the clustering process, you can then export the data, including the clustering results, in *.arff* format.

The following excerpt shows the first 15 instances of the Old Faithful dataset after clustering, in *.arff* format. Notice that the dataset includes four attributes including a **Cluster** attribute as the last column of the comma-separated dataset.

```
001   @relation old-faithful_clustered
002
003   @attribute Instance_number numeric
004   @attribute eruptions numeric
005   @attribute waiting numeric
006   @attribute Cluster {cluster0,cluster1}
007
008   @data
```

```
009    0,3.6,79,cluster0
010    1,1.8,54,cluster1
011    2,3.333,74,cluster0
012    3,2.283,62,cluster1
013    4,4.533,85,cluster0
014    5,2.883,55,cluster1
015    6,4.7,88,cluster0
016    7,3.6,85,cluster0
017    8,1.95,51,cluster1
018    9,4.35,85,cluster0
019    10,1.833,54,cluster1
020    11,3.917,84,cluster0
021    12,4.2,78,cluster0
022    13,1.75,47,cluster1
023    14,4.7,83,cluster0
024    15,2.167,52,cluster1
```

In the next chapter, you will explore how to use this saved *.arff* file to create the Old Faithful (Figure 5-37) Classifier app for mobile.

Figure 5-37. Old Faithful geyser in Yellowstone National Park (Courtesy of Tim Dimacchia, portfolio.timdimacchia.com)

CHAPTER 6

Integrating Models

ML models only become useful when you integrate them seamlessly into your Java applications. This chapter covers the following objectives:

- Manage ML models.

- Perform sensitivity analysis to make the best tradeoff between model accuracy and model size.

- Review the key aspects of the Weka Java API. The API allows you to open pretrained models and make predictions within Java.

- Use an Eclipse project to create a Weka API library you can use for both Java and Android applications.

- Present an overview of integration techniques for pretrained ML models with Android and the Raspberry Pi.

- Review Java code to handle sensor data on popular device platforms.

- Implement the Old Faithful ML app for Raspberry Pi.

- Implement the Activity Tracker ML Classification app for Android.

6.1 Introduction

It is amazing how many apps are available on the app stores today. In fact, there are so many, it has become difficult to cut through the noise and establish a presence. A small percentage of apps on the app stores today use ML, but this is changing.

Machine learning is the future of app development. Just as we have learned to design network performance into our apps, we must now learn to design ML performance into the app, including considerations for model size, model accuracy, and prediction latency.

297

© Mark Wickham 2018
M. Wickham, *Practical Java Machine Learning*, https://doi.org/10.1007/978-1-4842-3951-3_6

In this final chapter, you will learn about model integration and deployment. Figure 6-1 shows the ML-Gates 1 and 0 steps for this critical phase.

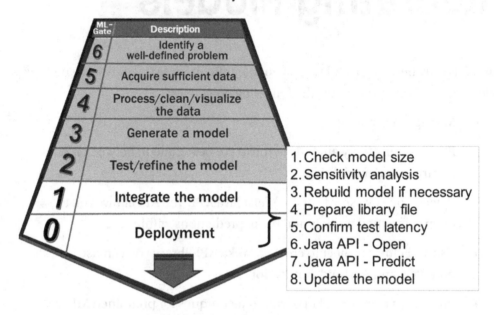

Figure 6-1. *ML-Gate 1/0, Model Integration/Deployment*

These final two ML-Gates represent the "business end" of the ML development pipeline. They represent the final steps in the pipeline where you realize the benefit of all the hard work performed in the earlier phases when you were working with data, algorithms, and models. Model integration and deployment are the most visible stages, the stages that enable you to monetize your applications.

6.2 Managing Models

In ML application development, the model is one of your key assets. You must carefully consider how to handle the model, including

- Model sizing considerations

- Model version control

- Updating models

Models can grow to be very large, and you need to start by making sure the models you create can physically reside on your target device.

Device Constraints

When you use ML models from the cloud providers, you simply rely on network connectivity and a cloud provider API to access models and make predictions. Storing prebuilt models on devices is a different approach, requiring you to understand the limitations of the target device. Table 6-1 shows the typical hardware storage specifications for two Java devices, Android and Raspberry Pi.

Table 6-1. *Device Processing/Storage Summary*

Specification	Android	Raspberry Pi
Device Category	Mid-tier device, such as Moto X4 (2018)	Pi 3B+ (2017)
O/S	Android 8.1 (Oreo)	Linux
CPU	Octa-core ARM Cortex-A53 2.2 GHz	4x ARM Cortex-A53, 1.2 GHz
GPU	Adreno 508	Broadcom VideoCore IV
Internal flash	32GB	N/A
RAM	3GB RAM	1 GB LPDDR2 (900 MHz)
External flash	microSD, up to 256GB	microSD, up to 256GB

While the devices have a somewhat similar architecture and CPU technology, the table shows the typical Android device has more processing power and storage capacity than the Pi 3B+.

The device specifications for Android vary widely. Table 6-1 shows a typical mid-tier device and the latest revision Raspberry Pi, the Pi 3B+. Both devices support external SD cards for storage. On the Pi, you must use this external storage for your application code and the ML model. On Android devices, there is also internal storage, typically 32GB, sometimes up to 64GB or higher on the flagship phones. There are several reasons to use Android internal storage for ML models:

- Internal storage outperforms external storage by a factor of 3x for read operations. For write operations, the difference is not usually as significant.

- Many Android devices do not support external SD cards.

- External storage permissions have become increasingly strict in recent Android builds.

It is common on Android devices to see applications with sizes greater than 300MB. This does not mean you should create models with sizes to match. Huge models are difficult to manage. The primary downside of huge models is the time it takes to load them. You will see with Android, the best approach is to load models on a background thread, and you would like the loading operation to be complete within a few seconds. In the chapter projects, you will load the ML models during app startup while the startup splash screen displays.

Optimal Model Size

In Chapter 5, you saw model accuracy, model training, and model testing times varied for each of the classification algorithms discussed. There is an additional factor, model size, which is equally important to consider. Table 6-2 shows the relative priority of these factors.

Table 6-2. *Model Creation Factors*

Factor	Priority	Reason
Model training time	Low	Training time is important; however, when you are deploying static models within applications at the edge, the priority is low because you can always apply more resources, potentially even in the cloud, to train the model.
Model test time	Medium	If an algorithm produces a complex model requiring relatively long testing times, this could result in latency or performance issues on the device when making predictions.
Model accuracy	High	Model accuracy must be sufficient to produce results required by your well-defined problem.
Model size	High	When deploying pretrained ML models onto devices, the size of the model must be consistent with the memory and processing resources of the target device.

Weka allows you to save models by right-clicking on a ***Result List*** item after a classification completes. Table 6-3 shows the size of several models created using the specified model options. There are two entries for RF algorithm, one representing ten iterations (i=10) and another representing one hundred iterations (i=100).

Table 6-3. *Model Size Summary, Various Classification Algorithms*

Algorithm	Options	Model size	Accuracy (%)
Random forest	i=10	5.5MB	87.7%
Random forest	i=100	55.2 MB	90.5%
KNN-KStar	Default	3.6 MB	82.8%
Naive Bayes	Kernel default	51 KB	72.9%
SVM/SMO	c=2	51.9 MB	83.4%

To understand how the factors interrelate, you can perform a sensitivity analysis. Consider the RF algorithm. You know the number of iterations, i, is a key variable for determining how deep or how many trees the algorithm produces. More iterations means more trees, which results in each of the following:

- Higher degree of accuracy
- Longer creation time
- Larger model size

You can use the Weka ML environment to run a series of model creations to see how these factors relate. Figure 6-2 shows a sensitivity analysis plotting model accuracy against model size for varying settings of the iteration (i) parameter.

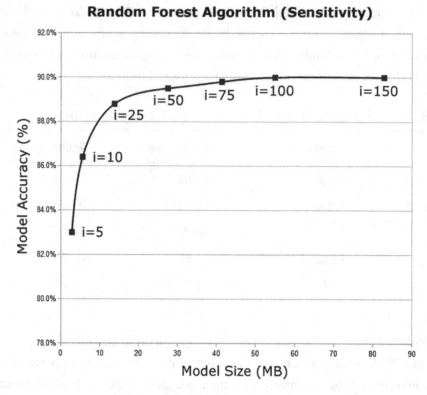

Figure 6-2. *Sensitivity analysis, model size vs. model accuracy*

One of the things you immediately notice when working with the RF algorithm is that the relationship between iterations (i) and model size is linear. For example, with all other parameters being equal, the size of the model with i=5 is 2.76 MB, and the size of the model with i=50 is 27.6MB. As Figure 6-2 shows, accuracy does not behave the same way. The RF model reaches a ceiling, in this example, at approximately 90% accuracy. In terms of model size, the 90MB model (i=150) does not produce any significantly greater accuracy than the 40MB model (i=75).

The optimal point on the curve is the tangent line at the knee of curve. You can see visually this point lies somewhere between the i=10 and i=25 values. The i=10 value yields a reasonably good accuracy with a model size at only 5.5MB, so let's proceed with this configuration. Note that these accuracy values do not include 10-fold training; adopting this test approach can further improve the accuracy.

Another factor influencing model size is the dataset size. The **PAMAP2_dataset** you used was large. **Subject101-cleaned.arff** contained 22,846 instances. You already performed **feature reduction** (also called dimensionality reduction) on the dataset when you removed columns (attributes) that were not useful. However, consider if you were to reduce the number of instances in the dataset. This would probably result in a reduced model size, possibly at the expense of accuracy.

Figure 6-3 shows a second sensitivity analysis to help you explore this effect. This chart plots the number of training instances vs. the model size, using a constant value of ten iterations (i=10) and reducing the training instances by filtering the dataset input file.

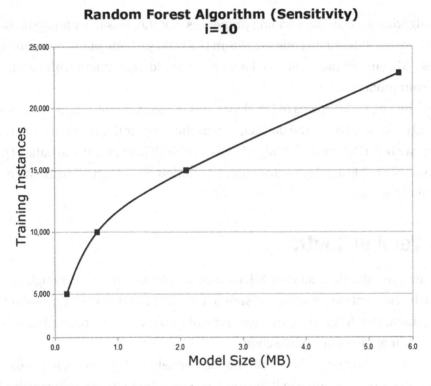

Figure 6-3. *Data size sensitivity analysis*

Figure 6-3 shows four models with varying training instance sizes. The three points on the left of the plot represent a subset of the complete dataset. The relationship to model size is not linear because you can observe a bend in the curve. The slope of the curve represents the utility of the training instances. As the slope decreases on the right-hand side of the plot, the utility of each training instance is lower. This also relates to the accuracy ceiling.

The question is, which instances should you delete? All of the ML environments, including Weka, have filters to assist with instance reduction which try to minimize dataset class integrity.

Of course, reducing the training data will eventually reduce accuracy. Finding the right balance is a trade-off decision, and you can use the sensitivity analysis to help you choose the most efficient point along the curves.

> *Optimizing model size for devices involves performing a sensitivity analysis for the critical parameter(s) of the chosen algorithm. Create models to observe their size, and then choose tangent points along the sensitivity curves for the optimum tradeoff.*

Each algorithm has its own scaling properties. For the sensitivity analysis shown here, you have considered just one algorithm (RF) and just one of its parameters (iterations). ML environments like Weka make it easy to experiment with parameters to optimize your models.

One of the huge advantages of DL algorithms is that generally, their size does not scale linearly with the size of the dataset, as was the case for the RF algorithm. DL algorithms such as CNN and RNN algorithms use hidden layers. As the dataset grows in size, the number of hidden layers does not. DL models get "smarter" without growing proportionally in size.

Model Version Control

Once created, you should treat your ML models as valuable assets. Although you did not write code in the creation process, you should consider them as code equivalents when managing them. This infers that ML models be placed under version control in a similar manner as your application source code.

Whether or not you store the actual model, a serialized Java object in the case of Weka's model export, depends on if the model is reproducible deterministically. Ideally, you should be able to reproduce any of your models from the input components, including

- Dataset

- Input configuration including filters or preprocessing

- Algorithm selection

- Algorithm parameters

For deterministic models that are reproducible, it is not necessary to store the model itself. Instead, you can just choose to store the input components. When creation times are long, such as with the KNN algorithm for large datasets, it can make sense to store the model itself, along with the input components.

The following tools are free and open source, and promise to allow you to seamlessly deploy and manage models in a scalable, reliable, and cost-optimized way:

- **https://dataversioncontrol.com**

- **https://datmo.com**

These tools support integration with the cloud providers such as AWS and GCP. They solve the version control problem by guaranteeing reproducibility for all of your model-based assets.

Updating Models

One of the key aspects to consider when you begin to deploy your ML app is how you are going to update the model in the future. The example projects later in the chapter will simply load the ML model directly from the project's asset directory when the app starts. This is the easiest approach when starting with ML application development, but it is the least flexible when it comes time to upgrade your application-model combination in the future.

A more flexible architecture is to abstract the model from the app. This provides the opportunity to update the model in the future without the need to rebuild the application. Table 6-4 summarizes some of the approaches for model management.

Table 6-4. *Model Management Approaches*

Approach	Description	Pros/Cons
Embedded	Include the model in the project assets.	Easy, but the least flexible approach.
Download	Rather than store the model on the device, download it from the cloud at application initialization.	Network connectivity required. Suitable for very small models.
Lazy loading	You can apply the standard image-loading approach to ML models. This is a hybrid combination of the first two approaches.	Many libraries are available. Flexible, but not ideal for large models.
SyncAdapter and *ContentManager*	You can use the built-in Android network synchronization (*SyncAdapter*) and content sharing (*ContentManager*) classes.	High flexibility. Background service architecture.
Push messaging	Deliver model updates with push services, such as Google's Firebase Cloud Messaging (FCM), or open source alternatives such as MQTT.	Low latency. Background service architecture.
Real-time streaming	With this approach, models update progressively as new data becomes available.	Distinctly different architecture from pre-built models.

If you wish to pursue the lazy loading or the push messaging approach, there are sample projects for each of these in the author's Android project book that can easily be adapted to support ML models:

https://github.com/apress/practical-android

In the chapter projects that follow, you will use the embedded model approach for simplicity. For production applications, the more advanced approaches in Table 6-4 are preferred.

Managing Models: Best Practices

A summary of best practices for creating and handling prebuilt models for on-device ML applications:

- Optimal model size depends on the input dataset size, attribute complexity, and target device hardware capabilities.

- Prepare a model sensitivity analysis plotting model accuracy vs. model size. Choose a point on the curve well to the left of the algorithm ceiling.

- Prepare a model sensitivity analysis plotting number of training instances vs. model size. Choose a point on the curve where the slope is higher.

- For Android and Raspberry Pi devices, a good guideline for model size is 5MB -50MB. If you are considering larger CML models, make certain you gain sufficiently greater accuracy to justify the larger size.

- Use version control to manage all of the source data, algorithm choices, algorithm parameters, and deployed models.

- Decide which architecture you will use for updating the model used by your application.

In the next sections, you will explore the Weka Java API, how to load models, and how to make predictions on devices.

6.3 Weka Java API

You have seen how easy it is to access the Weka classifiers and clusterers from the Simple CLI and from the various Weka GUI applications, including Explorer and KnowledgeFlow. The real power is unlocked when you can access the Weka classes from within your Java code. All of the Weka classes can be accesses from the Java APIs.

The Weka Java APIs allow you to do the following from Java code:

- Set options.

- Create and manage datasets attributes and instances.

- Load and save data in ARFF or CSV formats.

- Load and save serialized models.

- Apply any of the large number of Weka filters to datasets.

- Classify or cluster datasets using any of the many Weka algorithms.

- Select attributes as labels for classification.

- Visualize datasets, although this functionality is not available for the Android platform.

It takes just a few lines of Java code to replicate most of the tasks you performed using the Weka Explorer.

Next, I will review some of the most important Java API operations, first using the general Java API, and then specifically for the Android platform.

Loading Data

Your approach to place ML models at the edge means you typically will be loading pretrained models created on higher capability desktop or server machines. However, there may be occasional situations when you need to load datasets at the edge.

The Weka API allows you to load CSV or ARFF data files, just as you did in the Weka desktop environment. The following code demonstrates loading CSV and ARFF files using the API:

```
001    import weka.core.converters.ConverterUtils.DataSource;
002    import weka.core.Instances;
003    //
004    // Load ARFF file
005    //
006    DataSource sourceARFF = new DataSource("/your-directory/your-data.
       arff");
007    Instances dataARFF = sourceARFF.getDataSet();
008    //
009    // Load CSV file
010    //
011    DataSource sourceCSV = new DataSource("/your-directory/your-data.csv");
012    Instances dataCSV = sourceCSV.getDataSet();
```

You use the *Instance* object to store the data. You can apply filters to the data before running classification or clustering algorithms. The Weka API supports the same filter and algorithm options you used in the GUI-based desktop environment.

Working with Options

The Weka API supports options using *String Arrays* with the following two approaches:

```
001    // Manually create the String Array of options:
002    //
003    String[] options1 = new String[2];
004    options1[0] = "-R";
005    options1[1] = "1";
006    //
007    // or, you can automatically create the options String Array using
       splitOptions:
008    //
009    String[] options2 = weka.core.Utils.splitOptions("-R 1");
```

Once you have defined option *String Arrays*, you can apply them to filters or algorithms, as shown in the next examples.

Applying Filters

You can apply filters to *classes*, *attributes*, or *instances*. If you have an *Instances* object containing the dataset called *data*, you can apply a filter as follows:

```
001    import weka.core.Instances;
002    import weka.filters.Filter;
003    import weka.filters.unsupervised.attribute.Remove;
004    import weka.core.converters.ConverterUtils.DataSource;
005
006    // Load Data
007    DataSource source = new DataSource("/your-directory/your-data.arff");
008    Instances data = source.getDataSet();
009
010    // Set the options for "range" and "first attribute"
```

```
011    String[] options = new String[2];
012    options[0] = "-R";
013    options[1] = "1";
014
015    // Create a new instance of the "remove" filter and set the options
016    Remove remove = new Remove();
017    remove.setOptions(options);
018    remove.setInputFormat(data);
019
020    // Apply the filter to the data object
021    Instances newData = Filter.useFilter(data, remove);
```

In this example, you are removing the first attribute (column) from *data*, and the update is stored in the *newData* object.

Setting the Label Attribute

As you saw in Chapter 2, the label attribute can be any of the attributes in the dataset. Often, it is the first attribute, while some datasets include it as the last. It is a best practice to specify the label attribute in your Java code. The Weka API provides the *setClassIndex* to set the label attribute for classification:

```
001    // Set the class attribute (Label) as the first class
002    dataTest.setClassIndex(0);
```

Always double check that the data type of the class index is correct, especially when reading in CSV data. Recall earlier with the PAMAP2_dataset, you needed to use a Weka filter to convert the label attribute (class index) to the correct nominal type. ARFF files specify the data type so conversion filters are not necessary.

Building a Classifier

Building a classifier with the Weka API is a simple process requiring only a few lines of code, first specifying the options and then passing the options and the data to the classifier's *buildClassifier* method.

```
001    import weka.classifiers.trees.J48;
002
003    // Set the option for "unpruned tree"
004    String[] options = new String[1];
005    options[0] = "-U";
006
007    // Specify the tree classifier
008    J48 tree = new J48();
009    tree.setOptions(options);
010    tree.buildClassifier(data);
```

All of the Weka classifiers are available in the API, including the four most important ones discussed in Chapter 4.

Training and Testing

The Weka API allows you to train and test classifiers. You can train a classifier by passing training data (*Instances* object) to the *buildClassifier* method. The *evaluateModel* method allows you to test a trained classifier.

```
001    import weka.core.Instances;
002    import weka.classifiers.Evaluation;
003    import weka.classifiers.trees.J48;
004    import weka.classifiers.Classifier;
005
006    Instances train = <your training data>
007    Instances test =  <your testing data>
008
009    // Train classifier
010    try {
011        Classifier cls = new J48();
012        cls.buildClassifier(train);
013
014        // Evaluate the classifier
015        Evaluation eval = new Evaluation(train);
016        eval.evaluateModel(cls, test);
```

```
017        System.out.println(eval.toSummaryString("\nResults\n======\n",
           false));
018    } catch (Exception e) {
019        // Handle Weka exception
020        e.printStackTrace();
021    }
```

You will not typically be training classifiers on devices at the edge, but it is nice to have this capability.

Building a Clusterer

Building a clusterer with the Weka API is also straightforward. You can use the *buildClusterer* method of the *clusterer* object to train the clusterer.

```
001    import weka.clusterers.EM;
002
003    // Set the options for max iterations
004    String[] options = new String[2];
005    options[0] = "-I";
006    options[1] = "10";
007
008    // Instantiate the EM Clusterer instance
009    EM clusterer = new EM();
010    clusterer.setOptions(options);
011    clusterer.buildClusterer(data);
```

You can evaluate a clusterer using the *evaluateClusterer* method.

Loading Models

In Chapter 5, you saw how to save models created in the Weka ML environment. Now you can use the Weka API to load these pretrained models. Use the Java *InputStream* class to specify the model filename, and then provide the stream to the Weka API *SerializationHelper* class.

```
001    // Define a Weka Classifier Object
002    Classifier mClassifier = null;
003
004    // Load the Classifier from local storage
005    try {
006        File wekaModelFileUnix = new File("/path/modelname.model");
007        FileInputStream fis = new FileInputStream(wekaModelFileUnix);
008        mClassifier = weka.core.SerializationHelper.read(fis);
009    } catch (Exception e) {
010        // Handle Weka model failed to load
011        e.printStackTrace();
012}
```

Later in the chapter, you will leverage this approach for loading models with the Weka library for Android.

Making Predictions

You can use the Weka API to make predictions, or to say it more formally, to classify a sample. The *classifyInstance* method is available for all of the classifiers.

```
013    import weka.core.Instances;
014    import weka.core.converters.ConverterUtils.DataSource;
015    import weka.classifiers.Classifier;
016
017    // Load unlabeled data
018    DataSource source = new DataSource("/your-directory/your-unlabeled-
       data.arff");
019    Instances unlabeled = source.getDataSet();
020
021    Classifier mClassifier = null;
022
023    // set class attribute
024    unlabeled.setClassIndex(unlabeled.numAttributes() - 1);
025
026    // classify the instances
```

```
027    for (int i = 0; i < unlabeled.numInstances(); i++) {
028        double clsLabel = mClassifier.classifyInstance(unlabeled.
           instance(i));
029
030    }
```

You will use this logic later in the chapter to implement the Activity Tracker Android app.

6.4 Weka for Android

The most useful way to use the Weka ML library on Android devices is to port the library to Android. The task is not trivial, but once completed, a **Weka.jar** file for Android is a gift that keeps on giving.

It is important to use the same version of Weka throughout the ML-Gates pipeline. If you use the latest stable version of Weka on the desktop to create ML models, you must use the same version of Weka on the device to ensure compatibility, especially for opening serialized pretrained models. Weka is stable so this should not pose a major problem.

The main issue with porting Weka to Android is Weka's integration with the following Java packages:

- AWT: A Java interface to native system GUI code

- Swing: A pure Java GUI that uses AWT to create windows and then manipulate objects within the windows

- Net Beans: A platform of modular components used for developing Java applications

Weka relies on these packages for GUI-related functionality. One of the reasons Android is so wonderful is that it does not use any of these GUI packages. Of course, that is also the reason it is difficult to port Weka to Android.

Fortunately, you do not need the GUI capabilities of Weka on Android. You just require access to the data utilities, filters, algorithms, and serialization methods. However, before you can build a Weka library for Android, you need to resolve the build issues on Android caused by use of these packages.

The book resources include the Weka jar file you will use for Android projects:

Weka-Android-3-8-1.jar

The easy approach is to grab the Weka jar file and simply add it to your Android Weka projects.

To demonstrate how to build the ***Weka-Android-3-8-1.jar*** library for Android, the book resources include a complete Eclipse project. The project is also available at the author's GitHub page:

Weka-Android-3-8-1.zip

https://github.com/wickapps/Weka-Android-3-8-1

The Eclipse project is useful to explore the code updates required to resolve the many GUI-related compile errors when porting the Weka library to Android. The project can also act as a guide if you need to create a library file for a different Weka version.

Creating Android Weka Libraries in Eclipse

You have two approaches to port Weka to Android.

- **Bottom-up approach**: Decide which exact functionality you require, such as the seven most useful ML algorithms. Start from the bottom, identifying the specific classes for these algorithms and begin including just those classes, working your way up to resolve any needed dependency issues. When all dependencies are resolved, you will have a bare minimum set of functionality for your library.

- **Top-down approach**: Start at the top and include all of the obvious Weka classes (excluding KnowledgeFlow) for the Android build. When you import the project into Eclipse as an Android project, a large number of errors will require manual resolution.

This section will demonstrate the latter approach. The top-down approach requires more effort than the bottom-up approach, but once you resolve all the issues, you will have a more flexible, capable library for your Android projects. The library will support all of the Weka filters and algorithms, and you will not need to rebuild the library until the release of a new version Weka version.

The following steps summarize the initial setup process for porting Weka to Android:

- Start with the latest version of Weka that supports Java 7 (more on this later), version 3.8.1. Navigate to the *weka-src.jar* file. Unzip the file with the *7Zip* utility. Navigate to *src->main->java->weka*. You will import this base directory into Eclipse after making a few changes.

- Delete all of the *gui* directory, except for the following files which you need to keep because of the high degree of dependency on objects contained within them:

  GenericPropertiesCreator.excludes

  GenericPropertiesCreator.java

  GenericPropertiesCreator.props

  HierarchyPropertyParser.java

  Loader.java

  Logger.java

  TaskLogger.java

- Delete the entire *knowledgeflow* directory. The *KnowledgeFlow* application is not required on Android.

- Delete the two files in the base directory, *PluginManager.props* and *Run.java*.

- Open Eclipse.

- Create a new Android project named *Android-Weka-3-8-1*.

- Set the project as a *Library Project.* The setting is in the *Java Build Path* settings.

- With the new project highlighted, select *Import->General->File system*. Import the *weka* base directory created earlier.

The Android Weka project is now set up, but there are many errors to resolve before you can successfully build a Weka library for Android.

The latest versions of Weka require the Matrix Toolkit for Java (*mtj*) library. The Matrix Toolkit for Java is an open-source Java software library for performing numerical linear algebra. The following is the link for the GitHub repository for Matrix Toolkit for Java:

https://github.com/fommil/matrix-toolkits-java

Copy the *mtj-1.0.1.jar* library file from the book resources, or download the library file from the Maven repository:

https://mvnrepository.com/artifact/com.googlecode.matrix-toolkits-java/ mtj/1.0.1

The Maven repository also includes instructions for Maven or Gradle builds. Add the *mtj-1.0.1.jar* to the Eclipse project as an external library file.

You may notice that there are many errors related to the Java handing of *Vectors* and *ArrayLists* in the code. The latest versions of Weka rely heavily on *ArrayLists*. Table 6-5 shows the Weka Java requirements. Java 7 (1.7) is the minimum Java version required for the Weka version 3.8.1. The newest stable version of Weka is 3.8.2 which requires Java 8 (1.8).

Table 6-5. *Weka Version Java Requirements*

		Java version				
		1.4	1.5	1.6	1.7	1.8
Weka version	<3.4	X	X	X	X	X
	3.4.x	X	X	X	X	X
	3.5.x	3.5.0-3.5.2	>3.5.2	X	X	X
	3.6.x		X	X	X	X
	3.7.x		3.7.0	>3.7.0	>3.7.13	X
	3.8.x				3.8.1	>3.8.1
	3.9.x				3.9.1	>3.9.1

However, keep in mind that Android does not yet support full Java 8 (1.8). Android does support some Java 8 features. The latest on Android's Java 8 support can be found here:

https://developer.android.com/studio/write/java8-support

The highlighted cells in the table show the optimal settings: Weka version 3.8.1 running on Java version 1.7, which Android does support.

To minimize the compile errors for Weka on Android, set the Eclipse compiler compliance level to Java version 1.7 as shown in Figure 6-4. The default value is usually Java 6 (1.6).

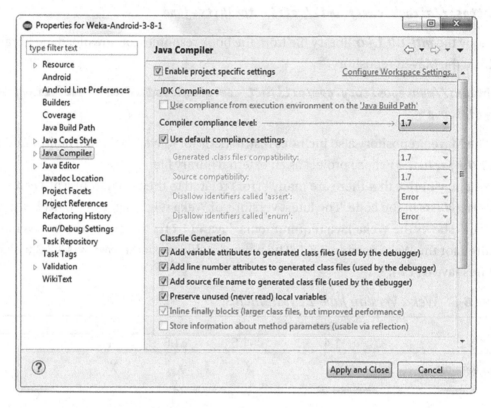

Figure 6-4. *Eclipse Java Compiler settings*

At this point, you have resolved many build errors, but there are still many build issues that you need to manually resolve. Most of the remaining errors are due to dependencies on the ***PackageManager*** or ***PluginManager*** classes. The errors can be resolved with the following resolution hierarchy:

- Delete the offending file.

- Delete the method or function in the class.

- Resolve the error by modifying the code within the offending method or function. This is the last resort and is required when the two prior approaches result in an even greater number of dependency issues.

With all errors in the Android Eclipse project resolved, you are ready to export the Weka library for Android. Choose *File➤Export➤Jar Library* from the Eclipse main menu. Figure 6-5 shows the export.

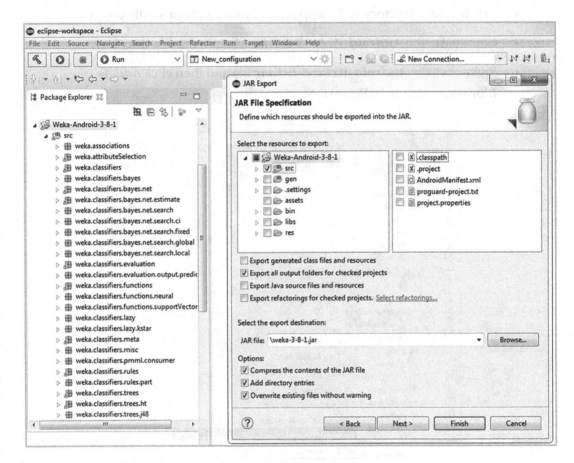

Figure 6-5.   *Eclipse exporting the Weka library file*

The size of the library file is only 3.3MB, even though it contains all the Weka Java API classes you will need for Android. The library's light memory footprint makes it perfect for mobile devices. The library can rival any ML library for mobile in terms of the size/performance trade-off.

Next, you will explore how to use the library for device ML applications.

Adding the Weka Library in Android Studio

Add the Weka ML library to Android Studio with these steps:

- Create a *libs* directory at the *app* level of your Android Studio project.

- Copy/paste the *Android-Weka-3-8-1.jar* file into the *libs* directory.

- Right-click the *Android-Weka-3-8-1.jar* file and then click *Add As Library*, as shown in Figure 6-6.

Figure 6-6. *Android Studio adding a library*

The Weka API will be available from the Android Java application.

Figure 6-7 shows a project in Android Studio after the library has been imported. On the left side you can see the exploded Weka directory structure, and at the top of the right side panel you can see several library imports required by the application to handle the requested Weka API classes.

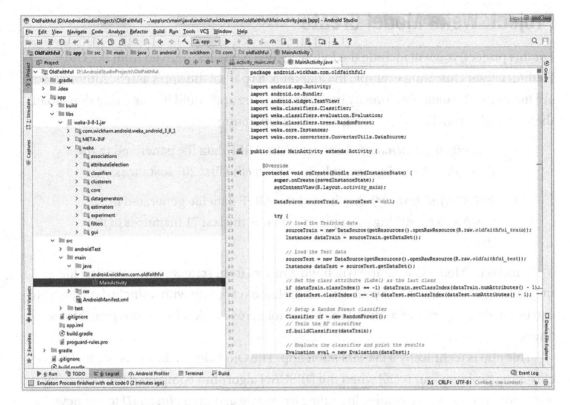

Figure 6-7. *Weka library for Android Studio*

6.5 Android Integration

The Android Weka library makes it easy to integrate ML for Android. In this section, you will implement two simple Android apps to demonstrate the following basic ML integrations:

- **Weka Model Create**: This app will demonstrate creating ML models in Android directly from data.

- **Weka Model Load**: This app will load a pretrained ML model and test the model with batch dataset instances.

The first project is a useful demonstration of the Weka API capability. The second project is a more practical architecture for the reasons discussed in earlier chapters.

Project: Weka Model Create

For this project, you will include the following two data files, derived from the Old Faithful geyser clustering example in Chapter 5, as part of the app's assets. Although you are including the data files directly in the project, the app could just as easily download these text files from the cloud using a network operation.

- *oldfaithful_train.arff*: A subset of the ARFF data file generated in the Chapter 5 clustering example, it contains the first 201 instances.

- *oldfaithful_test.arff*: A subset of the ARFF data file generated in Chapter 5 clustering example, it contains the last 71 instances of the dataset.

This Weka Model Create app will build a model from scratch, using the first file as the training data. Note that if you want to implement the app with a single data file, you can use a filter to perform a split of the file. K-fold cross-validation is also possible using filters.

This app is technically a classification app. The Old Faithful data was originally a clustering problem, but recall when the DBSCAN algorithm completed the clustering operation, you saved the results, including the newly assigned *clusterID* to the new ARFF file. When you test the model, you use the known cluster assignments to determine the classifier accuracy.

Table 6-6 shows the project summary.

Table 6-6. *Weka Model Create Project Summary*

Project Name: Weka Model Create	
Source: `weka_model_create.zip`	
Type: Android	
Notes: Create a random forest model, train it with a training dataset, evaluate the classifier with a test dataset, and display the results in a TextView.	

File	Description
app->libs-> *Weka-Android-3-8-1.jar*	The Weka jar file for Android generated from the Eclipse project.
app->src->main->java-> *MainActivity.java*	The main Java source code file. The project has a single activity.
app->src->main->res->layout *activity_main.xml*	The layout file for the single screen display output.
app->src->main->res->raw *oldfaithful_train.arff*	The training dataset, 201 instances in ARFF format.
app->src->main->res->raw *oldfaithful_test.arff*	The test dataset, 71 instances in ARFF format.
app->src->main->res *AndroidManifest.xml*	The manifest file.

You can use a simple copy-and-paste to import the three external files (Weka jar library and ARFF files) into their appropriate Android Studio directories. You will use one of the ARFF files to train the model, and the second file to test the model. This is the same approach as when you chose the ***Split Test Option*** in the desktop Weka Explorer.

The key points of ***MainActivity.java*** are as follows:

- The Weka imports at lines 6-10, courtesy of the ***Android-Weka-3-8-1.jar*** file.

- The ***setClassIndex*** method used at line 31 and line 32 sets the Attribute label as the last class for both the training and testing datasets.

- Data is loaded in ***Instances*** objects for each of the dataset files at lines 24 and 28.

- The RF model is created at line 40.

- The RF model is trained at line 42.

- The RF model assumes default options because you did not specify any additional options as shown earlier in the chapter.

Listing 6-1 shows the complete *MainActivity.java* code.

Listing 6-1. Weka Model Create MainActivity.java

```
001    package android.wickham.com.WekaModelCreate;
002
003    import android.app.Activity;
004    import android.os.Bundle;
005    import android.widget.TextView;
006    import weka.classifiers.Classifier;
007    import weka.classifiers.evaluation.Evaluation;
008    import weka.classifiers.trees.RandomForest;
009    import weka.core.Instances;
010    import weka.core.converters.ConverterUtils.DataSource;
011
012    public class MainActivity extends Activity {
013
014        @Override
015        protected void onCreate(Bundle savedInstanceState) {
016            super.onCreate(savedInstanceState);
017            setContentView(R.layout.activity_main);
018
019            DataSource sourceTrain, sourceTest = null;
020
021            try {
022                // Load the Training data
023                sourceTrain = new DataSource(getResources().
                   openRawResource(R.raw.oldfaithful_train));
024                Instances dataTrain = sourceTrain.getDataSet();
025
026                // Load the Test data
```

```
027        sourceTest = new DataSource(getResources().
           openRawResource(R.raw.oldfaithful_test));
028        Instances dataTest = sourceTest.getDataSet();
029
030        // Set the class attribute (Label) as the last class
031        if (dataTrain.classIndex() == -1) dataTrain.
           setClassIndex(dataTrain.numAttributes() - 1);
032        if (dataTest.classIndex() == -1) dataTest.
           setClassIndex(dataTest.numAttributes() - 1);
033
034        // Fill the summary information for the dataTrain set
035        int attrs = dataTrain.numAttributes();
036        int classes = dataTrain.numClasses();
037        int insts = dataTrain.numInstances();
038
039        // Setup a Random Forest classifier
040        Classifier rf = new RandomForest();
041        // Train the RF classifier
042        rf.buildClassifier(dataTrain);
043
044        // Evaluate the classifier and print the results
045        Evaluation eval = new Evaluation(dataTest);
046        eval.evaluateModel(rf, dataTest);
047
048        // Show the results
049        TextView tv_attrs = (TextView) findViewById(R.id.attrs);
050        tv_attrs.setText(String.valueOf(attrs));
051        TextView tv_classes = (TextView) findViewById(R.
           id.classes);
052        tv_classes.setText(String.valueOf(classes));
053        TextView tv_insts = (TextView) findViewById(R.id.insts);
054        tv_insts.setText(String.valueOf(insts));
055        TextView results = (TextView) findViewById(R.id.results);
056        results.setText((CharSequence) eval.toSummaryString());
057
```

```
058                } catch (Exception e) {
059                    e.printStackTrace();
060                }
061         }
062    }
```

In this example, you create a RF classifier because of its generally superior performance, but you have a complete Weka jar file, so you could choose any of the classification or clustering algorithms. The following code excerpt shows how to use the Weka API to instantiate each of the seven most useful CML algorithms presented in Chapter 4:

```
001    // Set up a Random Forest classifier
002    Classifier rf = new RandomForest();
003
004    // Other classifiers or clusterers can be defined as follows
005    Classifier nb = new NaiveBayes();
006    Classifier knn = new KStar();
007    Classifier svm = new SMO();
008    Clusterer EM = new EM();
009    Clusterer KMeans = new SimpleKMeans();
010    Clusterer DBSCAN = new MakeDensityBasedClusterer();
```

Figure 6-8 shows a screenshot of the app when run in the Android Studio emulator or on a device.

The **numAttributes**, **numClasses**, and **numInstances** methods of the **dataTrain** class provide a summary of the training data set. The **evaluateModel** method (line 46) of the classifier provides the classifier results.

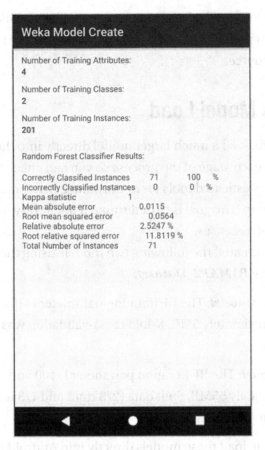

Figure 6-8. *Android app: Weka Model Create*

The classifier achieved a 100% classification result- impressive work by the RF algorithm on this dataset!

Note the app size was only 1.7MB and only contained 62 lines of Java code (much of which was only necessary to display the results). This illustrates the efficiency of CML for devices at the edge. The RF model was in memory when it evaluated the testing data. It would be possible to save the serialized model, or even to upload the model created from the source data to the cloud.

In the next example, you'll take a step up in complexity, working with a much larger dataset, and loading a pretrained model instead of creating the model on the device directly from a data source.

Project: Weka Model Load

In this project, you will load a much larger model directly into the app. You will include some time stamps at each stage of the process so you can check the performance. Android has some sophisticated tools for performance benchmarking, but you will just use a simple time stamp. The goal is to determine if the library performance on Android is sufficient for typical use cases.

In Chapter 5, you created the following two models using the RF algorithm for *subject101* of the large *PAMAP2_Dataset*:

- *rf_i10_cross.model*: The RF iteration parameter i=10 and the model size is approximately 5MB. K-fold cross-validation was used to train the model.

- *rf_i100.model*: The RF iteration parameter i=100 and the model size is approximately 55MB. Split data (2/3 train and 1/3 test) was used to train the model.

In this app, you will load these models directly into Android using the Weka API. Table 6-7 shows the project summary for the app.

Table 6-7. *Weka Model Load Project Summary*

Project Name: Weka Model Load

Source: `weka_model_load.zip`

Type: Android

Notes: Load a pretrained model into the app and perform a batch classification of 5,000 instances loaded from a file to test the classifier.

File	Description
app->libs-> Weka-Android-3-8-1.jar	The Weka jar file for Android generated from the Eclipse project.
app->src->main->assets-> rf_i10_cross.model	RF pretrained model.
app->src->main->java-> MainActivity.java	The app's main Java file. The project has a single activity.
app->src->main->res->layout activity_main.xml	The layout file for the single screen display output.
app->src->main->res->raw-> rf_i10_cross.model	A second copy of the pretrained RF model to demonstrate access from the raw directory.
app->src->main->res->raw-> subject101_cleaned_5k.arff	ARFF file with 5,000 instances to test the classification model.
app->src->main->res AndroidManifest.xml	The manifest file.

After you create models in the Weka desktop environment, you can directly copy them into the Android Studio project. Remember, the desktop version of Weka must match the Android library file, in this case, the Weka release version 3.8.1.

There are two methods to load pretrained models in Android:

- **Asset Manager**: Use the Android Asset Manager and load the models from the project's *assets* directory.

- **Raw files**: Load the models from the app's raw storage space.

The following code excerpt shows how to load models using each approach. In each case, you use the Weka *SerializationHelper* class.

```
001    // In Android, we have two ways we can load models directly from the
       file system
002
003    // The following code uses the AssetManager to load the model
004    // from the app->src->main->assets folder
005
006    AssetManager assetManager = getAssets();
007    InputStream is = assetManager.open("rf_i10_cross.model");
008    rf = (Classifier) weka.core.SerializationHelper.read(is);
009
010    // Alternatively, use the next line to load the model
011    // directly from the app->src->main->res->raw folder
012
013    rf = (Classifier) weka.core.SerializationHelper.read(getResources().
       openRawResource(R.raw.rf_i10_cross));
```

When naming saved models, it is a good practice to include the algorithm used as part of the filename. This makes it easier when you open the model, and need to instantiate a matching algorithm classifier or clusterer. It is possible to derive the algorithm type from a .model file using *ArrayList* operations.

Because of the large model size, for this app, you wish to benchmark the following operations:

- Elapsed time to load the model

- Elapsed time to load a file with 5,000 instances of testing data (ARFF format)

- Elapsed time to evaluate the model with the 5,000 test instances (batch testing)

You will use the following function for time-stamping the operations performed by the app:

```
001    public String getCurrentTimeStamp() {
002        return new SimpleDateFormat("HH:mm:ss.SSS").format(new Date());
003    }
```

The timestamp provides millisecond resolution, so you will get a good indication of how quickly the classifier performs.

Listing 6-2 shows the *MainActivity.java* of the application. The key code highlights:

- The app reads the Training dataset from local storage at line 26.

- The label attribute is set at line 30.

- The app loads the model into a RF object at line 38.

- The app evaluates the classifier at line 49.

- The *StringBuilder* class builds the application output. The app finally displays the output at line 56. The *StringBuilder* class retrieves the classifier capabilities at line 55.

Listing 6-2. Weka Model Load MainActivity.java

```
001    package android.wickham.com.WekaModelLoad;
002
003    import ...
004
005    import weka.classifiers.Classifier;
006    import weka.classifiers.evaluation.Evaluation;
007    import weka.core.Instances;
008    import weka.core.converters.ConverterUtils;
009
010    public class MainActivity extends Activity {
011
012        @Override
013        protected void onCreate(Bundle savedInstanceState) {
014            super.onCreate(savedInstanceState);
015            setContentView(R.layout.activity_main);
016
017            ConverterUtils.DataSource sourceTrain, sourceTest = null;
018
019            StringBuilder builder = new StringBuilder();
020            TextView results = (TextView) findViewById(R.id.results);
021
```

```
022             try {
023                 // Load the Test data
024                 builder.append("\n" + getCurrentTimeStamp() + ": Loading
                    test data");
025                 sourceTest = new ConverterUtils.DataSource
                    (getResources().openRawResource(R.raw.subject101_
                    cleaned_5k));
026                 Instances dataTest = sourceTest.getDataSet();
027                 builder.append("\n" + getCurrentTimeStamp() + ": Test
                    data load complete");
028
029                 // Set the class attribute (Label) as the first class
030                 dataTest.setClassIndex(0);
031
032                 Classifier rf;
033
034                 builder.append("\n" + getCurrentTimeStamp() + ": Loading
                    model");
035                 // The following code utilizes the AssetManager to load
                    the model from the app->src->main->assets folder
036                 AssetManager assetManager = getAssets();
037                 InputStream is = assetManager.open("rf_i10_cross.model");
038                 rf = (Classifier) weka.core.SerializationHelper.read(is);
039
040                 // Alternatively, use the next line to load the model
                      from the app->src->main->res->raw folder
041                 // rf = (Classifier) weka.core.SerializationHelper.
                    read(getResources().openRawResource(R.raw.rf_i10_cross));
042
043                 builder.append("\n" + getCurrentTimeStamp() + ": Model
                    load complete");
044                 Toast.makeText(this, "Model loaded.", Toast.LENGTH_
                    SHORT).show();
045
046                 // Evaluate the classifier
```

```
047          builder.append("\n" + getCurrentTimeStamp() + ": Starting
             classifier evaluation");
048          Evaluation eval = new Evaluation(dataTest);
049          eval.evaluateModel(rf, dataTest);
050          builder.append("\n" + getCurrentTimeStamp() + ":
             Classifier evaluation complete");
051
052          // Show the results
053          builder.append("\n\nModel summary: " +  eval.
             toSummaryString());
054          // Add the classifier capabilities
055          builder.append("\nRF Model capabilities:\n" +  rf.
             getCapabilities().toString());
056          results.setText((CharSequence) builder.toString());
057
058      } catch (Exception e) {
059          e.printStackTrace();
060      }
061  }
062
063  public String getCurrentTimeStamp() {
064      return new SimpleDateFormat("HH:mm:ss.SSS").format(new Date());
065  }
066 }
```

The app is performing a batch classification of 5,000 instances using a pretrained model. If you can achieve decent performance with this batch operation, you can be confident the architecture will be sufficient to classify a single instance.

Figure 6-9 shows a screenshot of the app after it has finished its task.

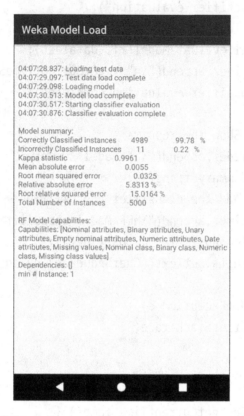

Figure 6-9. *Weka Model Load*

The application as shown ran in the Android Studio emulator. The model loaded in about 1.5 seconds and the evaluation completed in less than a half second. These seem like excellent results. You will explore the performance further in the next section.

The accuracy of the batch classification was very high: only 11 out of 5,000 incorrectly classified instances. This is most likely due to the fact the testing data was a subset of the training data originally used to build the model.

The Weka Model Load Android app proves that you can load large, pretrained models and batch classify efficiently on Android.

6.6 Android Weka Model Performance

Several factors contribute to the overall performance of ML models on devices, including

- Model size

- Model complexity

- CPU and memory capacity of the device

- Application code integration of the model

The Weka Model Load app provides timestamps. You can run the app on different devices to benchmark the relative performance. Table 6-8 shows a calculated summary of the timestamps for three operations:

- Test data load time (load 5,000 instances of testing data)

- Model load time (load the 5MB RF PAMAP2 subject101 model)

- Classifier evaluation

A special version of the app was created to run on the Amazon Fire Phone and Raspberry Pi. The app also ran in the Android studio Emulator and on a few devices, including the Moto X4, Sony Xperia, and an older Nexus tablet.

Table 6-8. *Android Weka ML Model Performance Comparison*

Device	Test data load time (5K) (sec.)	Model load time (5MB) (sec.)	Classifier evaluation time (sec.)
Android Studio Emulator	0.28	1.56	0.36
Motorola X4	0.20	1.27	0.64
Sony Xperia	0.16	1.16	0.45
Nexus 7 Tablet	1.51	3.52	1.71
Amazon Fire Phone	0.47	2.76	0.93
Raspberry Pi 3b+	0.62	3.44	0.82

Summary of the performance results:

- Classification times were less than .5 second for the newer devices that have faster CPUs.

- Memory was not an issue on any of the devices. The 5MB model was easily loaded into memory, although not as quickly for devices with slower CPUs.

- The Amazon Fire Phone is no longer a relevant Android device. It is old, lacks a modern Android version, and the hardware specifications are outdated. However, the ability of your code to function reasonably well on this device proves an important point.

  There may be times when you need to deploy CML solutions onto Android devices that do not contain Google Play Services. The CML solution you have deployed for Android does not require any of the Google services and does not even require network connectivity.

- The Android Studio emulator performed the best at classifying the 5,000 instances. The result is surprising, as normally you do not expect the emulator to outperform actual hardware. However, keep in mind the classifier evaluation is mostly a CPU-intensive operation (algorithm processing), and the desktop has a much more powerful CPU than the target mobile devices.

- The model load time is very reasonable. Typical applications will classify a single instance incrementally, as you will see in the next example, and this will be a much faster operation than the batch classification of 5,000 instances.

So, what happens to the performance when you load even larger models? You may find situations where you want to gain the increased accuracy at the expense of larger model size.

When you built the RF model for i=10 iterations, you also built one for i=100 iterations. Recall it took much longer to create and the size was much larger, approximately 55MB. Table 6-9 shows a model load time comparison for the smaller and larger models.

Table 6-9. *Android Weka ML Model Performance Comparison*

Device	Model load time (5MB model RF i=10) (sec.)	Model load time (50MB model RF i=100) (sec.)
Android Studio Emulator	1.56	12.61
Motorola X4	1.27	9.98
Sony Xperia	1.16	9.42

There are several points to consider when creating and loading models of this increased order of magnitude:

- Although the model is ten times larger, the loading time does not scale linearly. In this case, for these devices, the loading times are about eight times longer.

- Models of this size take approximately ten seconds to load. This is too long to hide during app initialization. Large models will require one of the model management strategies discussed in Table 6-4.

- It is feasible to integrate models of this size order of magnitude, but you first need to establish that they are providing a sufficient increased accuracy benefit.

Now that you have some confidence in the performance of your models on Android mobile devices, let's expand the target audience to include other Java devices.

6.7 Raspberry Pi Integration

Back in Chapter 1, you saw that the market for Java devices is huge; over 3 billion devices run Java, according to Oracle. The Raspberry Pi is a very popular device that can run Java. In this section, you will deploy CML models to the Raspberry Pi.

Developers familiar with the Pi will also be familiar with Arduino. Arduino devices have a smaller footprint and are thus not suitable for running Java. However, if you have Arduino applications, you can control those devices with Java using the open source

RXTX library. Using this library, a Java-based master device, such as the Pi, could handle the ML operations and communicate to Arduino devices for data gathering or output of model results. The RXTX library and additional information are available at the following sites:

https://github.com/rxtx/rxtx

http://rxtx.qbang.org/wiki/index.php/FAQ

Table 6-1 showed the basic hardware specifications of the Raspberry Pi 3 model b+. A quick glance at the table shows that the Pi has about one-half the processing and storage capability compared to a mid-tier Android device. Figure 6-10 shows the Raspberry Pi 3 model b+ and highlights some of the key interfaces.

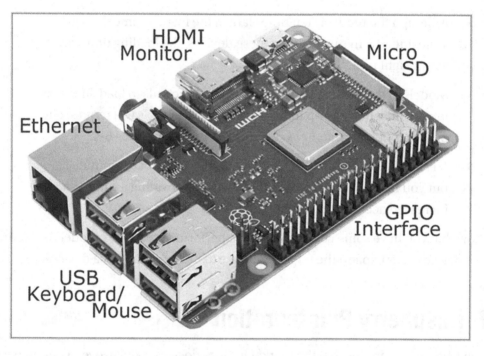

Figure 6-10. *Raspberry Pi 3 model b+ with interface summary*

The Raspberry Pi is extremely attractive because it is inexpensive and has so many useful features and interfaces, including HDMI, 4xUSB, USB powered, Micro SD card, GPIO pin interface, Wifi, Gigabit Ethernet, Bluetooth, and BLE. A complete list of the specifications can be found here:

www.raspberrypi.org/products/raspberry-pi-3-model-b-plus/

All of these features make the Pi an interesting choice for many ML applications.

- The Pi is an excellent choice for kiosk applications. You can connect HDMI monitors in portrait or landscape orientations and drive them directly from Java applications.

- You can connect small displays directly to the Pi. These can range from two-line LCD displays to 7-inch touchscreens.

- You can connect a myriad of buttons, sensors, LEDs, etc. to the GPIO interface and control them from Java applications. Sensors are available for motion, acceleration, temperature, water, wind, etc.

- The Raspberry Pi supports an external camera via the header connection next to the HDMI port. Adding a camera module to your Pi opens the door to picture and video data collection for use by ML applications.

- You can connect wireless USB keypads and keyboards to the Raspberry Pi. The devices can control the software application, even if the application does not have a monitor or display.

- There are countless potential uses for the Raspberry Pi. A quick Internet search reveals many amazing things developers are doing with the Raspberry Pi.

Raspberry Pi Setup for ML

Setting up the Raspberry Pi is easy, and there are many online support resources available. The official Raspberry Pi setup guide is available at

https://projects.raspberrypi.org/en/projects/raspberry-pi-setting-up.

Setting up Raspberry Pi 3 model b+ for ML integration does not require any special steps. The operating system and all application software are stored on the micro SD card. The Pi supports many operating systems, and you will choose the official *Raspbian* operating system during the installation. Raspbian is an unofficial port of Debian for ARM CPUs and it is the most popular OS for Raspberry Pi today. It is very similar to using Ubuntu and supports Apache, Nginx, Java, Python, and MySQL.

The steps below summarize the Raspberry Pi setup. Refer to the official link for the detailed setup steps.

1. Download the Raspberry Pi NOOBS (New Out Of Box Software) installation manager and copy it onto the micro SD card.

2. Insert the microSD card into the Pi.

3. Connect the monitor and keyboard, and power on the Pi with a USB power cable.

4. Follow the installation instructions. Choose **Raspbian** as the operating system. The good news is that Raspbian includes Java.

5. Set up the Wifi or Internet connection so you can update all the packages after the Raspbian install completes.

6. Set up an IP address if you would like to connect to the Pi from another networked device. This is not required because you will be able to copy files onto the Pi by simply inserting a flash drive and copying the files with the file manager.

7. Log into the admin user and confirm that the latest version of Java is available. Raspbian includes Java, but the following commands can upgrade Java on the Raspberry Pi if needed. The steps involve removing OpenJDK, obtaining a key, and then installing the latest Oracle Java 8.

```
001    // Install the latest Java version
002    // First remove OpenJDK
003    sudo apt-get purge openjdk*
004
005    // Add the digital key
006    sudo apt-key adv --recv-key --keyserver keyserver.ubuntu.com EEA14886
007    // Using an editor such as vi or vim, add the following lines to /
       etc/apt/sources.list
008    deb http://ppa.launchpad.net/webupd8team/java/ubuntu trusty main
009    deb-src http://ppa.launchpad.net/webupd8team/java/ubuntu trusty main
010
011    // install Java 8
```

```
012    sudo apt-get update
013    sudo apt-get install oracle-java8-installer
014    sudo apt-get install oracle-java8-set-default
015
016    // Remove the old Java(s)
017    sudo apt-get purge openjdk*
018    sudo apt-get purge java7*
019    sudo apt-get autoremove
020
021    // Check for success, we should only see Java 8
022    java -version
```

Raspberry Pi GUI Considerations

One of the main challenges when writing Java applications for the Raspberry Pi, especially for Android developers, is mastering the GUI limitation of pure Java. On the Raspberry Pi, you lack the following elements that make it so easy to implement GUI interfaces on Android:

- Android allows you to specify layouts in XML and has many graphical tools to make GUI design easy.

- Android supports a huge set of widgets and classes, such as Layouts, List Views, Constraint Layouts, and countless GUI elements and tools.

- The Android platform can automatically support various screen sizes, from small to very large devices.

- It offers support for 9-patch image files that make it easy for images, such as buttons to scale.

- Android Studio provides a "what you see is what you get" (wysiwyg) view for all XML layout files. You can easily create GUIs by simply dragging and dropping GUI widget elements.

For Java ML applications on the Raspberry Pi, you will use the *Swing* and *AWT* GUI classes available in Java. The Java GUI classes have several layout managers available. For the project, you will implement the *GroupLayout* Manager.

Placing ML capability at the edge on the Raspberry Pi device is an exciting new frontier, made possible by the Raspberry device capabilities and its support for Java and the lightweight Weka API library.

Weka API Library for Raspberry Pi

In order to use Weka on the Raspberry Pi, you need a Weka API jar file for Raspberry Pi that you can include in your application. You have two options, as shown in Table 6-10.

Table 6-10. *Raspberry Pi Weka API Library Comparison*

Library	Size (MB)	Description
weka-src.jar	10.6	The full-function Weka API distributed with each Weka stable release, such as Weka 3.8.1.
Weka-Android-3-8-1.jar	3.3	The stripped version of the Weka API you built for Android in Eclipse earlier in the chapter.

You have two options because the stripped version you build for Android can also work on Raspberry Pi. The advantage of this option is that it is smaller. One advantage of the full version is that you could potentially use the graphical functions of Weka, such as visualizations, on the Raspberry Pi. Next, you will implement ML on the Raspberry Pi, using the ***Weka-Android-3-8-1.jar*** library.

Project: Raspberry Pi Old Faithful Geyser Classifier

Printing out a screen filled with ML classifier statistics, as you did earlier for Android, is not a very compelling app.

The best ML apps are the ones that produce a compelling experience for the users, with the users never realizing that ML techniques were responsible for achieving the result.

The goal for this project is to implement a GUI-based app for Raspberry Pi that integrates a pretrained ML model to make predictions.

In Chapter 5, you reviewed the Old Faithful geyser dataset and saw how clustering helped you to identify a hidden pattern in the data. The geyser has two "modes" which we will call "hot mode" and "warm mode." Geologists probably have better terminology for this phenomenon. It makes sense that longer waiting times correlate to longer eruption times. What is interesting is that are two distinct modes.

If you have been to Yellowstone, you may recall that the park service maintains a simple handwritten information board suggesting when the next eruption might occur, roughly hourly.

For this project, you will create an app for the Raspberry Pi that can inform us of the current geyser mode based on the waiting time and eruption time. You could easily deploy this Pi app as a kiosk application to replace the handwritten information board.

In the app, you will implement some simple requirements:

- Users will enter the values for the waiting time and the eruption time.

- Users will press a Predict button to get a prediction of the geyser mode.

- The app will run on the Raspberry Pi.

- The app will load a prebuilt model to handle the prediction.

- The app will include some basic GUI elements.

The app runs manually, but you could automate the manual data input with a video camera to detect eruptions, or possibly add push buttons and timers to help facilitate data collection.

Table 6-11 shows the project summary.

Table 6-11. *Android Old Faithful Project Summary*

Project: Old Faithful
Source: *old_faithful.zip*
Type: Raspberry Pi ML Application
**Notes: This project is an Eclipse Java project to build and export the *OldFaithful.jar*
class, a classifier that can run on the Raspberry Pi device.**

File	Description
OldFaithful->srcOldFaithful.java	The main Java class. Contains everything including the GUI code. Loads the model and data file from the external Unix file system directory.
OldFaithful->libsWeka-Android-3-8-1.jar	The Weka API library file. You can use the Android version for the Raspberry Pi.
/home/pi/Java-proj/Weka/old_faithful_rf_ i10.model	RF model, external file
/home/pi/Java-proj/Weka/old_faithful_ single_instance.arff	Single instance of data. External file

In addition to the main Java file, the project also requires the Weka API library, the external Weka *.model* file, in this case a RF classifier, and an ARFF file I will discuss later.

App Overview

Before you review the project setup and Java code, you should launch the application to see how the app looks. You can launch the Java app on the desktop or on the Raspberry Pi with the following command:

```
001   pi@raspberrypi:/Java-proj/Weka $ java -jar OldFaithful.jar
```

You use the *-jar* option on the command line because this project build output is an executable jar file, *OldFaithful.jar*. When the jar file executes, the app displays the GUI shown in Figure 6-11. In this example, you entered two values and pressed the Predict button and the application informs you the geyser is in warm mode.

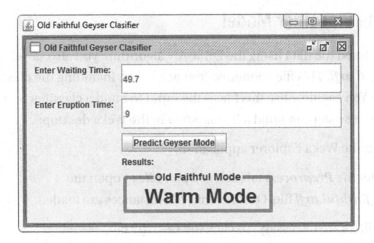

Figure 6-11. *Old Faithful Geyser app showing warm mode*

Entering some different data produces the hot mode result, as shown in Figure 6-12.

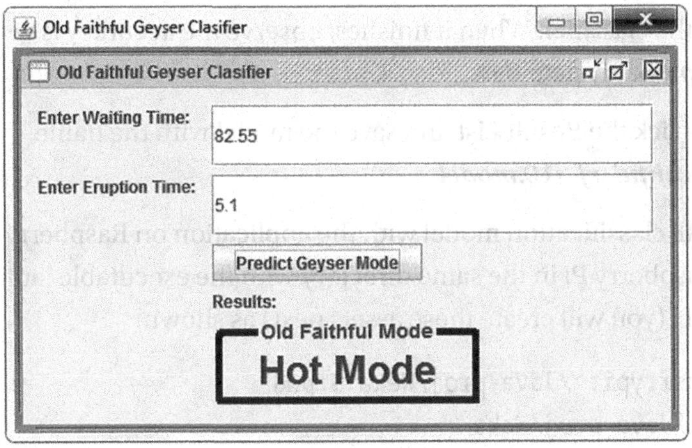

Figure 6-12. *Old Faithful Geyser app showing hot mode*

As you experiment with different values, you will notice the mode output by the app is very consistent with the clustering results you derived in Figure 5-20. In Chapter 5, you used the DBSCAN clustering algorithm to cluster the Old Faithful dataset.

Often times, classifiers are the most useful way to integrate ML models into device applications. In this case, clustering helped you identify that the geyser has two modes, and now you want users to be able to know in which mode the geyser resides. In other words, the application needs to classify new instances of data. Clustering the data was the first step to identify the hidden pattern; now you need to build a classifier.

Building the Classifier Model

When you clustered the data using the DBSCAN algorithm, you also saved the output file, *old_faithful.arff*. This file contained four attributes, including the *cluster_ID* for each instance. You can now use this file as the input to build a classifier for the Raspberry Pi app. Follow these steps to build a RF classifier in the Weka desktop:

1.   Open the Weka Explorer application.

2.   Under the *Preprocess* tab, select *Open File* to open the *old_faithful.arff* file. Observe that 272 instances are loaded.

3.   No filters are necessary, so click the *Classify* tab.

4.   Under *Classifiers*, choose the *Random Forest* algorithm from the *Trees* submenu. Click the algorithm and change *iterations = 10*.

5.   Under *Test Options*, select *Cross Validation Folds = 10*.

6.   *Start* the classifier. When it finishes, observe the accuracy is very high, probably near 99%.

7.   Right-click the Result List and save the model with the name *old_fiathful_rf_i10.model*.

To use this RF classification model with the application on Raspberry Pi, save the model on the Raspberry Pi in the same directory with the executable jar file and the external ARFF file (you will create these assets next) as shown:

```
001   pi@raspberrypi:~/Java-proj/Weka $ pwd
002   /home/pi/Java-proj/Weka
003   pi@raspberrypi:~/Java-proj/Weka $ ls -lsart
004   total 3184
005     40 -rw------- 1 pi pi   38599 Jul 27 19:27 old_faithful_rf_i10.
          model
006      4 drwxr-xr-x 4 pi pi    4096 Jul 27 23:32 ..
007      4 -rw------- 1 pi pi     207 Jul 27 23:54 old_faithful_single_
          instance.arff
008   3132 -rw------- 1 pi pi 3205683 Jul 28 00:03 OldFaithful.jar
009      4 drwxr-xr-x 2 pi pi    4096 Jul 28 00:11 .
010   pi@raspberrypi:/Java-proj/Weka $ java -jar OldFaithful.jar
```

Next, you will look at how to build the application software, including the GUI, loading the Weka model, and making predictions in Java.

Project Setup

To get started with the Old Faithful project for Raspberry Pi, import the Eclipse Java project (*OldFaithful.zip*) from the book resources, or follow these steps to create an Eclipse Java project from scratch:

1. Start a new Eclipse project by selecting *File➤New➤Java Project*

2. Enter the project name as *OldFaithful*.

3. In newly created project, create a *libs* directory under the main project folder.

4. Copy the *Weka-Android-3-8-1.jar* file into the *libs* directory.

5. In *Project Properties*, set the Java version to 1.8. For the Raspberry Pi, you are not restricted to Java 7, as is the case for Android.

6. In *Project Properties*, click *Build Path➤Manage Build Path*.

7. Click the *Libraries* tab. Click *Add Jar* to include the *Weka-Android-3-8-1.jar* file as a jar file.

8. In the *Src* directory, create the *OldFaithful.java* main class. All of the application code resides in this class, and you will review it in the next section.

9. Edit the launch configuration properties. The *main class* should be set to *OldFaithful*, as shown in Figure 6-13. If you fail to set the launch configuration *main class*, you will not be able to execute the Old Faithful app directly from the command line because the main class will be unknown.

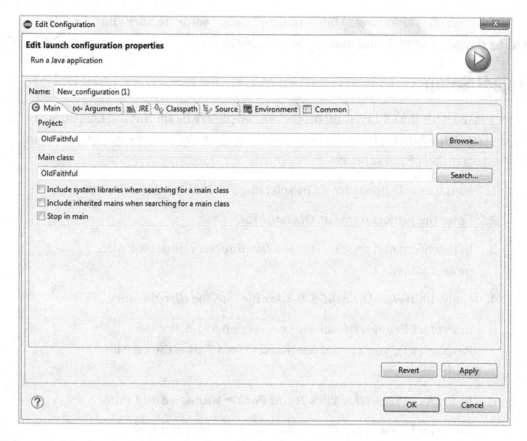

Figure 6-13. *Setting the project launch configuration*

Java Layout Managers

Java has seen gradual improvements in its GUI capabilities, starting with AWT, to Swing, and the most recent addition, JavaFX, which debuted in Java 8. JavaFX is a set of graphics and media packages that help developers design, create, test, debug, and deploy applications that operate consistently across diverse platforms. Java FX integrates well with the Web and rich media that is very popular today.

Unfortunately, Java FX is not a lightweight package, and it is not included in Java on the Raspberry Pi. It is possible to add, but it does not support all of the libraries and it is problematic to implement. For this reason, you will use the more mature Swing GUI library for the Old Faithful app. Swing fully supports all device platforms.

Swing has several *LayoutManagers*, including the following:

- *BorderLayout*

- *BoxLayout*

- *CardLayout*

- *FlowLayout*

- *GridBagLayout*

- *GridLayout*

- *GroupLayout*

- *SpringLayout*

The names provide some insight to the possible use cases, but the easiest way to understand the capabilities of these various layouts is to see them. Oracle maintains a helpful link at

https://docs.oracle.com/javase/tutorial/uiswing/layout/visual.html.

If you look closely at the GUI shown in Figure 6-12, you can see that it is comprised of labels, text entry boxes, a button, and large-font bordered text box to display the classification result. These GUI components are arranged in a 2-column by 5-row matrix.

You could choose several of the Swing layout managers to implement the Old Faithful GUI based on the desired layout. If you come from an Android background, you will find the Swing layouts difficult to use, mainly because they do not provide much control for the spacing, padding, and general styling required to make the GUI look nice. The GroupLayout manager tends to be the most flexible, so you will implement it.

If you find you are unable to implement Java FX, and the Swing layouts fail to meet your GUI requirements, there are external alternative layout managers you can consider. The *Mig Layout Manager* is an excellent choice. It is a lightweight Java library and is much more flexible than the built-in Swing layout managers. Details of the library are at

www.miglayout.com/.

GUI Implementation

All of the Java code for the app is contained in ***MainActivity.Java***. The filename retains the Android convention even though this is a Raspberry Pi app and technically is not an activity. You will review the code in two sections: first the GUI related code, followed by the ML logic.

The Java Swing GUI class works by allowing you to create ***JFrame*** objects. You can add components to any frame, such as ***JLabels***, ***JButtons***, and ***JTextFields***, in much the same way Android works. To control the way the components are arranged, Swing allows you to assign the layouts shown earlier to the ***JFrames***. For this project, you will use the ***GroupLayout***.

A summary of the key GUI code highlights:

- Create a GUI in Java Swing by extending ***JFrame*** (line 001).

- Define the components, including the ***JFrame***, ***GroupLayout***, ***JButton***, ***JLabel***, ***TitledBorder***, and ***JTextField*** (lines 002-011).

- Define the Constructor (line 013).

- The ***GroupLayout*** builds the GUI (lines 034-055).

- The private method ***setGeyserMode*** (lines 066-100) updates the GUI with new classification results from the ML model. You update the ***GroupLayout*** by calling the ***replace*** method (line 097).

Listing 6-3 shows all of the GUI-related code.

Listing 6-3. MainActivity.java: GUI-Related Code

```
001    public class OldFaithful extends JFrame {
002        static JFrame jf;
003        static GroupLayout layout;
004        static JTextField waitTime, eruptTime;
005        static JLabel priorLabel;
006        statis JButton classifyButton;
007        static TitledBorder tBorderWarm, tBorderHot, tBorderUnknown;
008        static Border borderOrange = BorderFactory.createLineBorder
           (Color.orange, 5, true);
```

```
009        static Border borderRed = BorderFactory.createLineBorder
           (Color.red, 5, true);
010        static Border borderGray = BorderFactory.createLineBorder
           (Color.gray, 5, true);
011        static String modeTitle = "Old Faithful Mode";
012
013        public OldFaithful() {
014            super("OldFaithful");
015            // Init Frame
016            JFrame.setDefaultLookAndFeelDecorated(true);
017            jf = new JFrame();
018            jf.setTitle("Old Faithful Geyser Clasifier");
019            jf.setResizable(true);
020            jf.setExtendedState(JFrame.MAXIMIZED_BOTH);
021            jf.setDefaultCloseOperation(EXIT_ON_CLOSE);
022            jf.setUndecorated(false);    // true for no title and menu
023            jf.setVisible(true);
024            layout = new GroupLayout(jf.getContentPane());
025            jf.getContentPane().setLayout(layout);
026            layout.setAutoCreateGaps(true);
027            layout.setAutoCreateContainerGaps(true);
028
029            // Setup the labels
030            JLabel labelWait = new JLabel("Enter Waiting Time:");
031            JLabel labelErupt = new JLabel("Enter Eruption Time:");
032            JLabel labelResult = new JLabel("Results:");
033
034            // Build the layout using the Swing GroupLayout
035            layout.setHorizontalGroup(layout.createSequentialGroup()
036                .addGroup(layout.createParallelGroup()
037                    .addComponent(labelWait)
038                    .addComponent(labelErupt))
039                .addGroup(layout.createParallelGroup()
040                    .addComponent(waitTime)
041                    .addComponent(eruptTime)
```

```
042                          .addComponent(classifyButton)
043                          .addComponent(labelResult)
044                          .addComponent(priorLabel))
045                );
046            layout.setVerticalGroup(layout.createSequentialGroup()
047                .addGroup(layout.createParallelGroup()
048                    .addComponent(labelWait)
049                    .addComponent(waitTime))
050                .addGroup(layout.createParallelGroup()
051                    .addComponent(labelErupt)
052                    .addComponent(eruptTime))
053                .addComponent(classifyButton)
054                .addComponent(labelResult)
055                .addComponent(priorLabel)
056                );
057
058            jf.pack();
059            jf.validate();
060            jf.repaint();
061        }
062
063        // The main class includes the ML logic and is not shown in this
           listing
064        public static void main(String args[]){}
065
066        private static void setGeyserMode(int mode) {
067            // Udate the results depending on the mode the RF classifier
               has returned
068            JLabel label = null;
069            if (mode == 2) {
070                tBorderHot = BorderFactory.createTitledBorder(borderRed,
071                        modeTitle,
072                        TitledBorder.CENTER,
073                        TitledBorder.CENTER,
074                        Font.decode("Arial-bold-14"));
```

```
075                 label  = new JLabel("   Hot Mode    ");
076                 label.setFont(Font.decode("Arial-bold-28"));
077                 label.setBorder(tBorderHot);
078             } else if (mode == 1) {
079                 tBorderWarm = BorderFactory.createTitledBorder(borderOrange,
080                         modeTitle,
081                         TitledBorder.CENTER,
082                         TitledBorder.CENTER,
083                         Font.decode("Arial-bold-14"));
084             label  = new JLabel("   Warm Mode   ");
085                 label.setFont(Font.decode("Arial-bold-28"));
086                 label.setBorder(tBorderWarm);
087             } else {
088                 tBorderUnknown = BorderFactory.createTitledBorder
                    (borderGray,
089                         modeTitle,
090                         TitledBorder.CENTER,
091                         TitledBorder.CENTER,
092                         Font.decode("Arial-bold-14"));
093             label  = new JLabel(" Unknown Mode ");
094                 label.setFont(Font.decode("Arial-bold-28"));
095                 label.setBorder(tBorderUnknown);
096             }
097             layout.replace(priorLabel, label);
098             // reset the priorLabel so it can be updated next time
099             priorLabel = label;
100         }
101     }
```

Single Instance Data File

Earlier in the chapter, you saw how to make batch predictions by loading a data file
containing many instances, 5,000 instances for the PAMAP2_Dataset example. For the
Old Faithful app, instead of batch classifying, you will be classifying a single instance
each time the button is pressed.

Loading a single instance ARFF file is a simple way to educate your application on the structure of the data. Think of the single instance data file as a type of data dictionary for the data, a best practice I discussed in Chapter 2. If you update your data structure or change any of the data types, you should update the single instance data file.

Using the single instance ARFF file has two advantages:

- The approach abstracts the data structure from the application code, making the code easier to maintain.

- The external file approach simplifies the ML code because it is not necessary to define all the attributes and data types in Java.

Listing 6-4 shows the *old_faithful_single_instance.arff* file. You can easily create the file from the original ARFF file by simply deleting all of the instances except for one.

Listing 6-4. old_faithful_single_instance.arff, a Single Instance ARFF File

```
001    @relation subject101-cleaned-weka.filters.unsupervised.attribute.
       NumericToNominal-Rfirst
002
003    @attribute activityID {1,2,3,4,5,6,7,12,13,16,17,24}
004    @attribute accelX numeric
005    @attribute accelY numeric
006    @attribute accelZ numeric
007    @attribute gyroX numeric
008    @attribute gyroY numeric
009    @attribute gyroZ numeric
010    @attribute magnetX numeric
011    @attribute magnetY numeric
012    @attribute magnetZ numeric
013
014    @data
015    1,2.30106,7.25857,6.09259,-0.069961,-0.018328,0.004582,9.15626,
       -67.1825,-20.0857
```

The alternative approach to loading the data structure from file is to define the structure manually in Java using the Weka API ***Attribute*** and ***Instances*** classes.

You need to deploy the single instance ARFF file packaged together with the executable jar file and the ML model file.

ML Code

Listing 6-5 shows all of the ML code. It is surprisingly brief. As promised, instead of writing vast amounts of code, you merely need to load the model and start making predictions.

Highlights of the ML code:

- The main class runs the constructor (line 003). The constructor in this example performs much of the GUI setup.

- It load the single instance ARFF file (lines 005-011).

- It load the classifier, a RF model created in Weka (lines 013-017).

- It sets up a button to perform the classification (line 019).

- It implements *predictButtonPressed* to read the values from the two GUI input fields (line 031)

- It create a new instance to classify, specifying *erupt* and *wait* values (lines 037-043).

- It classifies the instance (line 046).

- It sets the geyser mode according to the classification results (lines 048-050).

The ML code resides in the public main class.

Listing 6-5. MainActivity.java: ML-Related Code

```
001    public static void main(String args[]){
002        // Run the constructor
003        new OldFaithful();
004        try {
005            // Load a Test data instance so we can classify more easily
006            ConverterUtils.DataSource sourceTest = null;
007            String wekaDataStrUnix = "/home/pi/old_faithful_single_
                   instance.arff";
```

```
008            sourceTest = new ConverterUtils.DataSource(wekaDataStrUnix);
009            dataSet = sourceTest.getDataSet();
010            // Set the class attribute (Label) as the last class, the
               ClusterID
011            dataSet.setClassIndex(3);
012
013            // Load the model, a RF model created from the ARFF data and
               saved in Weka Explorer
014            File wekaModelFileUnix = new File("/home/pi/old_faithful_rf_
               i10.model");
015            FileInputStream fis = new FileInputStream(wekaModelFileUnix);
016            rf = (Classifier) weka.core.SerializationHelper.read(fis);
017            fis.close();
018
019            // Classify button
020            JButton classifyButton = new JButton("Predict Geyser Mode");
021            classifyButton.addActionListener(new ActionListener() {
022                public void actionPerformed(ActionEvent e) {
023                    predictButtonPressed();
024                }
025            } );
026        } catch (Exception e) {
027            e.printStackTrace();
028        }
029    }
030
031    private static void predictButtonPressed() {
032        // Get a prediction from the classifer and update the Geyser Mode
033        try {
034            double wait = Double.valueOf(waitTime.getText());
035            double erupt = Double.valueOf(eruptTime.getText());
036
037            // Create a new instance to classify
038            Instance newInst = new DenseInstance(4);
039            newInst.setDataset(dataSet);
```

```
040            newInst.setValue(0, 0);
041            newInst.setValue(1, erupt);
042            newInst.setValue(2, wait);
043            newInst.setValue(3, 0);
044
045            // Classify the Instance
046            double result = rf.classifyInstance(newInst);
047
048            if (result == 1.0) setGeyserMode(1);
049            else if (result == 0.0) setGeyserMode(2);
050            else setGeyserMode(0);
051        }
052    catch (NumberFormatException e) {
053            //Not a double so set unknown mode
054        setGeyserMode(0);
055    }
056    catch (Exception e) {
057            e.printStackTrace();
058    }
059  }
```

Exception Handling for ML Models

Exception handling is one of the more important aspects of application development. However, most developers do not spend enough time on it.

In ML applications, the model is a critical component of the application. The accuracy of the model is very important, but what if the model fails altogether, generating an exception? If the model fails, the app fails, and you need to know about it. In most of the examples, including Listing 6-5 above, you print out a stack trace in the event of a model exception, but fail to take any other actions. For commercial ML apps residing on Raspberry Pi devices or Android mobile phones, you need a more robust approach. Remote crash logging is a solution.

The idea behind remote crash logging is to collect the necessary information required to help developers resolve the problem and send it to a remote server before the application terminates from the crash.

On Android devices, there are many remote crash-logging services available. The most popular service is Google's Firebase Crashlytics. Detailed information on setting up Crashlytics for Android is available at

https://firebase.google.com/docs/crashlytics/.

There are also many third-party services, libraries, and backend servers available to implement Android crash logging. For a summary of all the services, refer to the crash logging chapter in the author's Android book at

https://github.com/apress/practical-android.

On devices like the Raspberry Pi, third-party services designed for log and sensor data collection work well for remote crash logging. One of the most popular is *LogEntries* from Rapid 7, which can accept any type of JSON-formatted data as the payload:

https://logentries.com

These services work by using the Java *UncaughtExceptionHandler* method. The following code shows how to use the handler to implement the *DefaultExceptionHandler*:

```
001    public class DefaultExceptionHandler implements
       UncaughtExceptionHandler{
002        private UncaughtExceptionHandler mDefaultExceptionHandler;
003
004        //constructor
005        public DefaultExceptionHandler(UncaughtExceptionHandler pDefault
           ExceptionHandler)
006        {
007            mDefaultExceptionHandler= pDefaultExceptionHandler;
008        }
009        public void uncaughtException(Thread t, Throwable e) {
010            //do some action like writing to file or upload somewhere
011
012            //call original handler
013            mStandardEH.uncaughtException(t, e);
014        }
015    }
```

This approach gives you the opportunity to perform some action before your application terminates due to an uncaught exception. To help understand why a model has generated an exception, it is usually sufficient to send the instance attribute data values at the time of the exception, up to the service.

Fortunately, Weka model failures are rare so long as the data and data type match, but when the inevitable crash does occur, you need remote crash logging to be able to see and analyze the problematic data so you can fix the problem. In many cases, the problem can be resolved by correcting the application code, while in some rare cases, you must rebuild the model to eliminate the anomaly.

Exporting Runnable jar Files for Raspberry Pi

Follow these steps to build the Old Faithful runnable jar file:

- Clean the project and confirm there are no build errors.

- Confirm that the Java Main class in the launch configuration is set as shown in Figure 6-13.

- In the Eclipse main menu, choose *File➤Export*, as shown in Figure 6-14.

Figure 6-14. *Exporting a runnable jar file*

- Click *Next*, and you will see the *Runnable JAR File Export* screen shown in Figure 6-15.

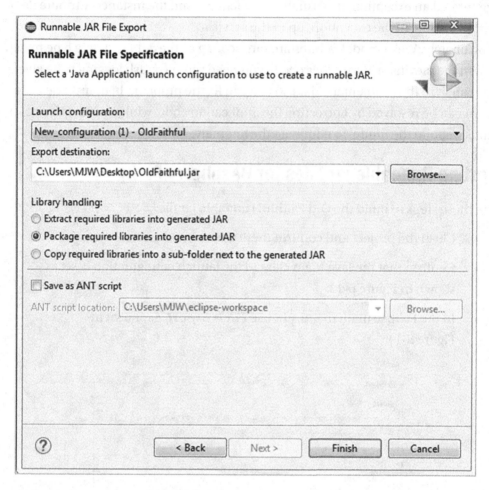

Figure 6-15. *Exporting OldFaithful.jar file*

- Make sure the *Library Handling* radio button selects the *Package required libraries into generated JAR* option. This is necessary so the Weka API library is included in the exported application.

With the export complete, the runnable jar file, along with the other required external files, will be sufficient to run the Old Faithful app on any Java compliant device.

Auto Starting ML Apps on Raspberry Pi

One of the requirements for the Old Faithful project is to create a kiosk-mode app. Such apps typically have two characteristics:

- Kiosk applications typically support a display or some type of visual output, but often do not have input devices such as a keyboard or mouse.

- Kiosk applications have a single purpose and are automatically initialize at power up or when reset.

On Raspberry Pi, there are several methods to achieve automatic start of the *OldFaithful.jar* file. You can use any of the following five Unix-based approaches to implement automatic start of any application:

- ***rc.local***: Add the application to launch at system startup.

- ***.bashrc***: Edit the bash shell startup file to start the application at startup.

- ***init.d tab***: Use ***init.d***, a directory that contains many start/stop scripts for system services.

- ***systemd***: Use ***systemd***, a standard process for controlling the processes that start in Unix.

- ***crontab***: Use ***cron*** jobs to schedule when applications run.

For running executable jar files, the first approach is the most simple and it works well. To configure automatic start on the Raspberry Pi for the ***OldFaithful.jar*** file, implement the following steps:

1. Place the required files,

   OldFaithful.jar,
   old_faithful_single_instance.arff, and
   old_faithful_rf_i10.model,
   into the ***/home/pi/Weka*** and another directory of your choosing.

2. Change into the */etc* directory and edit the **rc.local** file with the *nano* editor:

   sudo nano /etc/rc.local

   The *vi* editor is an alternative.

3. Add the following line to the end of the file, before the **exit 0**:

   java -jar /home/pi/Weka/OldFaithful.jar &
   exit 0;

4. Save the file. Do not forget the **&** at the end of the line. The **&** allows the command to run in a separate process. Without it, the boot process will not complete.

5. Add a dedicated IP address to the Pi by setting the **static_ip_address** in the */etc/dhcpcd.conf* file. This allows access to the device over the Ethernet connection to retain access to the kiosk device.

6. To disable the Raspberry Pi screensaver, edit the following file:

   sudo nano ~/.config/lxsession/LXDE-pi/autostart
   The file should match the following code:
   lxpanel --profile LXDE-pi
   #@xscreensaver -no-splash
   @point-rpi
   @xset s off
   @xset -dpms
   @xset s noblank

7. Use **sudo reboot** to reboot the Pi and test the changes.

Project Wrap-up

The Old Faithful project on Raspberry Pi was a simple ML application running in kiosk mode on the device. However, it illustrates a powerful device ML architecture that you can replicate for other potential applications.

Highlights of the Raspberry Pi ML architecture:

- The Pi is inexpensive and is loaded with connectivity options.

- The Pi runs Java, and libraries are readily available.

- The Weka API works well on the Pi. The memory and processing capabilities of the device make it more than capable to handle advanced CML problems.

6.8 Sensor Data

Sensor data is an excellent fuel for ML apps. In Chapter 2, I introduced the mobile phone as potentially the greatest data collection device ever invented. In this section, you will investigate device capabilities and explore how to implement ML for Android using sensors and the PAMAP2_Dataset covered in Chapter 2.

Android Sensors

You know that Android supports sensors, but a deep dive into the Android APIs reveals a surprising level of sensor coverage. Google divides the Android sensors into three categories: motion, environmental, and position. Table 6-12 shows a summary of the Android sensors. Most of the sensors have been in the platform since API level 14 (Android 4.0). Support for the proximity and humidity sensor is available beginning with API level 20 (Android 4.4).

Table 6-12. *Android Sensor Support*

Category	Sensor	Android sensor types
Motion	Accelerometers	TYPE_ACCELEROMETER TYPE_LINEAR_ACCELERATION
	Gravity	TYPE_GRAVITY
	Gyroscope	TYPE_GYROSCOPE
	Rotational Vector	TYPE_ROTATION_VECTOR
Environmental	Barometers	TYPE_PRESSURE
	Photometers	TYPE_LIGHT
	Thermometers	TYPE_AMBIENT_TEMPERATURE TYPE_TEMPERATURE TYPE_RELATIVE_HUMIDITY
Position	Orientation	TYPE_ORIENTATION TYPE_PROXIMITY
	Magnetometers	TYPE_MAGNETIC_FIELD

The Sensor framework allows you to use any of the Android sensors. It includes the following classes:

- ***SensorManager***: Use this class to create an instance of a sensor service. The class contains various methods for accessing, listing, registering, or unregistering sensors. The class also provides many of the constants used to set sensor accuracy and data acquisition rates.

- ***Sensor***: Use this class to create an instance of a specific sensor. The class also provides methods to determine a sensor's capabilities.

- ***SensorEvent***: A sensor event object allows you to collect raw sensor data.

- ***SensorEventListener***: Use this interface method to create callback methods that receive notifications when the sensor values change.

The Android sensors are hardware dependent, so sensor availability varies from device to device and between Android versions. Use the following code to determine sensor availability:

```
001   private SensorManager mSensorManager;
002   ...
003   mSensorManager = (SensorManager) getSystemService(Context.SENSOR_
      SERVICE);
004   ...
005   List<Sensor> deviceSensors = mSensorManager.getSensorList(Sensor.
      TYPE_ALL);
```

If you wish to narrow the search, you can replace the constant **TYPE_ALL** with another constant, such as **TYPE_GYROSCOPE** or **TYPE_GRAVITY**.

In the Android Activity Tracker project, you will examine in detail how to implement the Android sensors.

Raspberry Pi with Sensors

Figure 6-10 shows a picture of the Raspberry Pi. The GPIO interface makes the Pi an excellent device for ML with sensor data collection. The sensors are inexpensive, and you can connect many different types of sensors to the Raspberry Pi. Table 6-13 shows some of the sensor devices that you can connect.

Table 6-13. Raspberry Pi Sensor Summary

Category	Sensor	Description
Environment	DHT11/DHT22	Measure temperature and humidity.
	DS18B20/ DS18S20	Outdoor use temperature and humidity.
	BMP180	Barometer for air pressure, as well as temperature and altitude.
	MQ-2	Gas sensor. Methane, butane, and smoke.
Motion	PIR Motion	Low-cost motion sensor sends a signal only when something moves.
	HC-SR04	Ultrasonic motion sensor. Can also measure distances.
	MPU-6050	Gyroscope to detect rotation along three axes.
	HMC5883L/GY-271	Compass.
Water	YL-69 Soil hygrometer Moisture sensor	Ground moisture sensor. Useful for irrigation systems.
	SEN0193	Capacitive ground moisture sensor from DFrobot. More precise and does not erode over time.
	FC-37 +MCP3008	Raindrop sensor. Depending on the amount of water, the capacitance is increased.
	YF-S201C	Water flow meter.
Gravity	HX-711	Weight sensor and load scale.
Other	Pulsesensor.com	Heartbeat and pulse sensor.

The Raspberry Pi has sensors for almost anything you can imagine. The pulse sensor shown at the bottom of Table 6-13 was the result of a recent Kickstarter campaign. The mobile phone is a great data collection device, but for specialized dedicated data collection systems, the Pi takes it to another level.

For specialized sensor-driven data applications, the Raspberry Pi in conjunction with Java and the Weka API library makes a low-cost powerful machine learning platform.

To implement sensors on the Raspberry Pi, you need a Java library to interface with the sensors. There are two options available:

- PI4J: A Java-based API only for the Raspberry Pi

- Device I/O: A Java-based API that can support many devices

The PI4J project is an open source library (LGPL version 3.0) for Java that makes it easy to interface with the device from Java. Instructions for using PI4J including downloads are available at *http://pi4j.com/*.

Accessing the GPIO and other Raspberry Pi interfaces from Java is very simple, as shown by the following code:

```
001    import com.pi4j.io.gpio.GpioController;
002    import com.pi4j.io.gpio.GpioFactory;
003    import com.pi4j.io.gpio.GpioPinDigitalOutput;
004    import com.pi4j.io.gpio.PinState;
005    import com.pi4j.io.gpio.RaspiPin;
006
007    // create gpio controller
008    final GpioController gpio = GpioFactory.getInstance();
009
010    // provision gpio pin #01 as an output pin and turn on
011    final GpioPinDigitalOutput pin = gpio.provisionDigitalOutputPin(Raspi
       Pin.GPIO_01, "MyLED", PinState.HIGH);
012
013    // set shutdown state for this pin
014    pin.setShutdownOptions(true, PinState.LOW);
015
016    // turn off gpio pin #01
017    pin.low();
018
019    // toggle the current state of gpio pin #01 (should turn on)
020    pin.toggle();
```

There is some overlap between the PI4J library and Device I/O. PI4J is more feature rich. The Device I/O library is from Oracle and was originally part of the Java ME embedded library. It is also an open source Java-level API for accessing generic device peripherals on embedded devices. It is under the OpenJDK project, and documentation is available at

https://docs.oracle.com/javame/8.0/api/dio/api/index.html.

The Device I/O library has a configuration file for each board, so you can write code once and use it on any Java device, not just limited to Raspberry Pi. The main difference between PI4J and Device I/O is the GPIO mapping.

The following is a Java code example using the Device I/O library:

```
001   //
002   // Accessing the GPIO Pin number 12.
003   //
004
005   GPIOPin led = (GPIOPin)DeviceManager.open(12);
006
007   led.setValue(true) //Turns the LED on
008   led.setValue(false) //Turns the LED off
009   boolean status = led.getValue() //true if the LED is on
```

To use Device I/O library you will need to download the Mercurial configuration management system and then clone the project. The name of the actual library is *dio.jar*:

```
001   sudo apt-get install mercurial
002   hg clone http://hg.openjdk.java.net/dio/dev
```

To run an application using Device I/O, you will need the following:

- Any standard Java class with a main method

- *java.policy*, a file that contains the permissions configuration

- The *dio.jar* library file

- *libdio.so*, a linked library that contains native code interfaces

- *dio.properties*, the configuration file that contains a board-specific configuration

Sensor Units of Measure

When working with sensor data, it is important to keep close track of the unit of measure of the data. Sensor manufacturers can use a variety of different units of measure depending on many factors, including accuracy, local standards, country of origin, etc. Table 6-14 shows the unit of measure for some of the Android sensors.

Table 6-14. *Android Sensors Unit of Measure*

Android sensor name	Unit of measure	Data description
TYPE_MAGNETIC_FIELD	uT	Magnetic field strength in micro-Tesla along three axes
TYPE_LINEAR_ACCELERATION	m/s^2	Acceleration along three axes
TYPE_GYROSCOPE	rad/sec	Angular velocity along three axis
TYPE_AMBIENT_TEMPERATURE	°C	Ambient air temperature
TYPE_LIGHT	lx	Illuminance, measured in lux units
TYPE_PRESSURE	hPa or mbar	Ambient air pressure
TYPE_RELATIVE_HUMIDITY	%	Ambient relative humidity
TYPE_TEMPERATURE	°C	Device temperature

When working with data from outside sources, you need to make sure the units are consistent before mixing with your own device data. If the units are not the same, you need to provide a conversion to the base data format.

In the Android Activity Tracker project, you will use the data collected for the PAMAP2_Dataset. The cleaned data you used to build your model contained accelerometer, gyroscope, and magnetic field data. The units of measure used by the original collection devices match the Android sensor units, so no conversion is necessary.

Project: Android Activity Tracker

In this project, you are creating an Android application that uses the RF model together with the Android sensors to provide a near real-time prediction of the current activity of the user. Table 6-15 shows the project summary.

Table 6-15. *Android Activity Tracker Project Summary*

Project: Activity Tracker	
Source: *acticity_tracker.zip*	
Type: Android Studio Project	
Notes: This project uses a trained model from the PAMAP2_dataset in conjunction with near real-time Android sensor data to determine the current activity of the device user.	

File	Description
app->libsWeka-Android-3-8-1.jar	The Weka API library file for Android.
app->src->main->javaMainActivity.java	The main application source code is included in this single file.
app->src->main->res->layoutactivity_main.xml	The main GUI layout file for the application.
app->src->main->res->rawrf_i10_cross.model	The RF model used by the application to make predictions.
app->src->main->res->rawsubject101_single.arff	The single instance ARFF file used by the application to set up the data attribute properties.

In this project, you want to create an application that gives you a near real-time display of the current activity. Figure 6-16 shows the screenshot of the application.

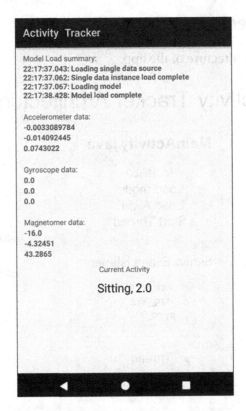

Figure 6-16. *Activity Tracker Android application screenshot*

The app shows a real-time readout of the current sensor values for the accelerometer, gyroscope, and magnetometer. At the bottom of the screen, the app shows the current activity and the current activity ID, an integer between 1 and 12. As you monitor the app, you will see the sensor values update in real time, while the current activity updates twice per second.

Application Architecture

Figure 6-17 shows the architecture of the app.

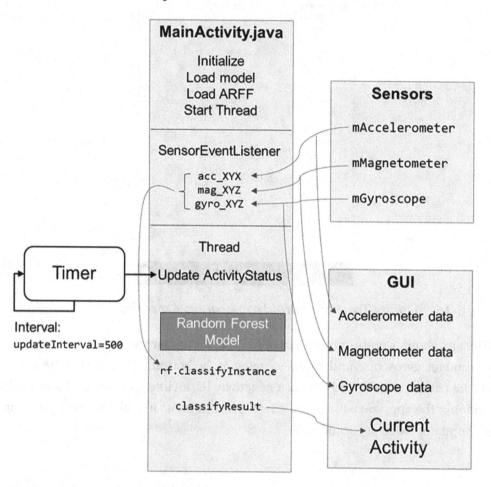

Figure 6-17. *Activity Tracker architecture*

The structure of the app is similar to the previous examples in terms of loading the model and making the prediction, but contains two additional constructs:

- Implements *SensorEventListener* to handle the incoming sensor data from the accelerometer, gyroscope, and magnetometer.

- Implements a *Thread* to handle the timing for the classification processing.

In this app, you will load the RF model you created in Chapter 5, *rf_i10_cross.model*. You created the model from a cleaned version of the *subject101* dataset. As a result, the model allows you to track the following activities. You define these activities as the *String[]*, named *activityID*.

```
001    activityID = new String[] {
002            "Other (transient)",     // 0
003            "Lying",                  // 1
004            "Sitting",                // 2
005            "Standing",               // 3
006            "Walking",                // 4
007            "Running",                // 5
008            "Cycling",                // 6
009            "Nordic Walking",         // 7
010            "Ascending Stairs",       // 8
011            "Descending Stairs",      // 9
012            "Vacuum cleaning",        // 10
013            "Ironing",                // 11
014            "Rope jumping"            // 12
015    };
```

You use this *String[]* to print out the resulting activity. Recall, the original dataset contained 24 activities. It would not be fair to expect your model to classify all of these activities because half of them were not included in the training dataset. You excluded some of the activities because the chosen subject did not perform them and you excluded others in the cleaning process.

Implementing Android Sensors

A key function of the app is to collect current data from the Android sensors. This is a two-step process:

- Initialization
- Implementing the sensor listener

373

The initialization process involves creating objects for each of the three required sensors in the application ***onCreate*** method. The following code shows how to create these objects in Android and how to register the ***SensorEventListener***. Keep in mind that you also need to register and unregister the ***SensorEventListener*** in the ***onPause*** and ***onResume*** methods (not shown).

```
001    private SensorManager mSensorManager;
002    private Sensor mAccelerometer, mGyroscope, mMagnetometer;
003
004    mSensorManager = (SensorManager) getSystemService(SENSOR_SERVICE);
005
006    mAccelerometer = mSensorManager.getDefaultSensor(Sensor.TYPE_LINEAR_
       ACCELERATION);
007    mGyroscope = mSensorManager.getDefaultSensor(Sensor.TYPE_GYROSCOPE);
008    mMagnetometer = mSensorManager.getDefaultSensor(Sensor.TYPE_MAGNETIC_
       FIELD);
009
010    mSensorManager.registerListener(mSensorEventListener, mAccelerometer,
       SensorManager.SENSOR_DELAY_NORMAL);
```

In line 006, you create the accelerator object. In Android, there are two choices:

- ***Sensor.TYPE_LINEAR_ACCELERATOR***

- ***Sensor.TYPE_ACCELERATOR***

The difference between the two is the inclusion of a gravity component. The linear accelerator removes the impact of gravity on the readings. Analysis of the initial data shows this measurement approach is consistent with the initial data gathering protocol, so you use this sensor in the application.

In line 010, you use the ***SENSOR_DELAY_NORMAL*** constant in the ***registerListener*** method. This value specifies the rate at which you receive samples from the sensors. Table 6-16 shows the options. When using sensors, there is some internal latency, so the typical observed sample rate is higher than the Android-specified value. In the app, you want to update the user's current activity every 500 milliseconds (1/2 second). You have seen that you can classify a single sample at this rate, so ***SENSOR_DELAY_NORMAL*** is sufficient for the app. Note that the Android also uses the ***SENSOR_DELAY_NORMAL*** for some system functions, such as determining when the user rotates the device from portrait to landscape.

Table 6-16. *Android Sensor Delay Constants*

Constantname	Default constantvalue (microseconds)	Typical observed sample rate (milliseconds)
SENSOR_DELAY_NORMAL	200,000	225
SENSOR_DELAY_UI	60,000	78
SENSOR_DELAY_GAME	20,000	38
SENSOR_DELAY_FASTEST	0	20

To receive sensor events, you need to implement the ***SensorEventListener***. Android calls this listener to report sensor events for all of the registered sensors. In this app, you have three sensors registered. Even though you are using the least frequent sampling rate, ***SENSOR_DELAY_NORMAL***, there will still be many events passed to this listener.

```
001   private final SensorEventListener mSensorEventListener = new
      SensorEventListener() {
002       @Override
003       public void onSensorChanged(SensorEvent event) {
004           if (event.sensor.getType() == Sensor.TYPE_LINEAR_
              ACCELERATION) {
005               acc_X = event.values[0];
006               acc_Y = event.values[1];
007               acc_Z = event.values[2];
008               tv_acc_X.setText(Float.toString(acc_X));
009               tv_acc_Y.setText(Float.toString(acc_Y));
010               tv_acc_Z.setText(Float.toString(acc_Z));
011
012           } else if (event.sensor.getType() == Sensor.TYPE_GYROSCOPE) {
013               gyro_X = event.values[0];
014               gyro_Y = event.values[1];
015               gyro_Z = event.values[2];
016               tv_gyro_X.setText(Float.toString(gyro_X));
017               tv_gyro_Y.setText(Float.toString(gyro_Y));
018               tv_gyro_Z.setText(Float.toString(gyro_Z));
019
```

```
020                } else if (event.sensor.getType() == Sensor.TYPE_MAGNETIC_
               FIELD) {
021                    mag_X = event.values[0];
022                    mag_Y = event.values[1];
023                    mag_Z = event.values[2];
024                    tv_mag_X.setText(Float.toString(mag_X));
025                    tv_mag_Y.setText(Float.toString(mag_Y));
026                    tv_mag_Z.setText(Float.toString(mag_Z));
027                }
028            }
029
030        @Override
031        public void onAccuracyChanged(Sensor sensor, int i) {
032        }
033    };
```

Inside the listener, you decode the events by checking the ***event.sensors.getType()***
and then reading the values from the ***event.values[]*** array. Depending on the event type,
the listener stores the X, Y, and Z sensor values into the following local variables:

- **Accelerometer**: acc_X, acc_Y, acc_Z (lines 005-007)

- **Gyroscope**: gyro_X, gyro_Y, gyro_Z (lines 013-015)

- **Magnetometer**: mag_X, mag_Y, mag_Z (lines 021-023)

In addition to updating the local variables that you will use as a classification
instance, the listener also updates the ***TextView*** fields on the main app GUI layout.
When you run the app, it is immediately apparent how many events the sensors generate
because you can see these values change so frequently.

The listener also requires you to implement the ***onAccuracyChanged*** method (line
031). You can leave this method empty.

Implementing the Timer

For this app, you would like to show a continuously updated activity prediction derived
from the most recently available sensor data. This requires that you constantly feed
instances into the ML model for predictions. You know that the sensor data update
interval is approximately 200 milliseconds, because you set the sensor sample rate to

SENSOR_DELAY_NORMAL. You also know that you can classify an instance using the Weka API with an RF model in approximately 300-500 milliseconds.

To accomplish the continuous classifications, you will implement a background thread and define the integer *updateInterval* = 500 milliseconds. The thread will run continuously until an error occurs. Each time through the main loop, a call is made to *updateActivityStatus()*, which performs the classification and displays the result. The timing is controlled by a call to the *Thread.sleep(updateInterval)* method. You are not actually using Java or Android *Timer* objects in this code, but the implementation is a simple and efficient way to implement continuously updating classifications.

```
001    Thread m_statusThread;
002    Boolean m_statusThreadStop;
003    private static Integer updateInterval = 500;
004
005    public void createAndRunStatusThread(final Activity act) {
006        m_StatusThreadStop=false;
007        m_statusThread = new Thread(new Runnable() {
008            public void run() {
009                while(!m_StatusThreadStop) {
010                    try {
011                        act.runOnUiThread(new Runnable() {
012                            public void run() {
013                                updateActivityStatus();
014                            }
015                        });
016                        Thread.sleep(updateInterval);
017                    }
018                    catch(InterruptedException e) {
019                        m_StatusThreadStop = true;
020                        messageBox(act, "Exception in status thread: " +
021                                        e.toString() + " - " +
022                                        e.getMessage(), "createAndRun
                                        StatusThread Error");
023                    }
024                }
025            }
```

```
026        });
027        m_statusThread.start();
028    }
```

The final part of the code is the model integration.

Model Integration

As with the examples shown earlier in the chapter, the first step in model integration is to load the single instance data source, set the class attribute label, and load the prebuilt RF classifier model. The following code block shows the initialization steps performed on the Android *onCreate* method:

```
001    // Load the Single Instance data source
002    sourceSingle = new ConverterUtils.DataSource(getResources().
       openRawResource(R.raw.subject101_single));
003    dataSingle = sourceSingle.getDataSet();
004
005    // Set the class attribute (Label) as the first class
006    dataSingle.setClassIndex(0);
007
008    // Load the pre-built Random Forest model
009    rf = (Classifier) weka.core.SerializationHelper.read(getResources().
       openRawResource(R.raw.rf_i10_cross));
```

With initialization complete, the only steps remaining are to build samples from the sensor data, classify them, and display the result. The actions are shown in *updateActivityStatus()*, which runs on the UI thread so it can display the result:

```
001    private void updateActivityStatus() {
002        //Toast.makeText(MainActivity.this, "Button pressed.", Toast.
           LENGTH_SHORT).show();
003        // Grab the most recent values and classify them
004        // Create a new Instance to classify
005        Instance newInst = new DenseInstance(10);
006        newInst.setDataset(dataSingle);
007        newInst.setValue(0,0);    // ActivityID
008        newInst.setValue(1,acc_X);  // Accelerometer X
```

```
009        newInst.setValue(2,acc_Y);   // Accelerometer Y
010        newInst.setValue(3,acc_Z);   // Accelerometer Z
011        newInst.setValue(4,gyro_X); // Gyroscope X
012        newInst.setValue(5,gyro_Y); // Gyroscope Y
013        newInst.setValue(6,gyro_Z); // Gyroscope Z
014        newInst.setValue(7,mag_X);   // Magnetometer X
015        newInst.setValue(8,mag_Y);   // Magnetometer Y
016        newInst.setValue(9,mag_Z);   // Magnetometer Z
017
018        // Classify the instance and display the result
019        try {
020            double res = rf.classifyInstance(newInst);
021            classifyResult.setText(activityID[(int) res] + ", " + String.
               valueOf(res));
022        } catch (Exception e) {
023            e.printStackTrace();
024        }
025    }
```

You use the **setValue** method to load the most recent sensor values into the new instance, and then use the Weka API **classifyInstance** method to retrieve a result from the model.

Improving the Results

While running the app and monitoring the continuous classifier result, several things are apparent:

- The sensor data updates rapidly, every 200 milliseconds. This is evidence the **SensorEventListener** is working hard.

- At times, the activity result does not appear to update. This is an effect of the classifier returning the same result as a previous classification, such as when the device is stationary and not moving. In such a state, the sensors may show very small changes.

- The activity classification is not very accurate. While the classifier showed an accuracy of approximately 90% with the training and test data, real-world experience as you move with the device does not seem to exhibit this degree of accuracy.

- The app is very responsive, even with the sleep time set at 500 milliseconds. It is possible to reduce this sleep interval if you require a faster sampling rate.

This app illustrates a high performance CML app running on Android with a complex RF model. The size of the .apk file is only approximately 3MB, illustrating how lean the solution is.

A final step before deploying the app is to see if you can improve the classification results. Recall in Chapter 2, I mentioned the importance of leveraging academic research papers. Refer to the following paper:

A Comparison Study of Classifier Algorithms for Cross-Person Physical Activity Recognition by Saez, Baldominos, and Isazis.

`www.ncbi.nlm.nih.gov/pmc/articles/PMC5298639/`

This recent paper is an open access work distributed under the Creative Commons license on the National Institute of Health website. In the paper, the authors cover building classifiers for the PAMAP2_Dataset. While the authors do not implement a real-time classifier on Android, they have done some great research on classifiers for this dataset that could help improve your results.

A summary of the potential improvements for the Activity Tracker Android app:

- The classifier does not use time-series data. That is to say, each instance stands on its own. You could potentially define a window and implement time-series learning during the window.

- If the target Android device includes a heart rate sensor, you could include the heart rate data and increase accuracy. You did include magnetometer data in your classifier/app and it is not clear how much this helps accuracy.

- Body temperature data could be included if the target device includes temperature sensor.

- For the app, you built the classifier using training data from subject101. You could potentially include training data from the all of the subjects for a complete model.

- The original dataset included three sensors at different locations on the body. You chose only a single sensor at the hand location. You could include more than one sensor, or select data from another sensor, such as the foot, depending on which activities you are most interested in.

The spirit of machine learning involves the search for continuous improvement, starting from the beginning data collection, all the way through deployment of the application.

6.9 Weka License Notes

In Chapter 2, I discussed the potential for ML to help you monetize your apps. In this chapter, you produced integrated ML apps on mobile devices using a Weka Android library. When you produce integrated ML applications using Weka, or any other open source ML package for that matter, there is often confusion regarding licensing and commercialization issues.

First, the disclaimer: This section does not constitute legal advice. Consult an expert before deciding on your ML app licensing and distribution strategy.

You need to consider two important but separate issues:

- Copyright

- Licensing

With respect to copyrights, the copyright of anything you create (i.e. your contribution) remains with you, regardless of whether you officially register it or not. Registering your copyright makes it much easier to defend if someone infringes on your copyright.

With respect to licensing, due to the open source licensing conditions, it is more complicated situation. According to the GPL, once you produce a commercial application that incorporates open source components, you have to make all "derivative" works public or keep them completely private. By adhering to these terms, as you work with Weka, in your case licensed under the GPL, you contribute to the public domain. For example, the projects in this book are derivative works and contribute to the public domain.

The important question becomes, what is a derivative work? For example, when you exported the Old Faithful runnable jar file, you included the modified Weka API library in jar format. This library is certainly a derivative work, and the app itself becomes a derivative work through the jar fie inclusion.

Derivative works:

- A derivative work is something that depends on Weka.

- Data implemented in a derivative work does NOT have to be included under the GPL.

- Models produced by Weka are NOT derivative works.

- If applying the model depends on special classes you provide, which are derivative works of Weka, those classes must be included under the GPL or a compatible license.

Many individuals and companies are not comfortable releasing their classes into the public domain. If you do not wish to make your classes available under the GPL or a compatible open source license, there are two options:

1. You can obtain a Weka commercial license.

2. You can add a layer of abstraction between your package and the Weka-derivative work.

Commercial Weka licenses are available. They exclude the Weka parts that are copyright by external contributors, and there are many of them, such as the Simple Logistic Classifier. Potential Weka commercial licensees may be only interested in a subset of Weka, such as a specific classifier, and this should be a relevant part of the request.

If you wish to use Weka but do not wish to make the software subject to the GPL or obtain a commercial license, you can use a remote machine interface (RMI) to call it remotely. This added layer of abstraction can satisfy the GPL license terms because it removes the derivative status from the main application.

Weka is an amazing package. If you create something amazing with it, consider releasing under the GPL and growing the public domain. Your contribution can help all of us to become better developers.

Index

A

Access points (AP), 80
Amazon AWS
  advantages, 123
  cloud-based services, 123
  data schema, 128
  data validation, 127–128
  EC2 AMI, 131
  free tier pricing details, 147
  Java developers, 143
  ML model, 126
    evaluation, 130
    services, 124
    settings, 129
  process and experiment, 131
  regression algorithm, 130
  RMSE, 131
  SageMaker, 141
  S3 input data, 127
  Synergy Research Group, 123
  uploading ML data, 126
  Weka ML
    classification, 140–141
    deep learning packages, 135–136
    initial connection, 135
    Java, 136
    OpenJDK, 136–137
    Oracle JDK package, 137–138
    SSH client, 135
    weka-3-8-2 directory, 139

Amazon Linux, 132
AMR, 161
Android data visualization
  Android Studio, 97–98
  app screenshot, 102
  FrameLayout, 101
  mobile devices, 97
  project file summary, 97
  WebView class, 97–100, 102
Android SDK, 30
Android Studio, 36, 120
  download, 36–37
  features, 36, 37
  install, 37–38
  SDK Manager, 38
  version 3.1.2, 38
Apache MXNet, 21
Apache OpenOffice Calc
  advantgaes, 57–58
  CSV file, 59, 61
  installation, 58
  ML data, 61–62
API, ML
  API providers, 151
  cloud providers, 148
  high-level ML API
    comparison, 149
  REST APIs, 150
Artificial intelligence (AI), 3
  definition, 2
  with DL, 21

383

Printed in the United States
By Bookmasters